I0810299

IMAGES
of America

LOWELL
VOLUME II

IMAGES
of America

LOWELL
VOLUME II

Jay Pendergast

ARCADIA
PUBLISHING

ISBN 978-0-7385-6335-0

Published by Arcadia Publishing
Charleston, South Carolina

Printed in the United States of America

Library of Congress Catalog Card Number: 96174685

For all general information contact Arcadia Publishing at:
Telephone 843-853-2070
Fax 843-853-0044
E-mail sales@arcadiapublishing.com
For customer service and orders:
Toll-Free 1-888-313-2665

Visit us on the Internet at www.arcadiapublishing.com

Contents

Acknowledgments

Photograph credits for some of the following people are cited by the initials in parentheses at the end of each photograph caption. The acknowledgments include, as well as those who loaned photographs, those who suggested people with photos or brought other's photos to me.

Hank Garrity (HG)
Dean Contover (DC)
John Quinn (JQ)
Dracut Historical Society (DHS)
Paul Dunigan (PD)
Charlie Panagiotakos (CP)
Steve O'Connor (SOC)
Hidden Treasures (HT)
Illustrated History of Lowell (IHL)
Jim Cameron (JC)
Jack Flood
Huck Finneral (HF)
Armand Larmand (AL)
Armand Mercier
Bill Flanagan
Jim Millinazzo
Allen "Cappy" Thompson (CT)
Mrs. Alice Turcotte (AT)
Bill Koumantzelis (BK)
Pat Pendergast (PP)
Mehmet Ali
Guy Lefebvre
George Poirier (GP)
Ann Welcome (AW)
Paul Fanning (PF)

Introduction

This is the third collection of photographs of old Lowell and Dracut that I have published in the last two years, and I'm beginning to dream in sepia. In one of the more vivid dreams, Ben Butler and Lucy Larcom are dancing at the Holy Trinity on High Street, while Parker Varnum, who built the first bridge across the Merrimac in Lowell, is delivering ice to Dewey Archambault, who is enjoying a nut stick and coffee at the Dutch Tea Room with Kirk Boott and the shortstop from Marie's Oyster House Softball Team; Bette Davis is manning the cash register. In reality, as with the other two volumes, the task has been very pleasurable and enlightening. To come into contact with so many images of Lowell from so many time periods and locations, some representing well-known events and others depicting almost forgotten places and people, is a very unusual way to learn about the city—sort of like viewing an abstract painting or collage. Chronology, and most other forms of orderliness, has proven to be of little significance.

This eclectic process has created an image of the city for me which does not enhance an understanding of logical progressions, but has distilled an essence of Lowell and its uniqueness which somehow, I hope, transfers to the casual reader; nonchalantly is the only way to look through this little book. The reader browses through, thumbing from one page to the next; some things stand out more than others. I was most delighted to get good pictures from the thirties, forties, fifties, and even into the sixties, and on one or two occasions to the seventies, because people can still recognize either themselves, or friends, or the places. It's rewarding to hear the suspended respiration of pleasure as someone recognizes his aunt or milkman.

I met new enthusiasts this time—collectors like Paul Fanning and Alice Turcotte. Paul's c. 1856 photo of Jim Merrill's house on Christian Hill is probably the oldest image in the book. Mrs. Turcotte's photos, including the cover, of children in local parks in the teens remind one of Steichen or Louis Hines. Bill Koumantzelis came up with some remarkable old Lowell street scenes. Jim Cameron, a jazz saxophonist and member of the LHS Class of '57, gave me a picture of his grandfather's candy store on Middlesex Street. Jack Flood, a bit of history himself, gave me some great leads. Ann Welcome allowed me to include the one-hundred-and-twenty-two-year-old photograph of her grandfather. My brother Pat had a couple of pictures to offer. Huck Finneral offered his *Sasqua* poster and other shots. Dean Contover found a photograph of his iconographer grandfather. Steve O'Connor had a few photos for this volume as he did for the first one. John Quinn, my classmate at Keith Academy, loaned me a photo of his family's old oil business. Mehmet Ali, mailman and historian, offered suggestions and put me in touch with people and has proved a valued colleague and good friend. The Dracut Historical Society, as in the past, could not have been more helpful—generous and trusting. I have been holding onto some of Paul Dunigan's treasures for almost two years; now they can go home. Armand Mercier put me in touch with Jim Millinazzo at the Lowell Housing Authority. Jim put me in the capable hands of Bill Flanagan, who I knew back in the Acre in what seems a previous lifetime. Hank Garrity of Garrity Antiques offered photos of his family's association with the Old Washington House. Charlie Panagiotakos, whom a great number of people including me call "my best friend," spent a night with me in the old projection room developing glass plate negatives—a bit like the old days. I also tapped his extensive postcard collection heavily. George Poirier has proven to be the ultimate archivist of Lowell; not only does he have ancient Lowell photographic treasures which he has been gathering for half a century, but he has kept negatives of every photo he has taken since the mid-forties and knows every person in each, when and where it was taken, and the circumstances. A retrospective of George's work, from an historical as well as an artistic point of view, is something that will happen soon. He is a municipal treasure of the caliber of Charles Cowley or George O'Dwyer. At the last moment Guy Lefebvre pulled out spectacular fire photos of buildings across from city hall and a never-seen-before youthful Ben Butler engraving.

So, it would be incorrect of me take credit for the creation of this effort; I merely pieced it together, and with a good bit of ΧΑΟΣ at that. This has been the effort of a community of people interested in sharing a mutual feeling towards this unique bit of geography we live in where the Merrimac bends to the north. I don't know of any other place in the world where a river bends so dramatically, so sharply caressing the Wamesit Neck of land which held the promise for the future of America after it wrested its freedom, spiritually as well as physically, from its abusive mother country. From the days when it was known as *Sunneasitt, Augumtoocooke, Naamkeag, Mascuppic,* and *Wamesit,* when it served as the seat of the native population from here to the Saint Lawrence, to the time of East Chelmsford, Draycotte, Billericay, and Tewkesbury, when it sent the first farmers in the history of the world to successfully fight off the oppression of a king and keep him off, Lowell has been in the vanguard. Proportionately, more men from the Lowell area, then Dracut and Chelmsford, went to fight in the Revolution than any other community in the colonies. Abraham Lincoln notably designated General Ben Butler and the Lowell regiments as the saviors of the Union.

I would like to thank my son Ciaran for covering some of my many classes at Franklin Pierce College and New Hampshire College while I have been in the throes of this work. He is equally at home with Passaconaway and T.S. Eliot.

My daughter Cait is about to graduate high school, yet she has the editing skills and know-how of someone with twice her years. Her willingness, capability, and hard work has made my task easier and given me great pleasure.

Finally, I would like to thank my wife Maire, who always gives me the support needed for these efforts and who had enough confidence in me to leave her own exquisite country to share my life along the banks of the Merrimac.

Jay Pendergast
Tyngsborough 1997.

One

The People

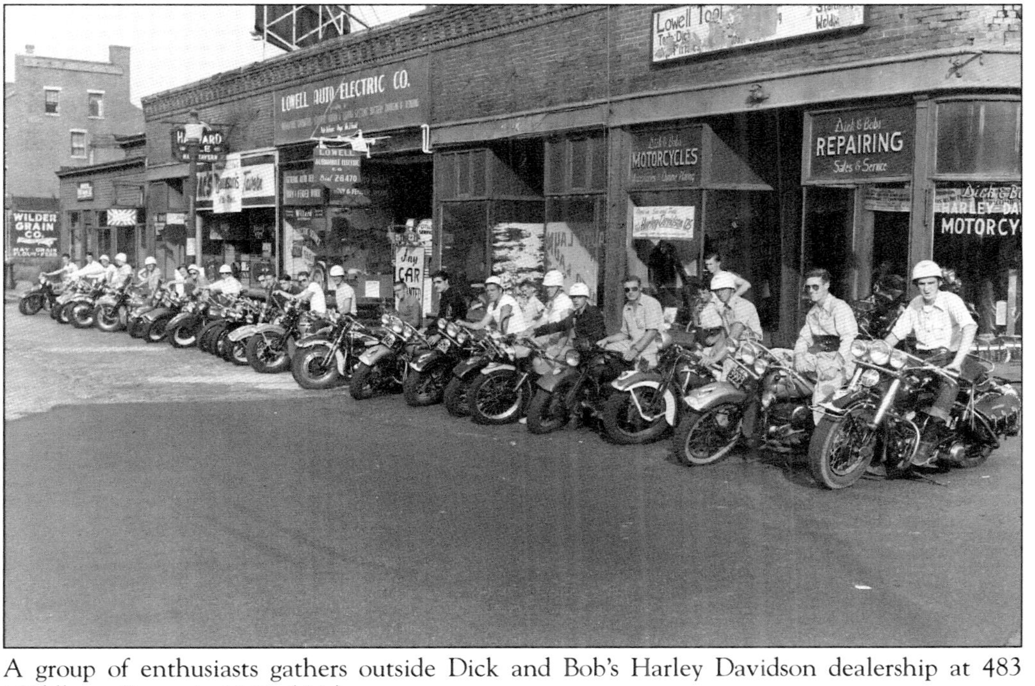

A group of enthusiasts gathers outside Dick and Bob's Harley Davidson dealership at 483 Middlesex Street in 1948. (AL)

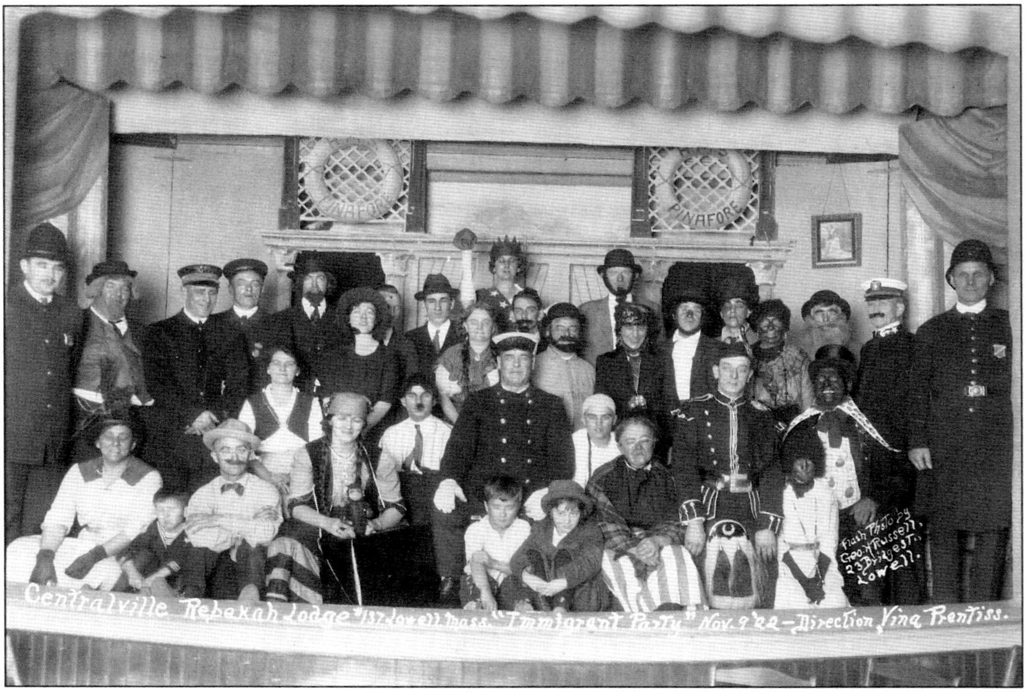

The Centerville Rebekah Lodge of the Knights of Pythias held its "Immigrant Party" on November 9, 1922. (DH)

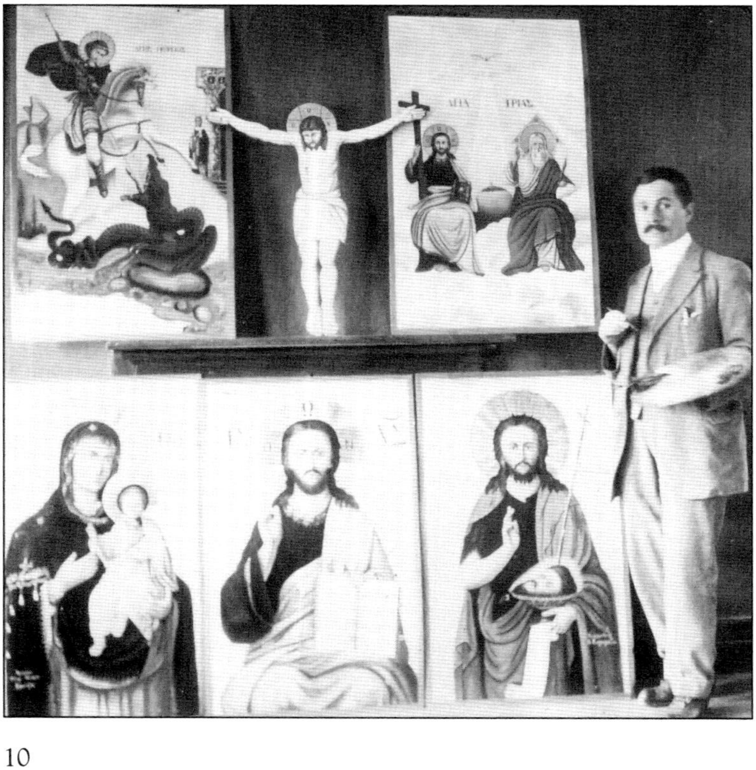

Athanasios Solominides, iconographer, stands beside his work prepared for the altar of the Transfiguration Greek Orthodox Church. He lived at 70 Rock Street. (DC)

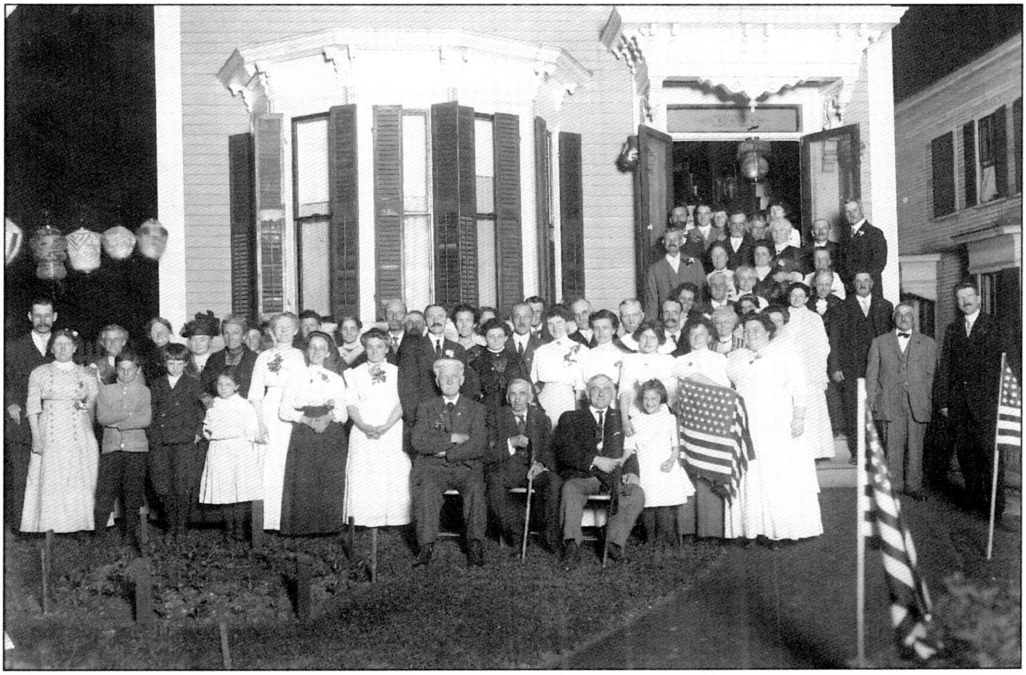

The Floyd Bible Class held its Fourth of July celebration at 351 Walker Street in the mid-twenties. (HG)

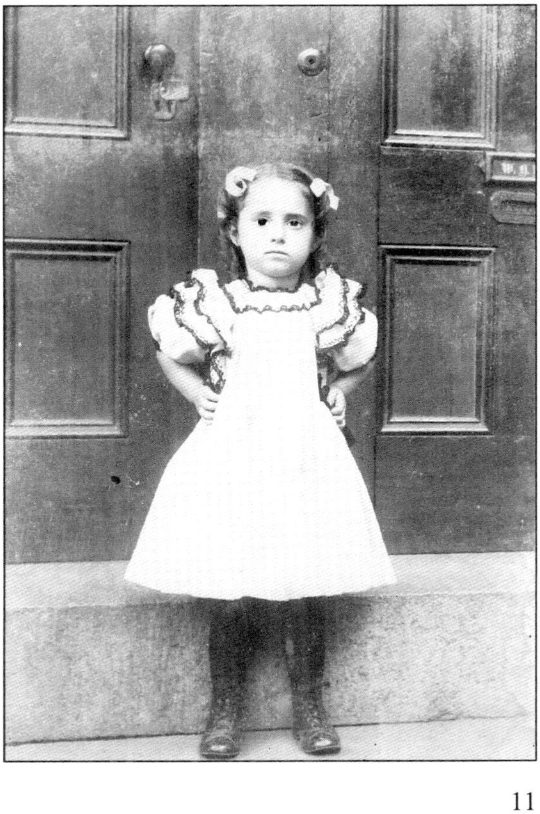

This picture of an unidentified Lowell lady was taken at Freeman's Photography Studio in the Hildreth Building on Merrimack Street. (JP)

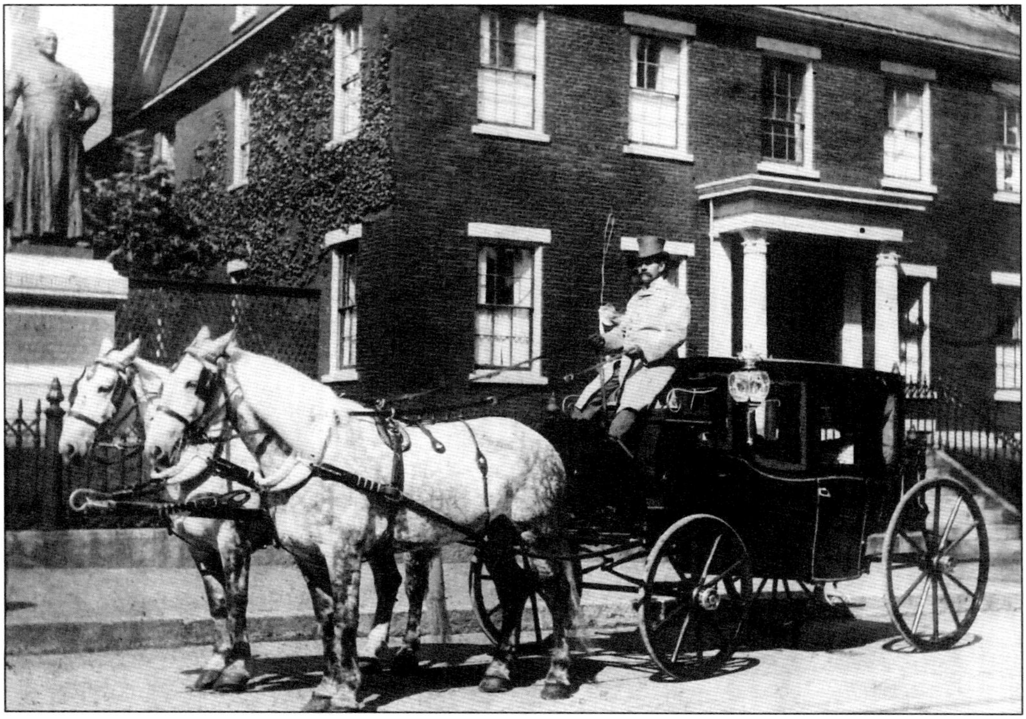

Joseph Albert drives his mourners funeral coach past the rectory at St. Jean d'Arc Church on Merrimack Street, 1912. Father Garin looks with approval from his pedestal in the background. Mr. Albert's parlors were at 171 Aiken Street. (DHS)

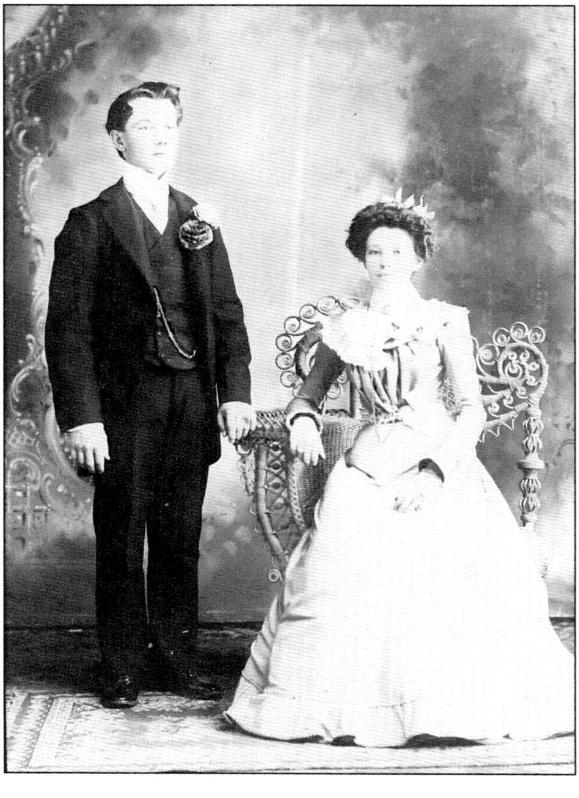

This portrait and the two on page 13 are of unidentified Lowellians. This couple was photographed at Fontaine's photo parlors on Merrimack Street. (JP)

This photo was taken at Loupret's on Central Street. (JP)

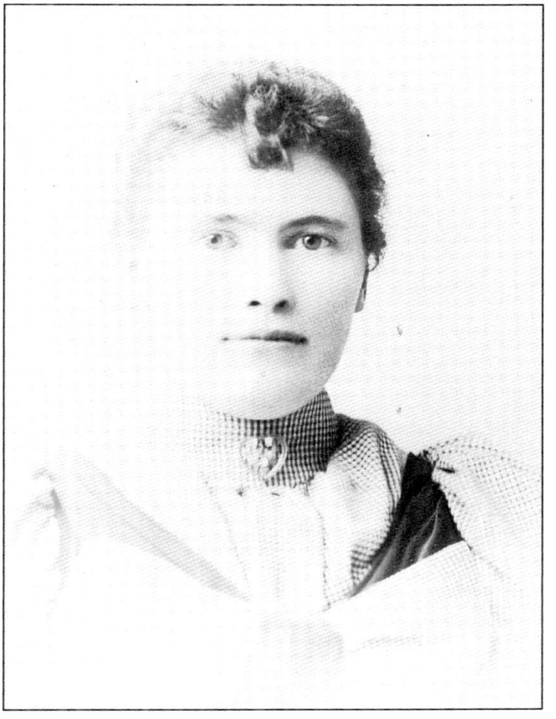

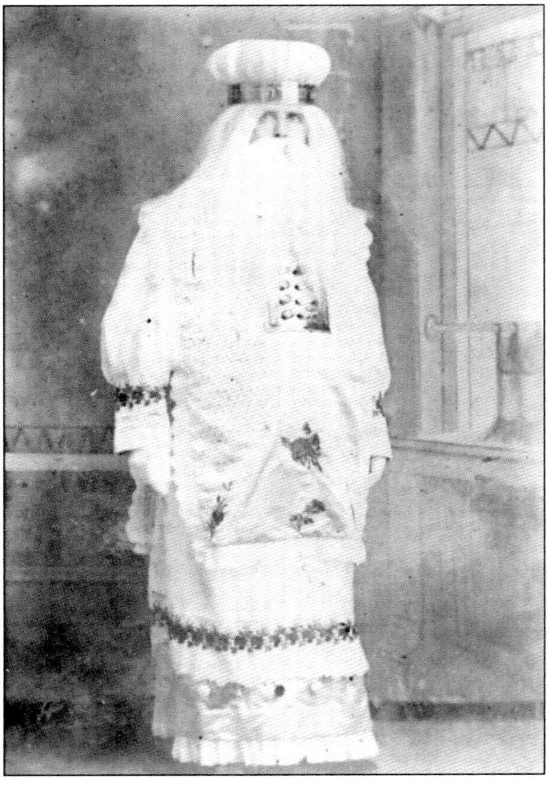

This photo was taken at Hayden's and Squire's parlors on Merrimack Street. (JP)

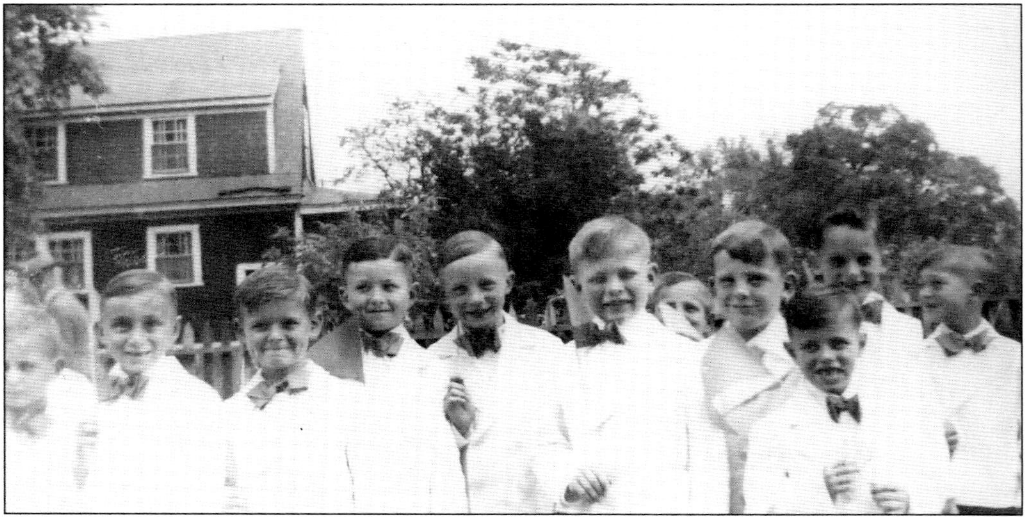

This photograph was taken after a procession at St. Patrick's Church on May 28, 1951. (JP)

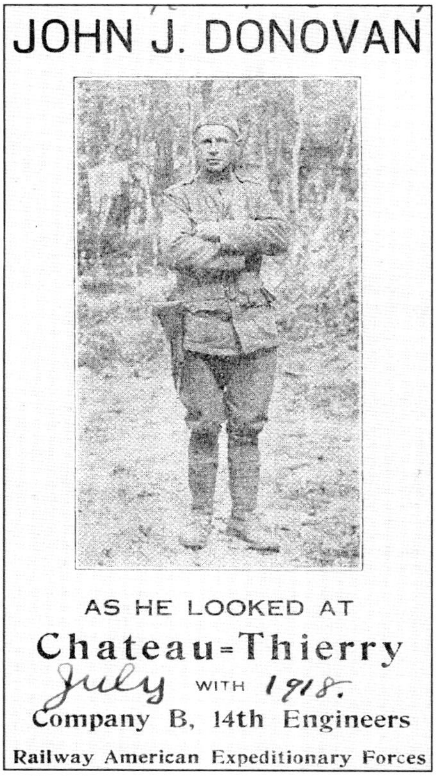

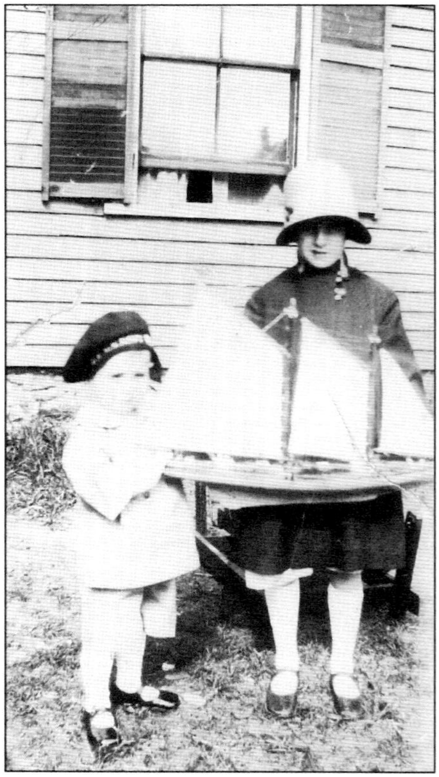

Left: John J. Donovan used this World War I photograph of himself on his campaign literature when he ran for mayor. He was a police officer in Lowell for many years. He was unsuccessful even though his name was the same as Lowell's first Irish mayor in 1882.(JP)
Right: Allen "Cappy" Thompson and his sister Ruth show off their beautiful clipper ship in their backyard on Epping Street in 1930. (AT)

Charlie Petroulas waves goodbye as he leaves an apartment in the Lowell Housing Project in the late 1950s. (JP)

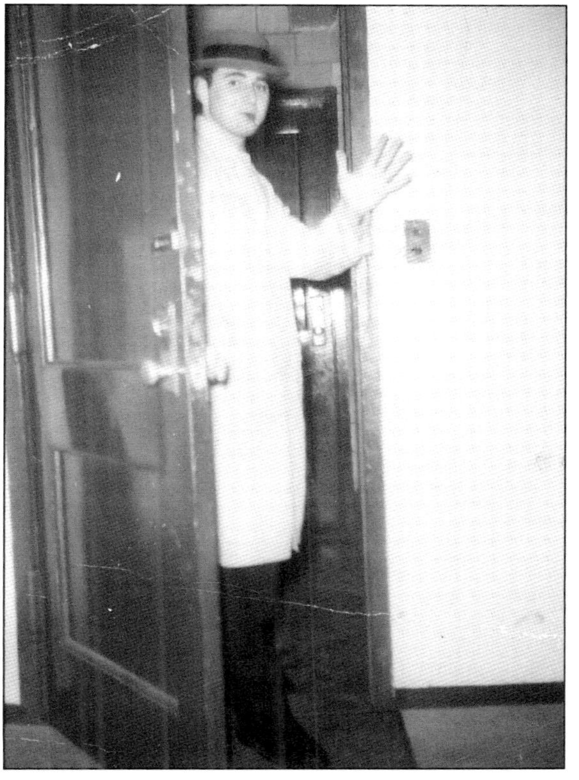

O'Brien Terrace is seen here from Market Street in 1956. The North Common Village was the first housing project of its size in the United States. It proved an overwhelmingly successful project. (LHA)

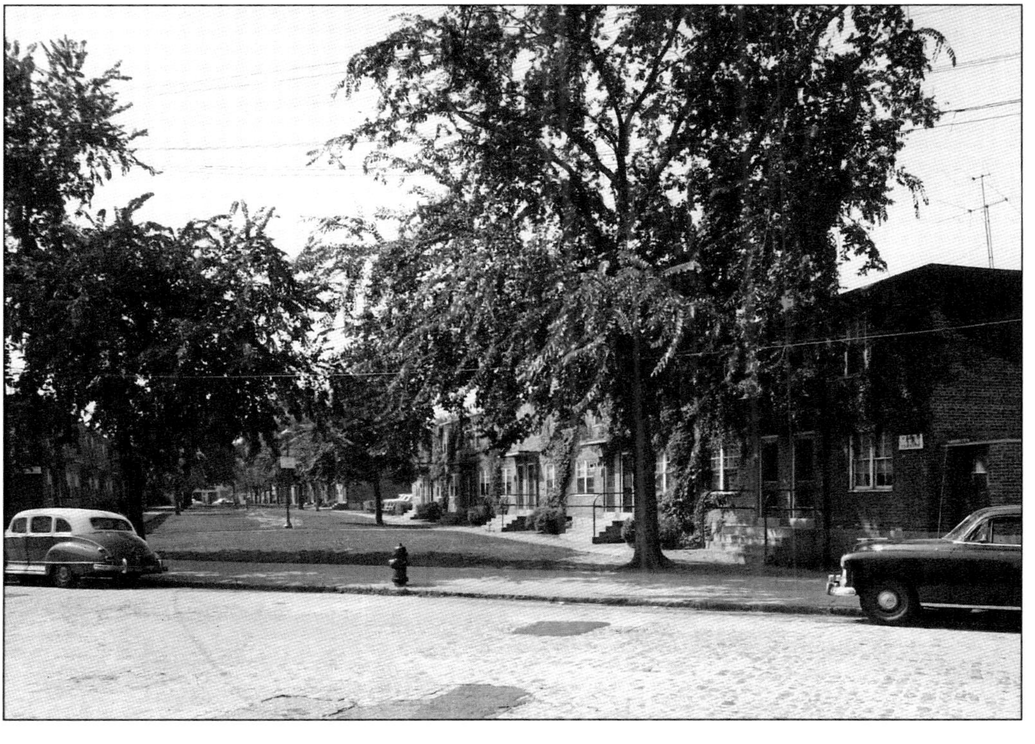

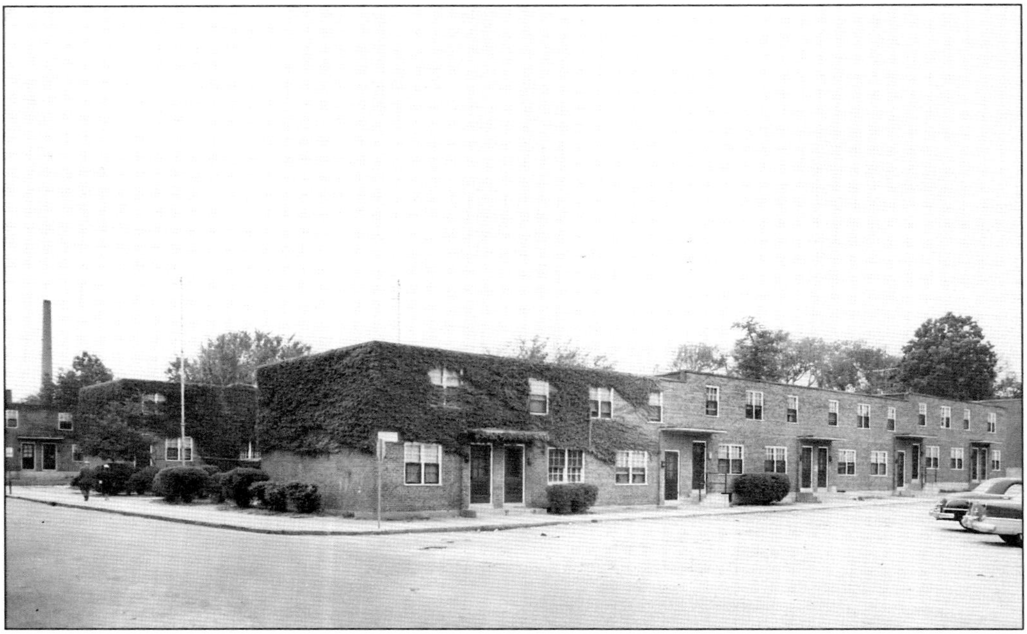

This view of the housing project looks from Salem Street to Hancock Avenue in 1956. The project displaced much of Lowell's Greek population. (LHA)

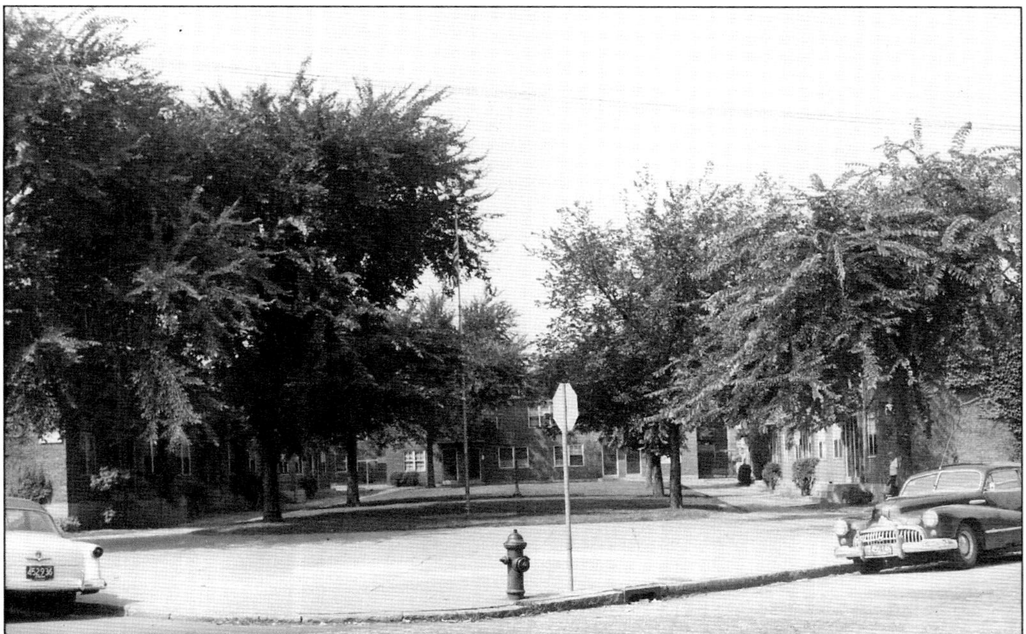

Conlon Terrace is photographed here from Cardinal O'Connell Parkway in 1956. (LHA)

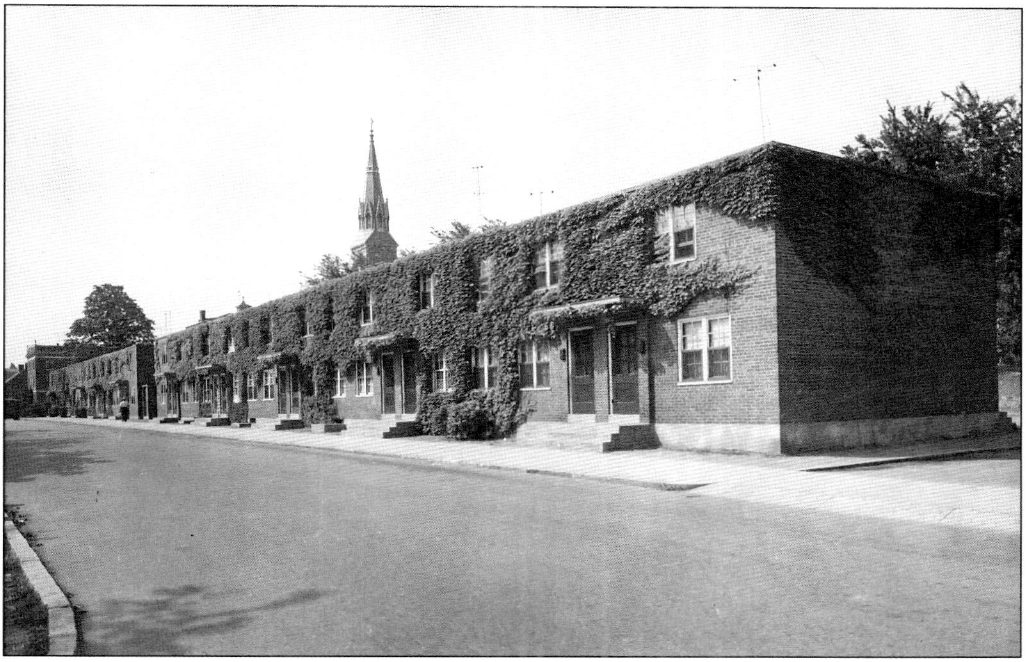

This photograph depicts Suffolk Street from Market Street in 1956. The spire of St. Patrick's Church is visible in the background. (LHA)

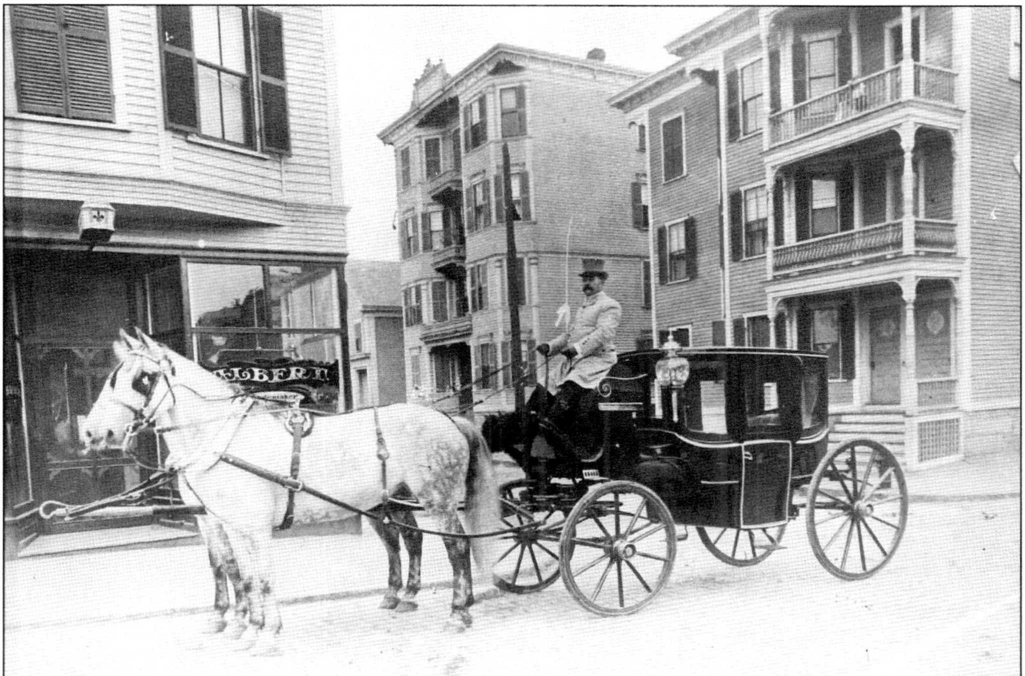

Mr. Joseph Albert, undertaker, is in front of his parlors on Aiken Street in May 1912. Notice the fleur-de-lis over the front door. (DHS)

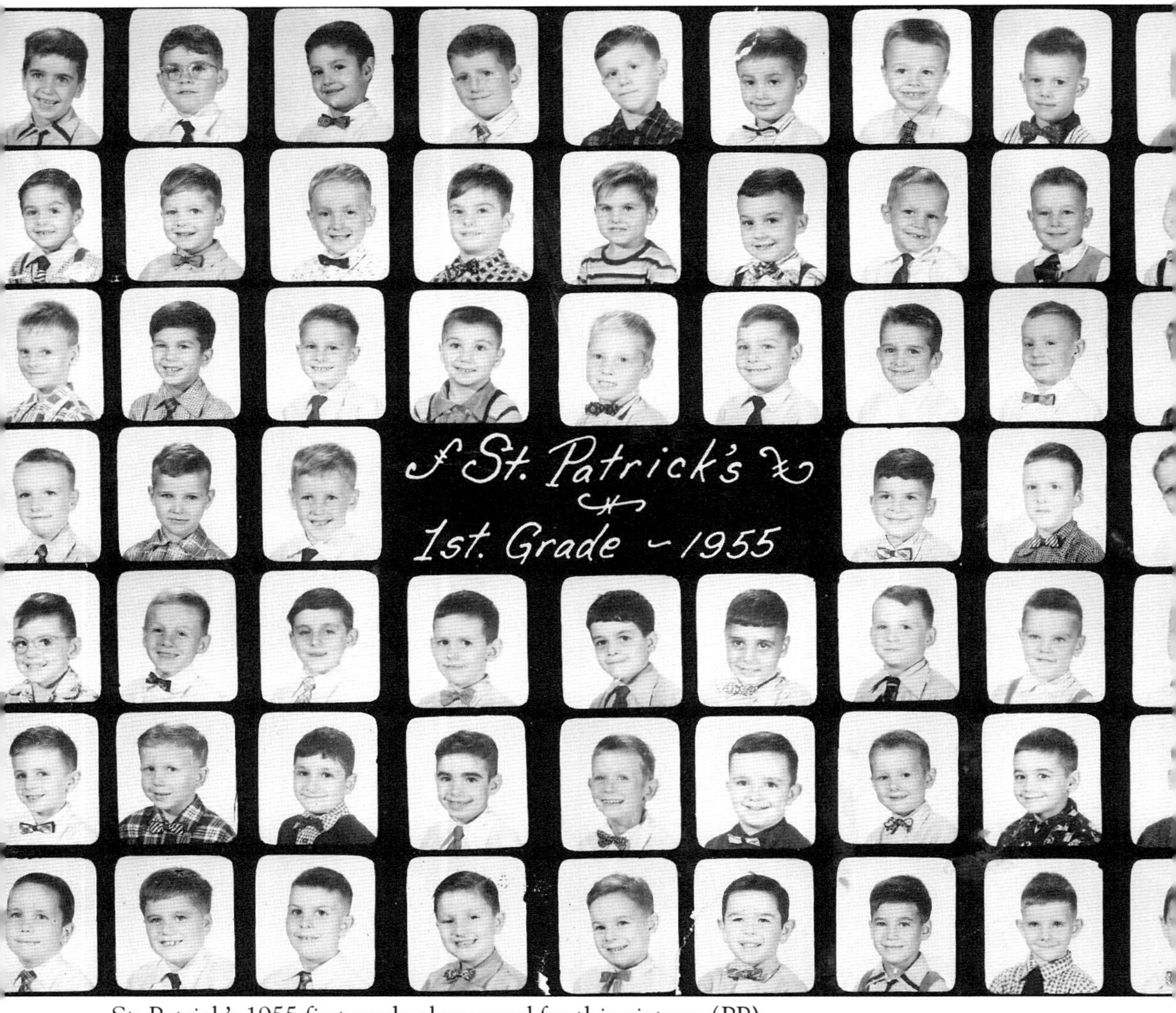

St. Patrick's 1955 first grade class posed for this picture. (PP)

Ben Butler, the Beast of New Orleans, has been the subject of extensive biographies, and his life merits such treatment. He was the defender of Irish-Catholic rights in Lowell and was promoted to colonel in the Irish Lowell Militia; he ultimately received the rank of brigadier-general. After the Baltimore riots, he captured the Naval Academy at Annapolis and the USS *Constitution*. He then captured Baltimore—which stopped the secession of Maryland—while the rest of his regiment proceeded to Washington. The Lowell regiment was the first group of volunteers to reach Washington. Abraham Lincoln personally thanked the Lowell men for saving the Union. (JP)

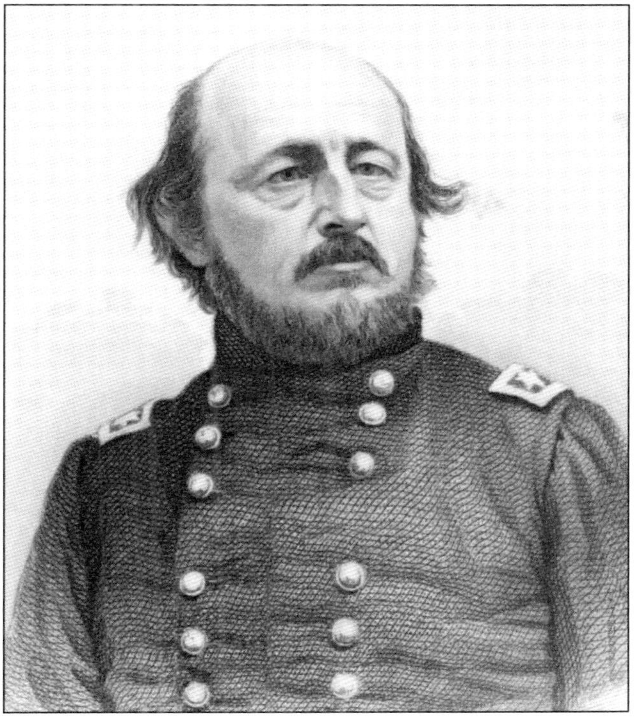

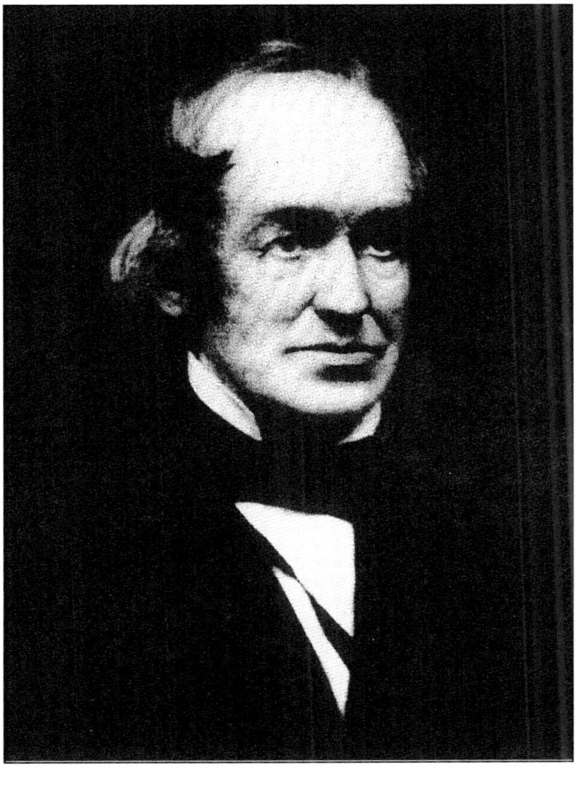

John Nesmith was born in Windham, New Hampshire, in 1793. He and his brother Thomas, after having been apprenticed locally, left for New York where they developed a considerable business. They arrived in Lowell in 1831 and invested largely in real estate, developing the section of the city known as Belvedere. John was the agent for many mills in the greater Lowell area. He secured the water rights to Lake Winnepesaukee and Squam Lake. He amassed a considerable fortune and became a valued benefactor of the city. His house on Andover Street is open to the public. (IHL)

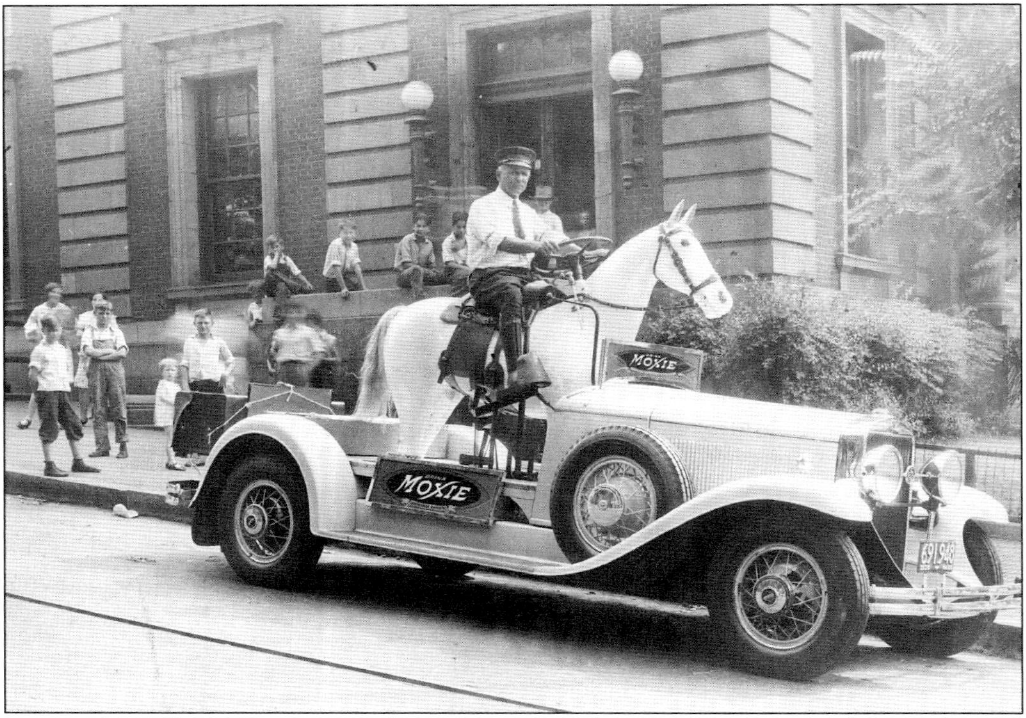

George Demers, in the saddle, lived on Fourth Avenue in Pawtucketville. The license plate on the gleaming Stutz reads, "1930." Moxie was invented in Lowell. (DHS)

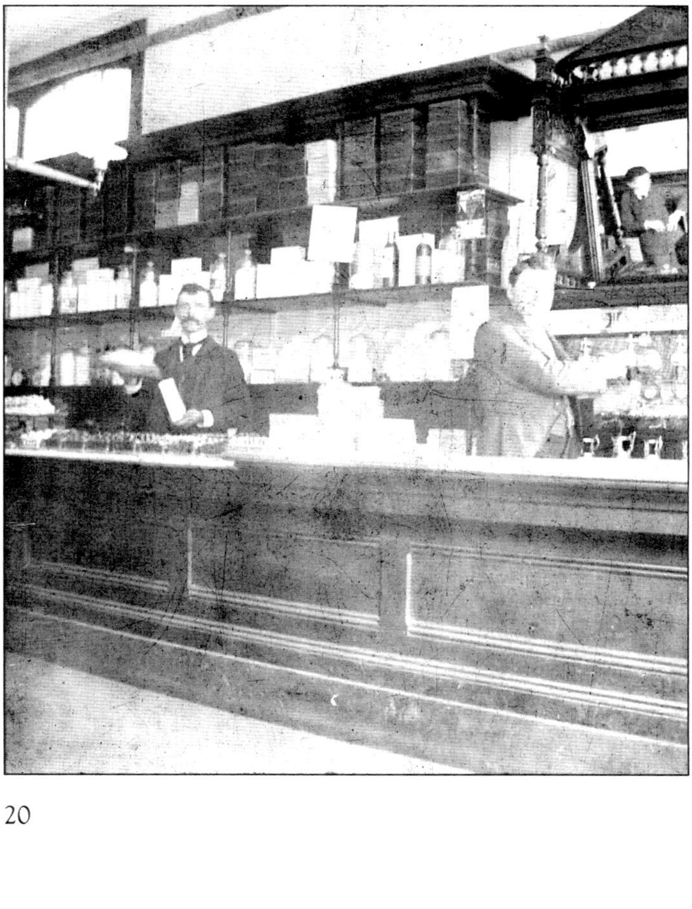

Albert and James Cameron owned the family confectionery store on 155–157 Middlesex Street. The business was established in 1889 and acted as a wholesale agency for Lenox Chocolates, Lowneys, Schraffts, and several others. The family had another shop at 183 Pine Street. Albert and his wife Catherine lived at 256 Stevens Street, while James and his wife Nellie lived at 105 Georgia Avenue. (JC)

The residence of Joshua Merrill was located on "Christian Hill" in Centralville, *c.* 1856. Merrill was a schoolteacher in Lowell and was born before the city was founded. In the *Illustrated History of Lowell* (1894), Merrill wrote extensively about Lowell schools and anecdotally about Kirk Boott and other famous Lowellians. (DHS)

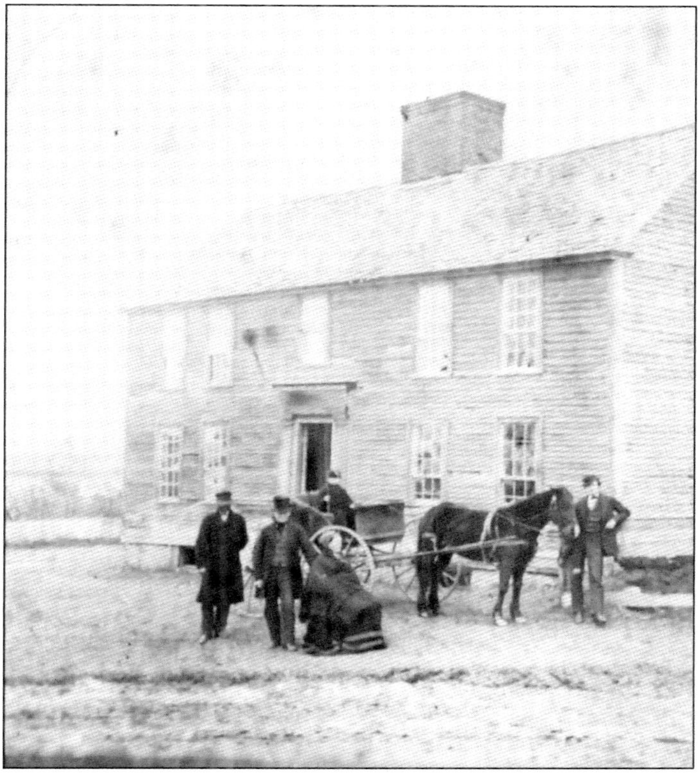

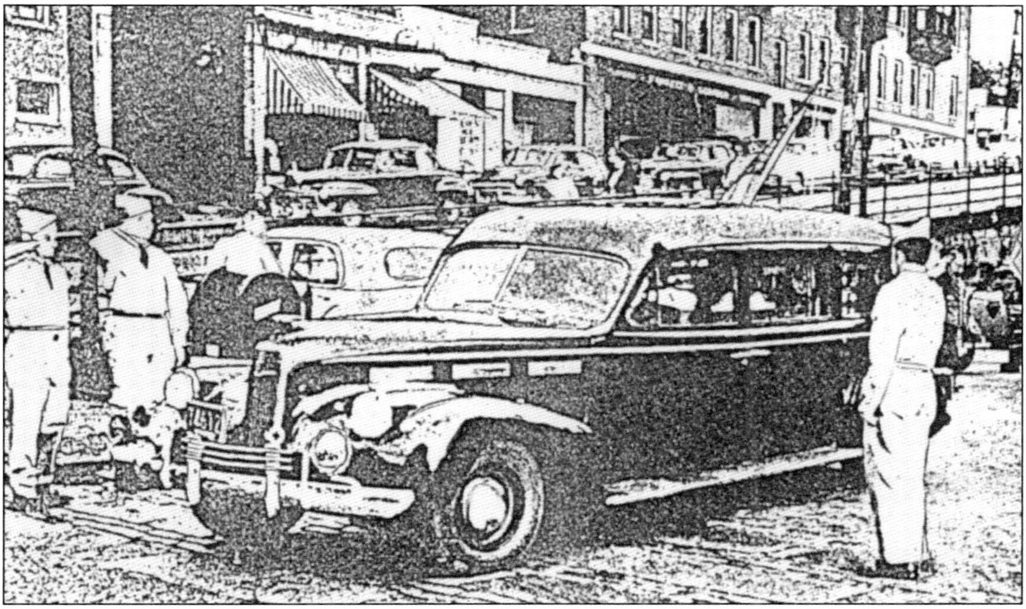

This *Lowell Sun* photograph is dated September 18, 1951. It depicts the return of the body of Joseph Ovellette, a nineteen-year-old Lowell soldier posthumously awarded the Congressional Medal of Honor during the Korean War. An honor guard from the American Legion and the Franco-American War Veterans meets the hearse at the Middlesex Street Railroad Station.

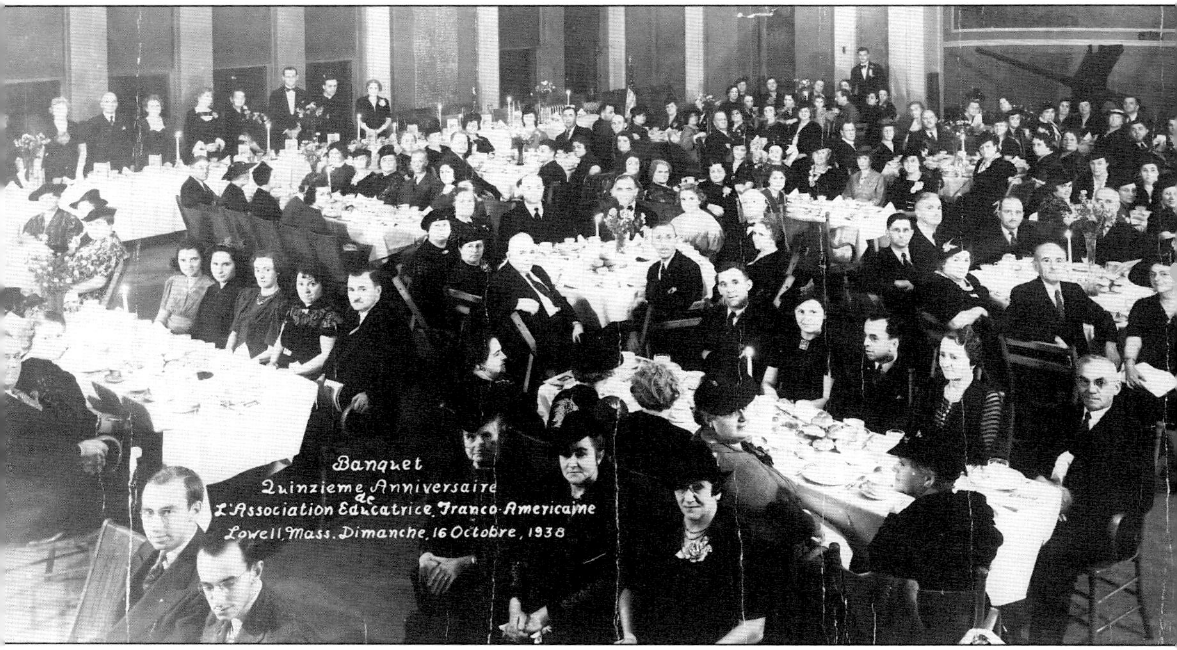

This banquet, held October 1938, commemorated the fiftieth anniversary of L'Association de Educatrice, Franco-Americaine. (DHS)

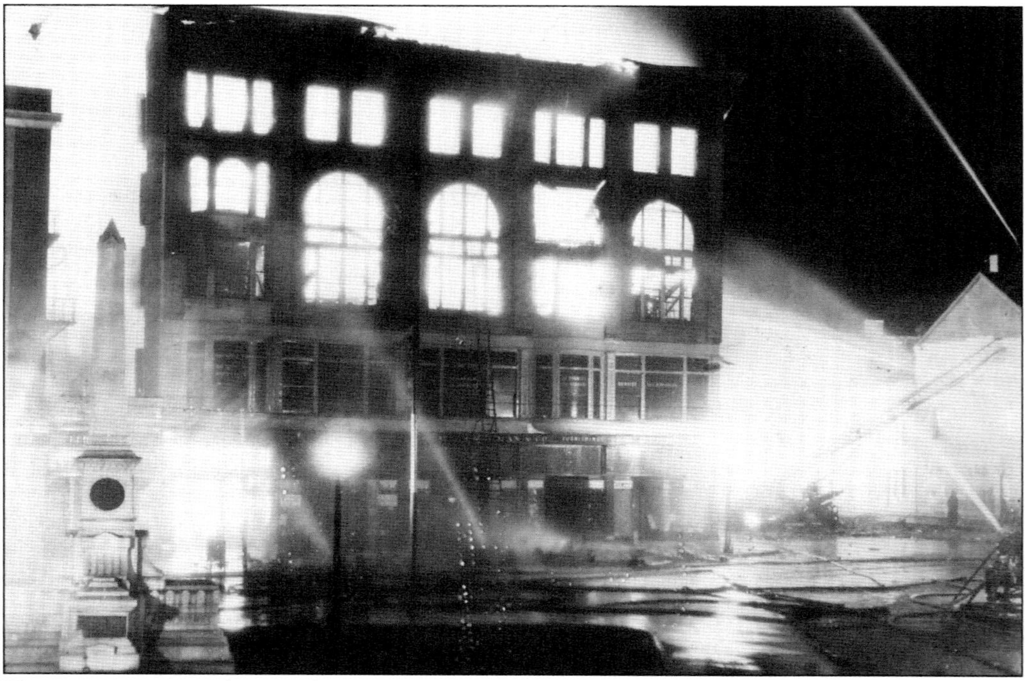

This is an image of one of Lowell's most devastating fires at the Associate's Building on Merrimack Street (note the Ladd and Whitney Monument in the foreground). Dances were held on the other side of those brightly lit arched windows on the third floor. One fireman lost his life and three were hospitalized.

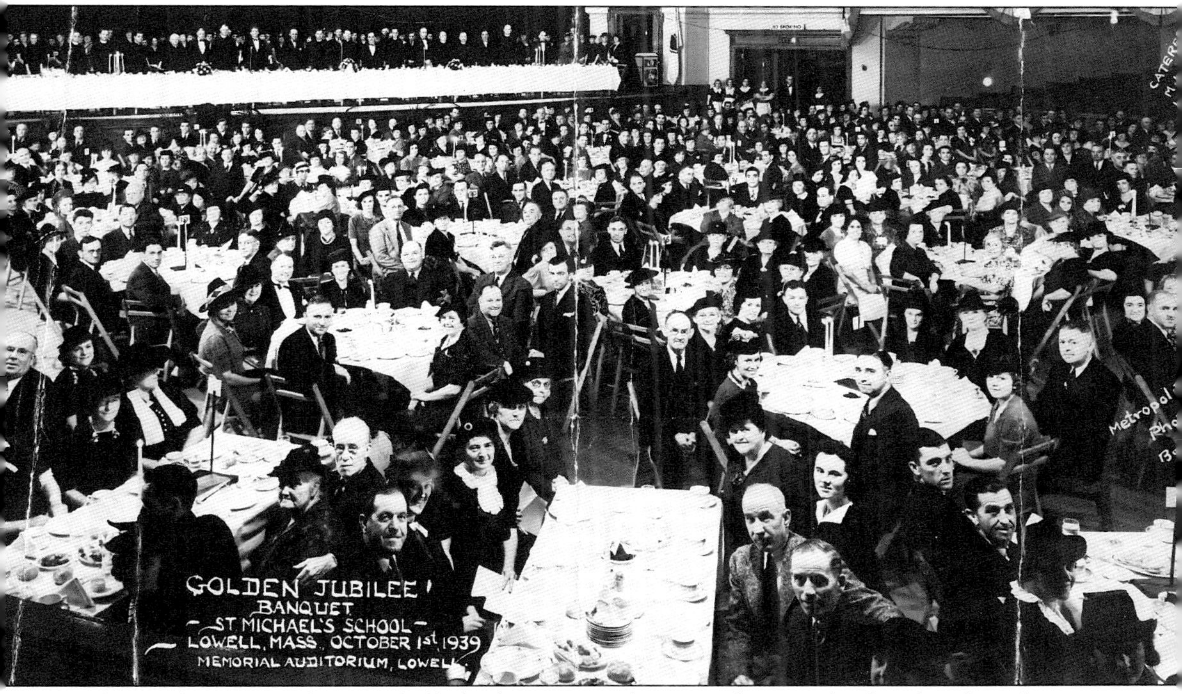

Residents of Dracut and Centralville both were parishioners of St. Michael's Church and are well represented in this photograph taken at Lowell Memorial Auditorium. It had the same caterer (Lydon of Lowell) and the same photographer (Metropolitan of Boston) as the Franco-Americaine banquet on page 22.

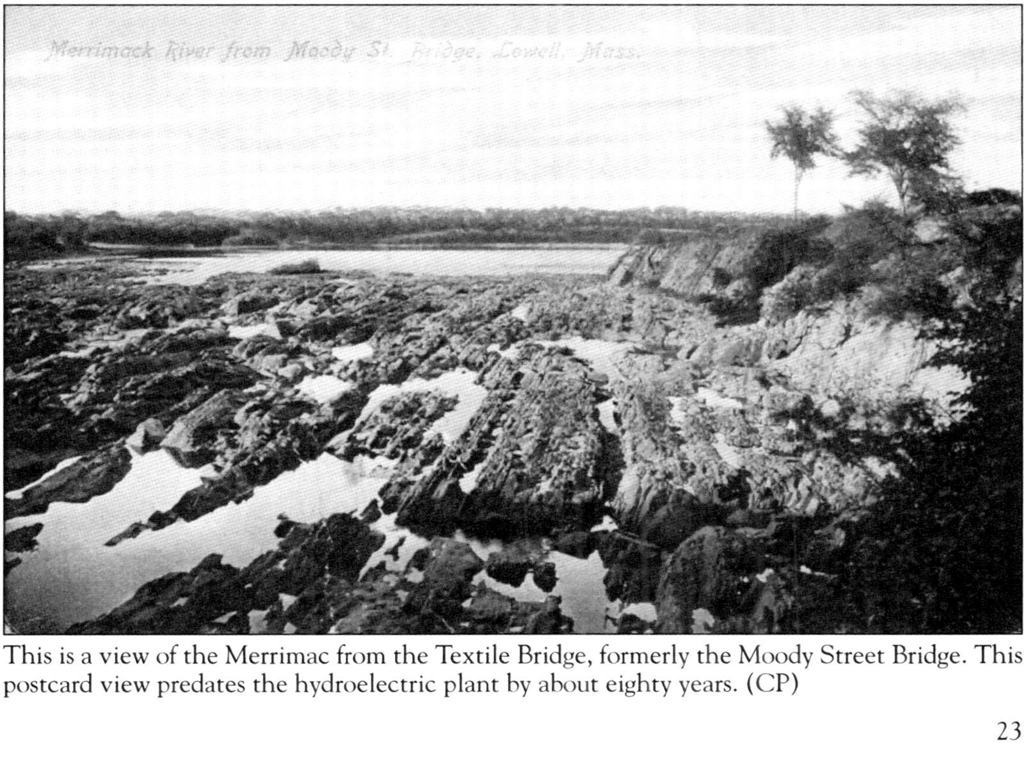

This is a view of the Merrimac from the Textile Bridge, formerly the Moody Street Bridge. This postcard view predates the hydroelectric plant by about eighty years. (CP)

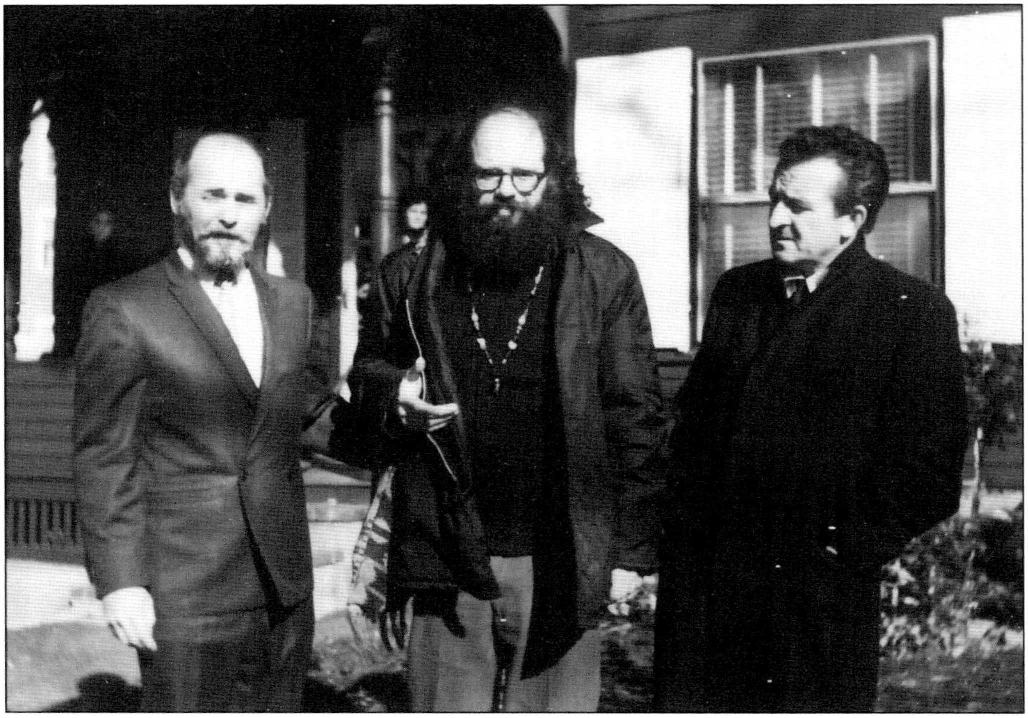

Huck Finneral, Allen Ginsberg, and Billy Koumantzeles interrupt a conversation for the camera after Jack Kerouac's funeral on October 12, 1969. (HF)

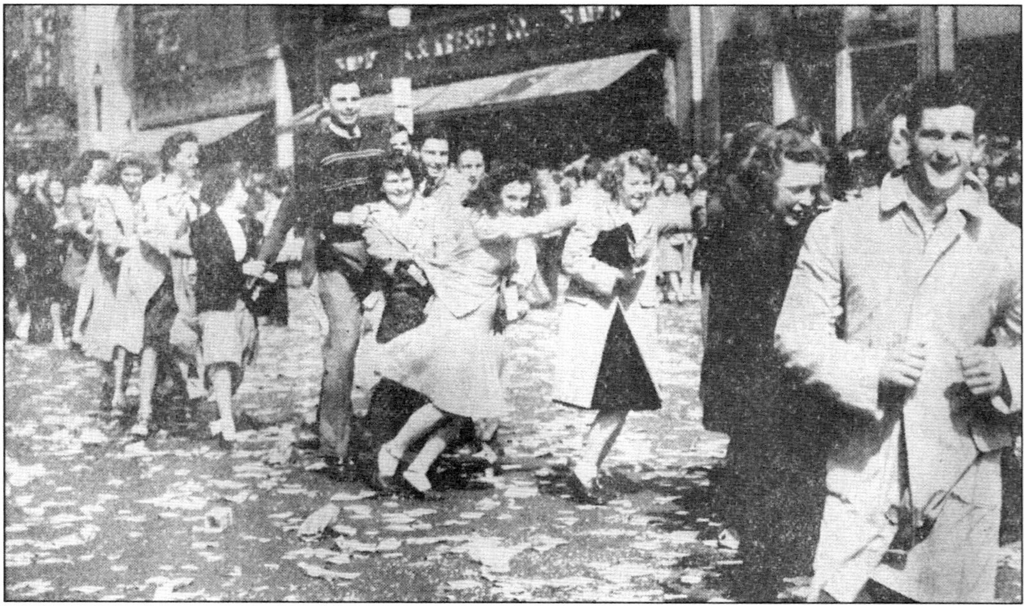

In this "snake dance for victory," the *Lowell Sun* photo depicts one of the many impromptu snake-dances and conga lines that broke out in Kearney Square at the height of celebration of V-E Day in 1945. This group was snapped in front of Kresge's and is comprised mostly of high school students.

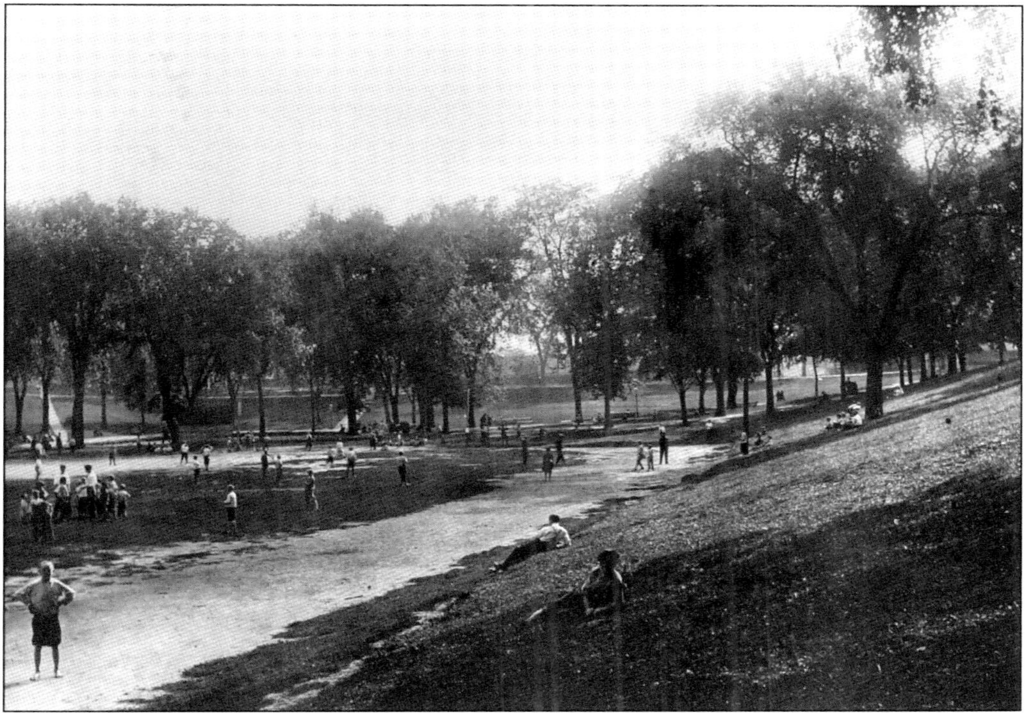

Today, Lowell folk festival audiences sit on this slope of the South Common to watch the performances. This photo was taken on August 10, 1912, at 3 pm. (AT)

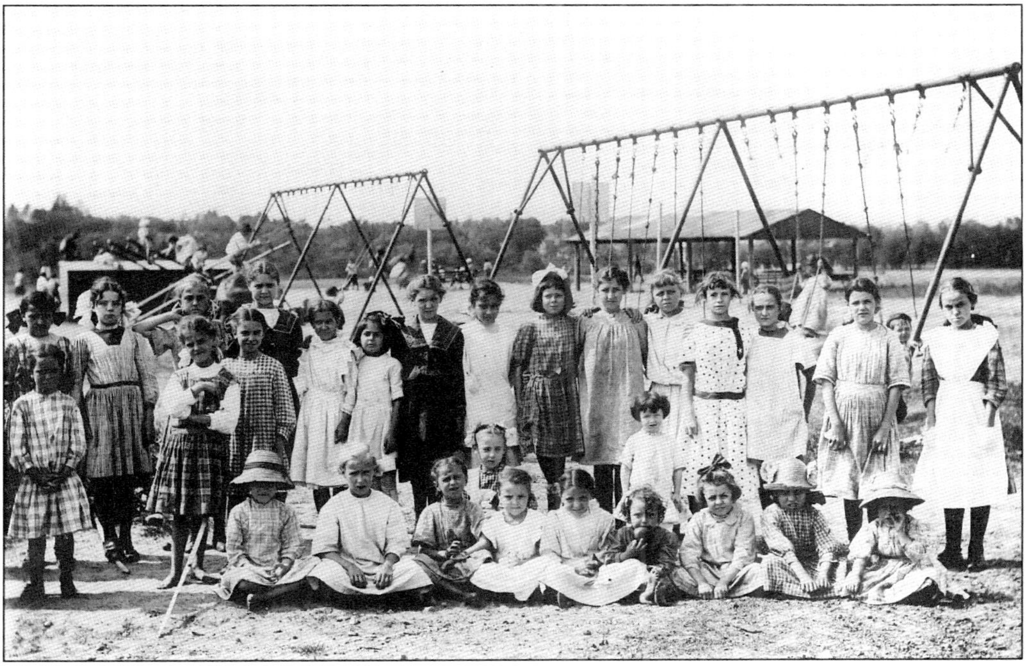

All play stops for this "girls only" photo at the Aiken Street Playground on August 16, 1912, at 2 pm. (AT)

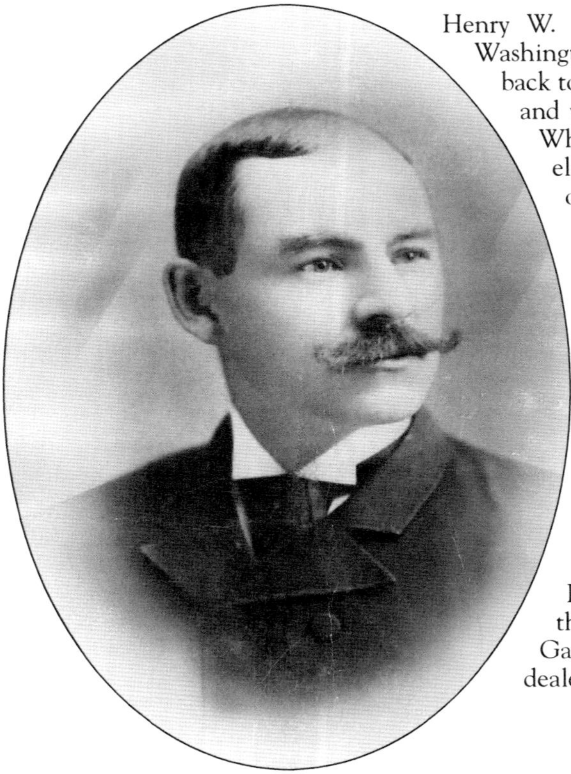

Henry W. Garrity was the proprietor of the old Washington Tavern on Central Street, which dates back to 1826 (the year of Lowell's first founding) and was the first stagecoach house in Lowell. When Andrew Jackson visited Lowell, an elected committee of twenty-four rode out to the Tewksbury line to meet the President. The famous parade of the mill girls began at the Washington House and extended down Central Street below the Boston and Maine depot (the Rialto Building). Every girl wore a white dress, a blue sash, and carried a green parasol. Commodore Hull, Martin Van Buren, and Franklin Pierce were also present. Kirk Boott covered all the expenses, which amounted to about $500. Josiah Peabody (mayor 1865–6) constructed the lower end of the tavern, which in those days consisted of three stories. It remained as the Farragut House when the rest of the building was razed. Mr. Garrity's grandson is presently an antique dealer in Lowell. (HG)

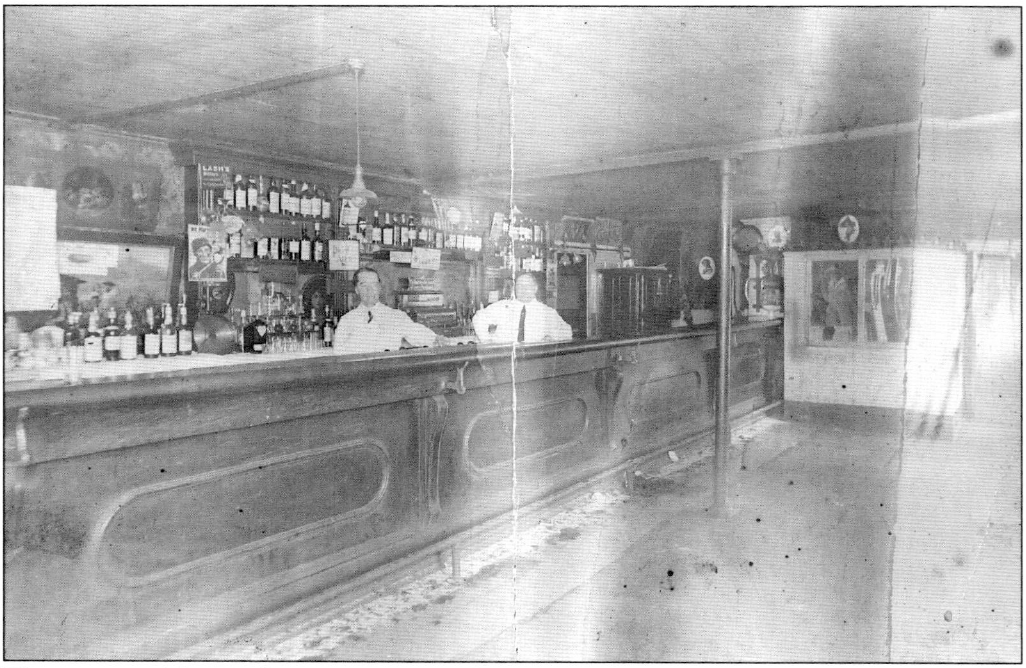

The interior of the Washington Tavern is shown here in later years during the period when it was owned by Mr. Garrity. (HG)

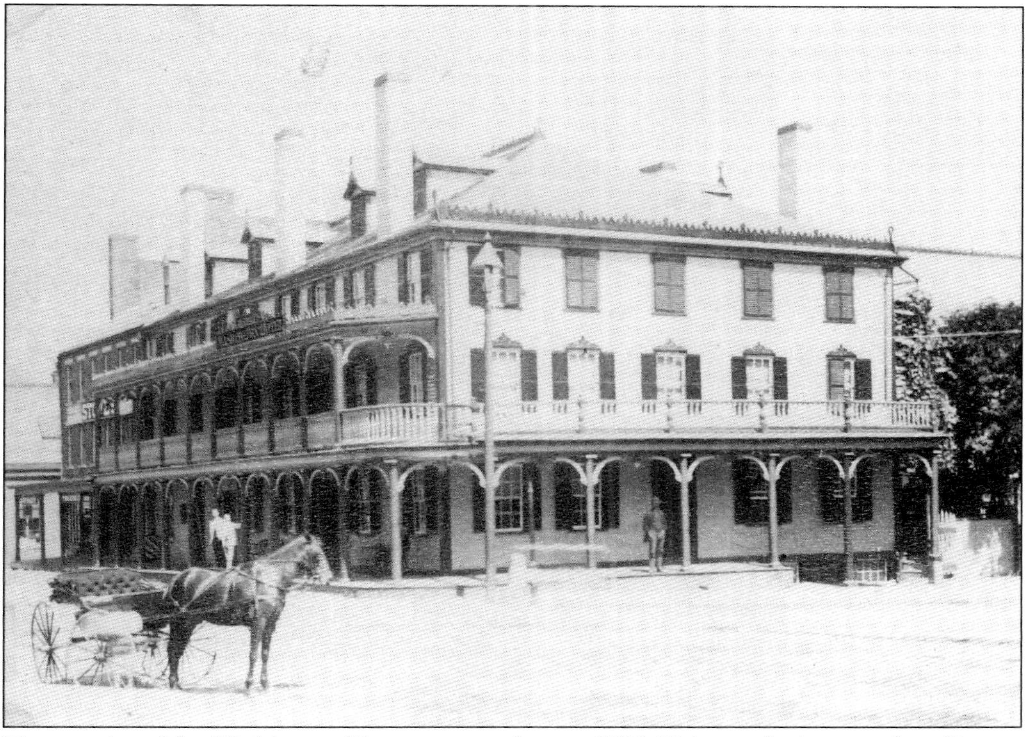

The exterior of the Washington Tavern appears here *c.* 1880. This was the last stop from Boston and points south before crossing the Merrimac at Bradley's Ferry, which later became the location of the Bridge Street Bridge, heading to New Hampshire and the North.

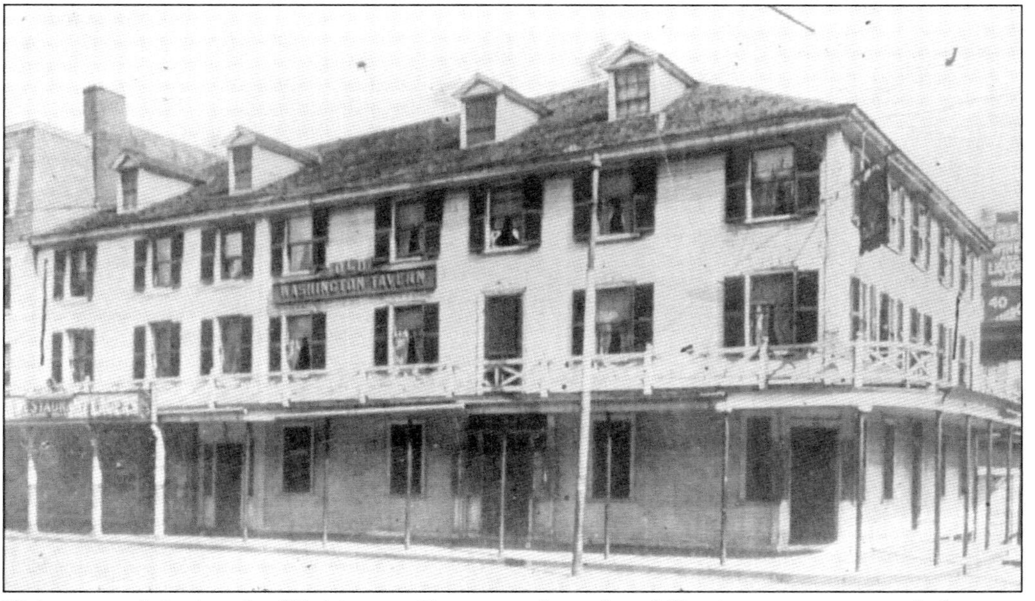

This postcard depicts the Washington Tavern at a later date following many structural changes. The chimneys and balconies were removed, but the four-story section on the far left still remained intact. (HG)

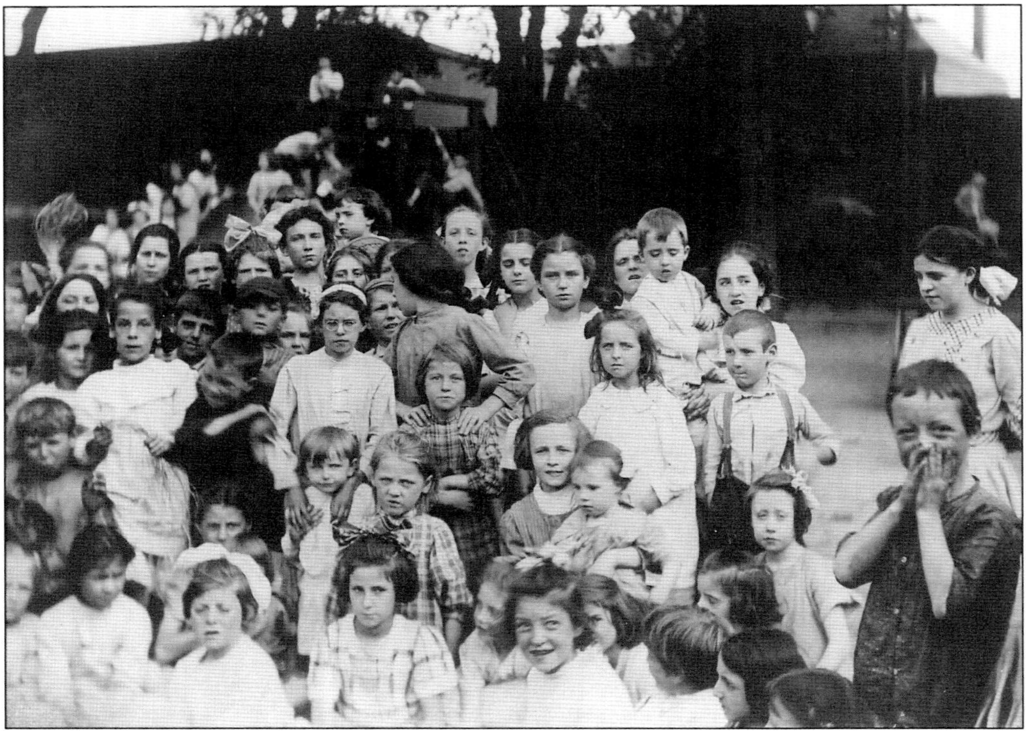

Acre children appear on the North Common in 1912. The North and South Common were laid out in 1845. (AT)

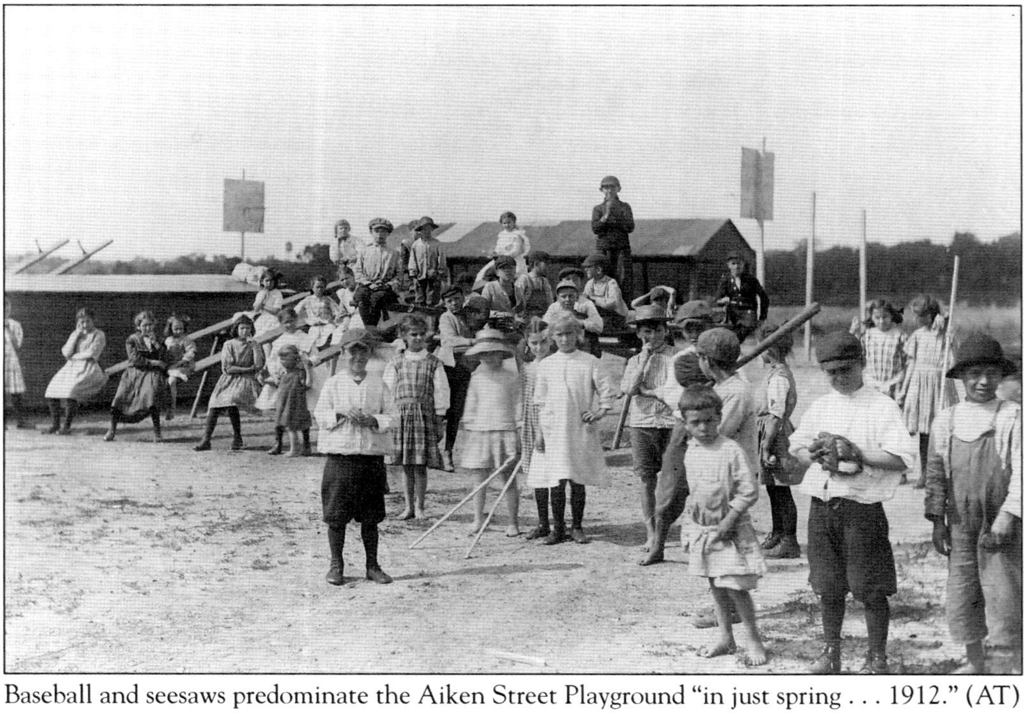

Baseball and seesaws predominate the Aiken Street Playground "in just spring . . . 1912." (AT)

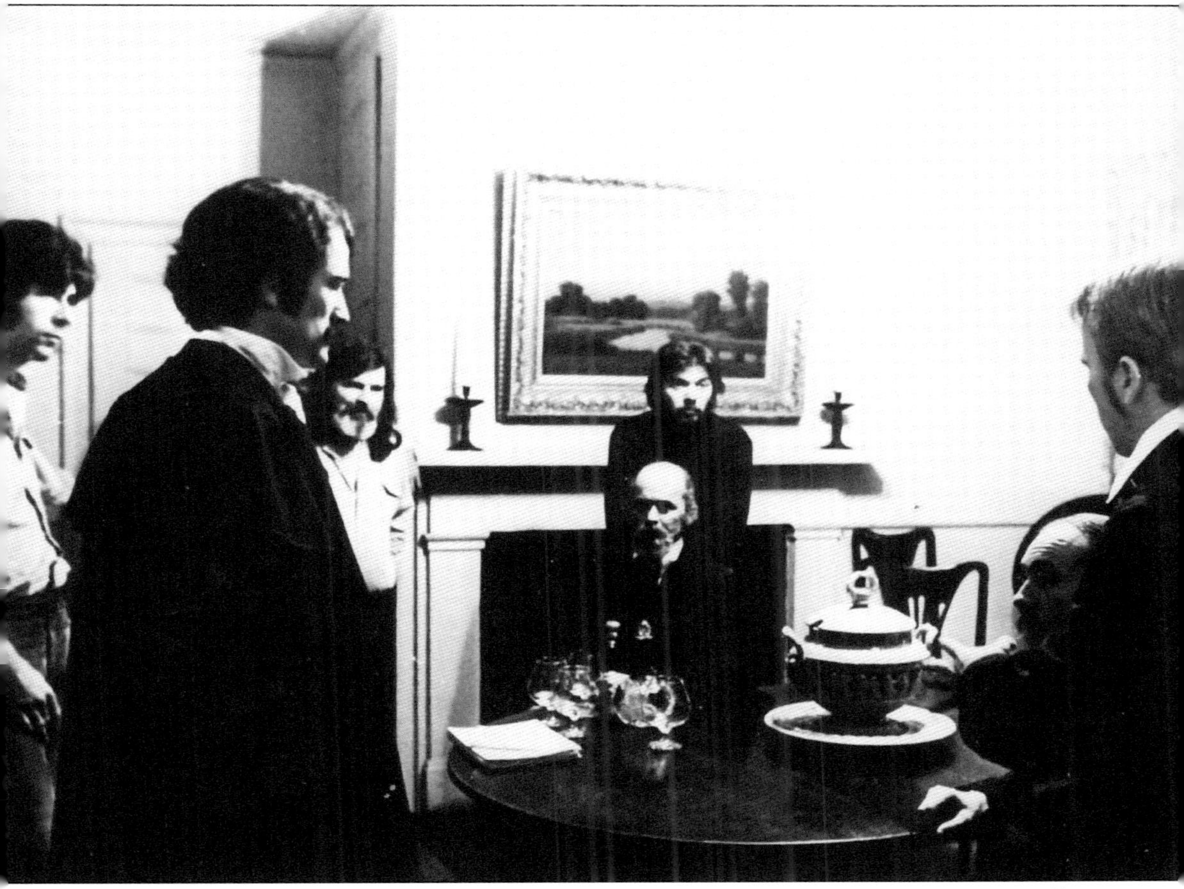

This scene is from a *c.* 1973 Lowell docudrama about Edgar Allen Poe's experiences in Lowell. In the foreground is Joe Finneral as Poe. In the background, from left to right, are: Boody Byers, cameraman; the author; Brian Dean, director (behind the chair), and Anthony "Huck" Finneral (seated). The two gentlemen on the right are unidentified. (JP)

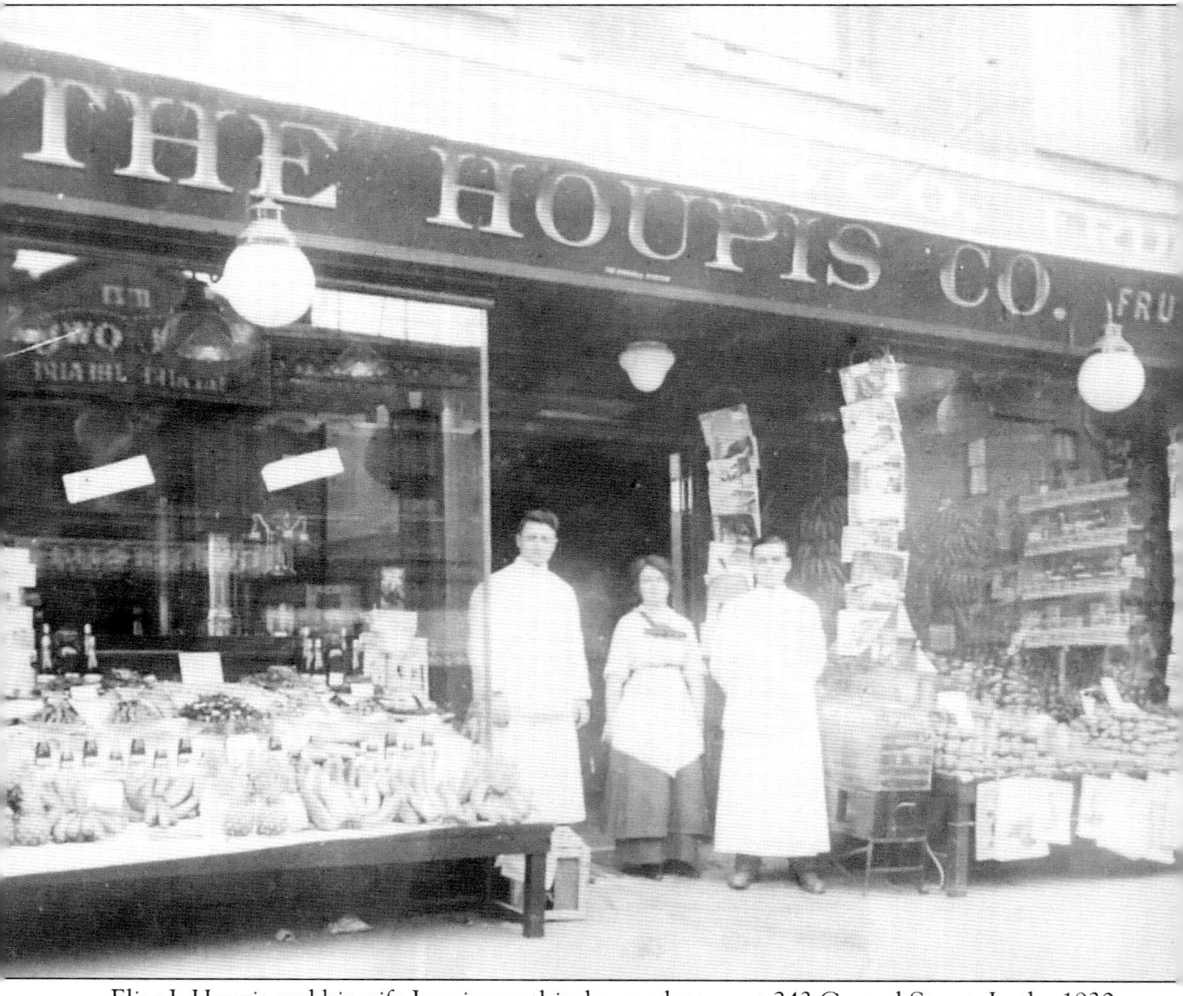

Elias J. Houpis and his wife Jennie ran this dry goods store at 243 Central Street. In the 1930s, the same family had a dry goods store at 404 Market Street. We know this is the Central Street store and can also date the photo within seven years because we can see the marquee of the Owl Theater reflected in the window. The Owl Theater was opened on Christmas Day in 1912 and closed on January 18, 1919. (DHS)

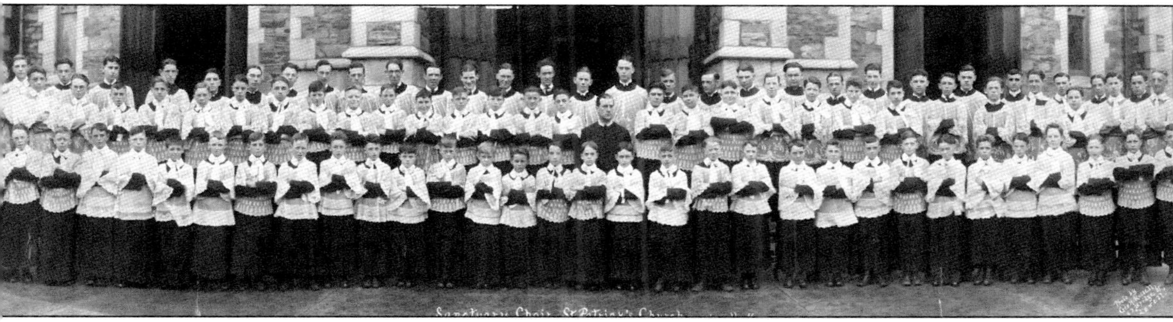

This is a photograph of the Sanctuary Choir from St. Patrick's Church, June 18, 1922. (JP)

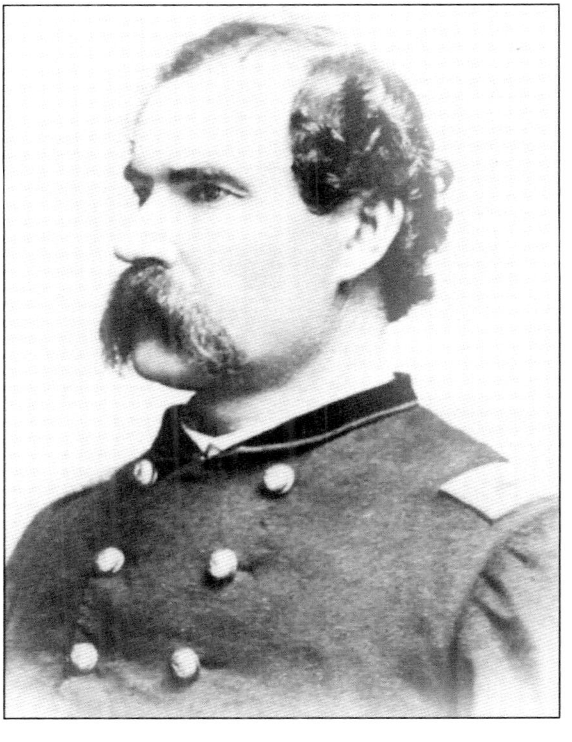

Captain A.B. Follansbee led the Lowell troops into the first encounter of the Civil War as they passed through the streets of Baltimore. Follansbee later became Colonel of the Massachusetts Sixth Regiment.

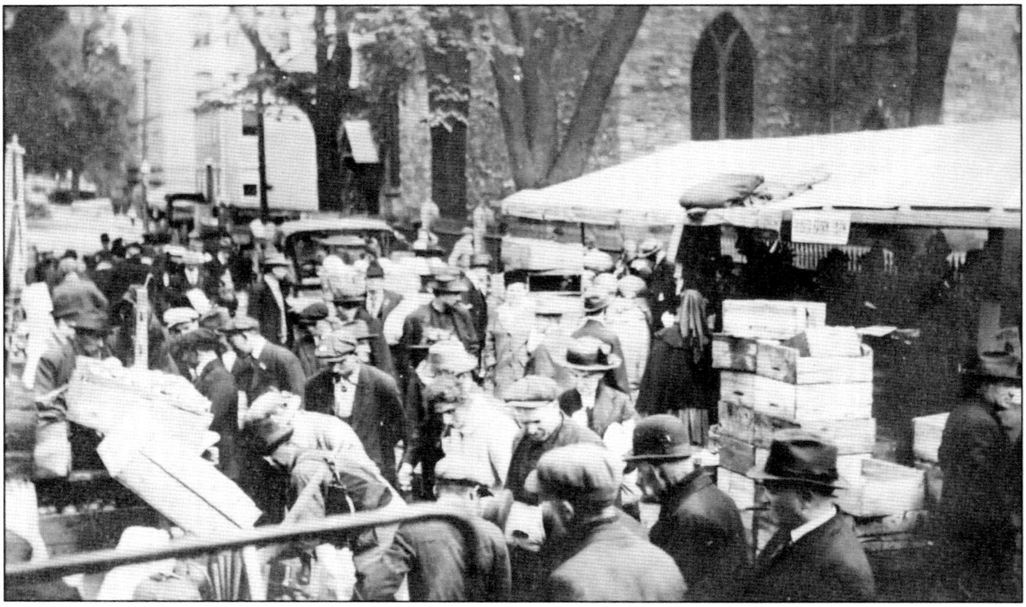

In this *c.* 1915 scene of Market Day in Lucy Larcom Park, Justus Richardson, owner of Beaver Brook Farm in Dracut, has a stand on the right. (DHS)

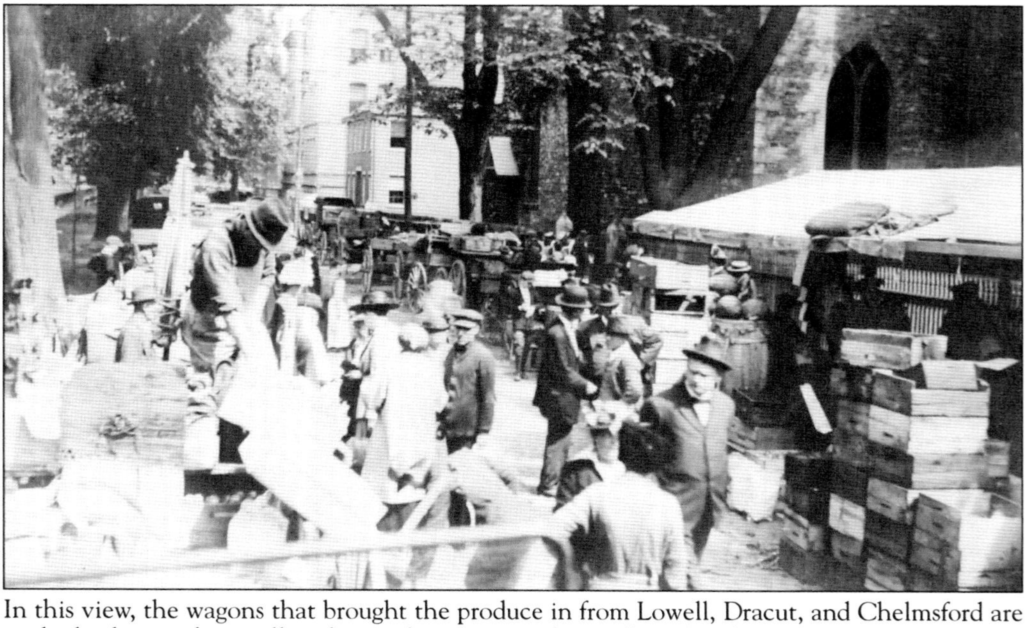

In this view, the wagons that brought the produce in from Lowell, Dracut, and Chelmsford are in the background, as well as the newly constructed Lowell High School. (DHS)

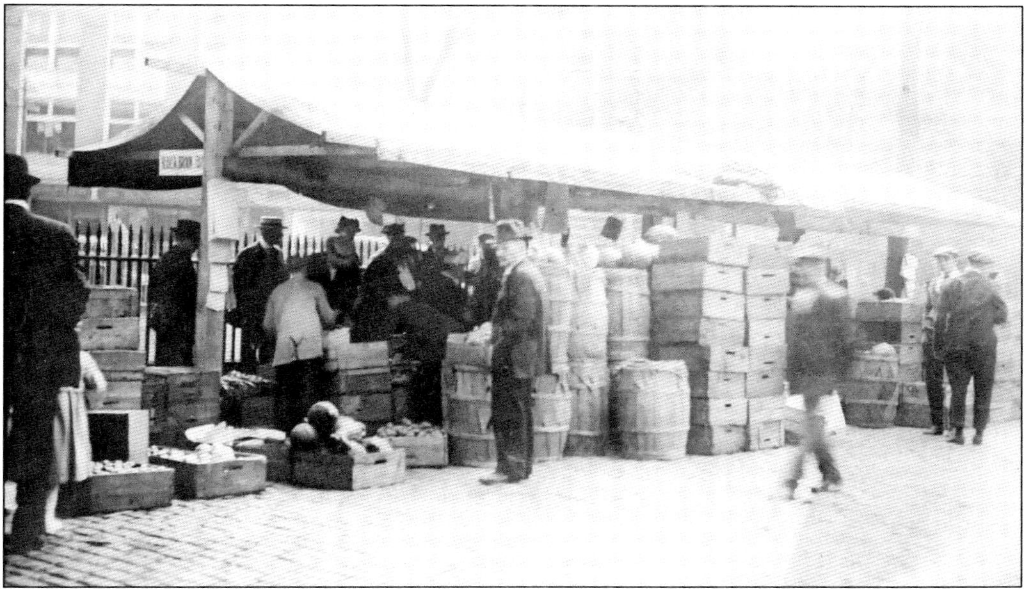

This image provides another view of the *c.* 1928 Farmer's Market at Lucy Larcom Park. The picture is looking towards Merrimack Street. (DHS)

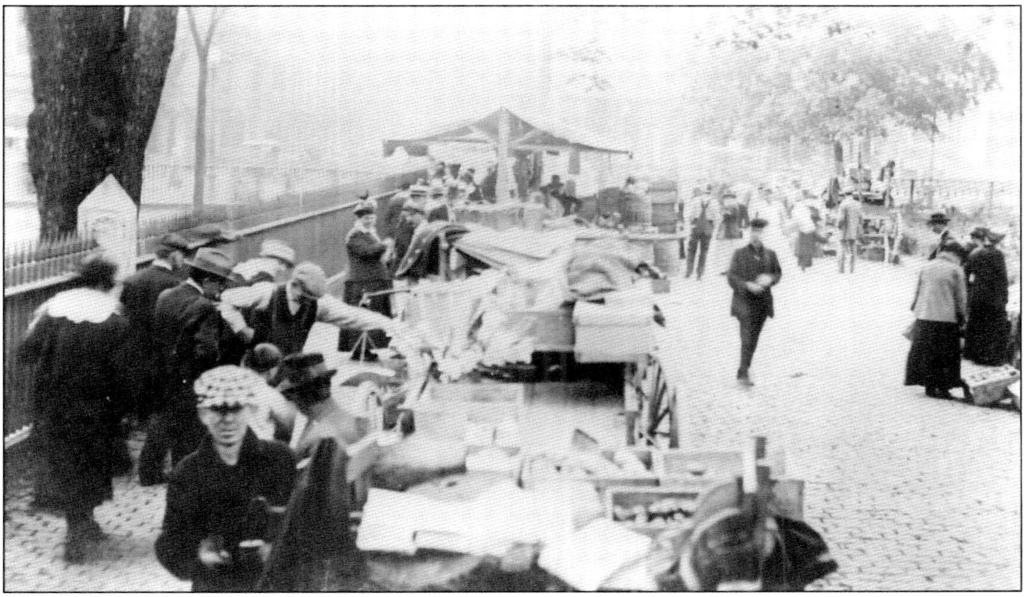

In this 1915 view towards Merrimack Street, we can see that the distinctive crisscross canal railing was the same as it is today. (DHS)

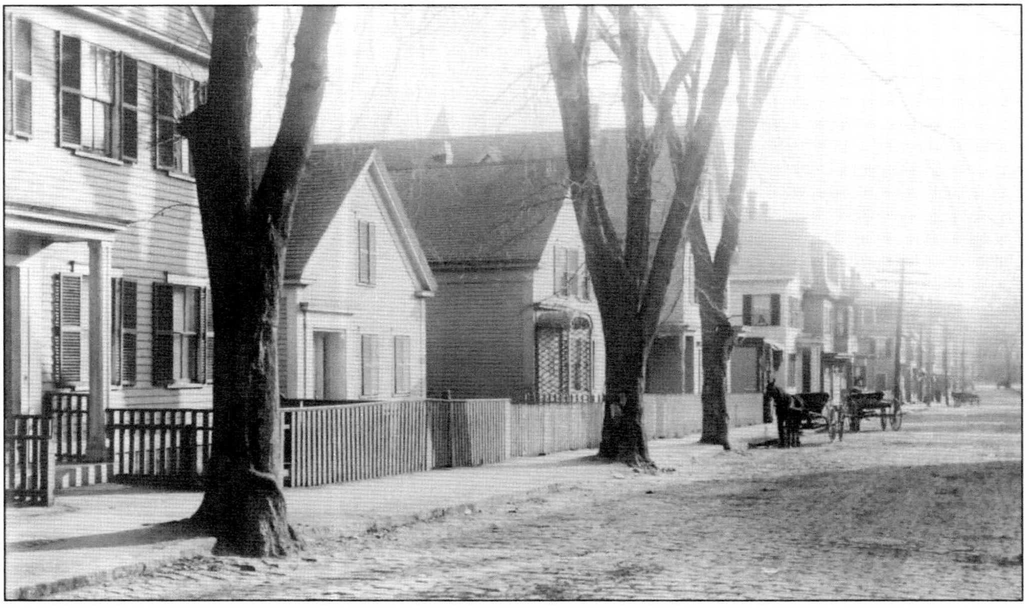

Salem Street was opposite Whitney Street (which no longer exists). Here, we look down toward Market and Adams Streets on December 1, 1904. (AT)

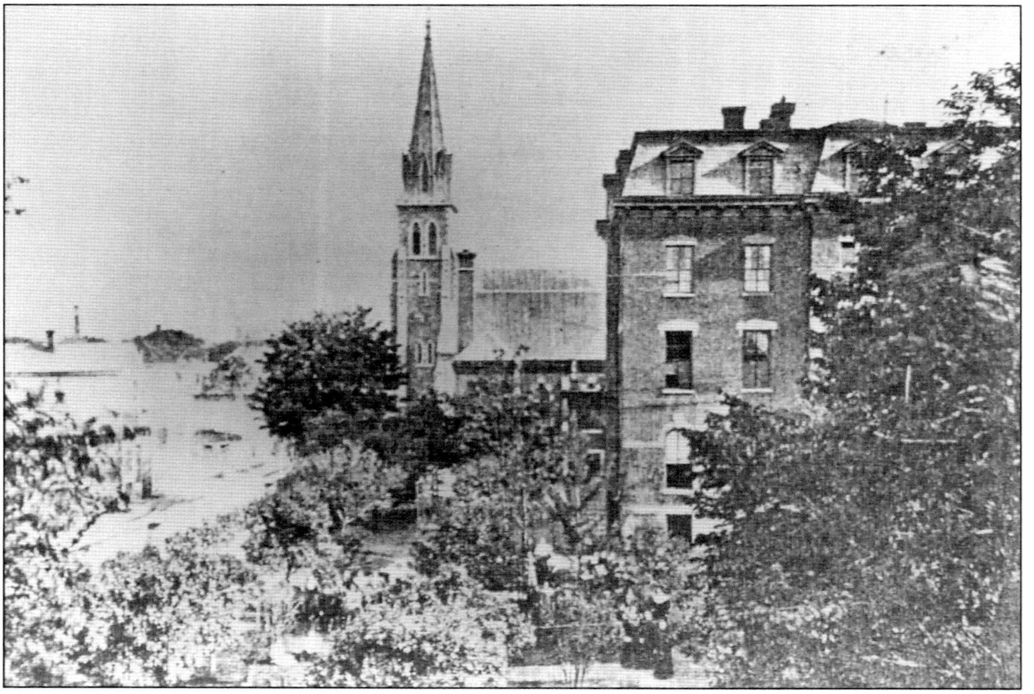

This undated photograph depicts St. Patrick's Church and the gardens around the girls' high school. Close examination shows a small group of Notre Dame nuns in the foreground. (JP)

Two

Their City

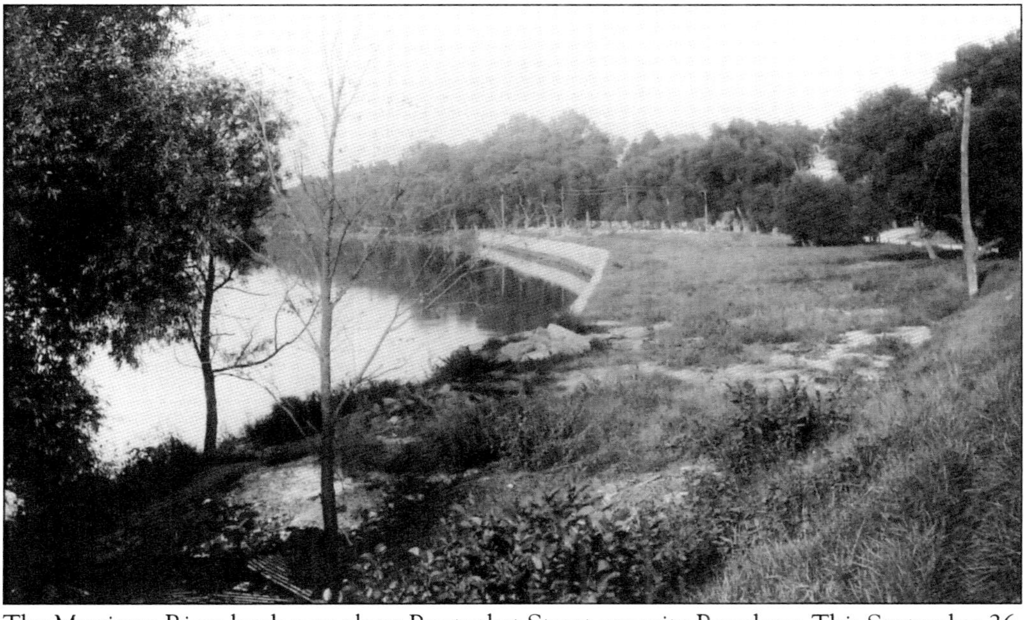

The Merrimac River bank runs along Pawtucket Street opposite Broadway. This September 26, 1912 photograph looks east. (AT)

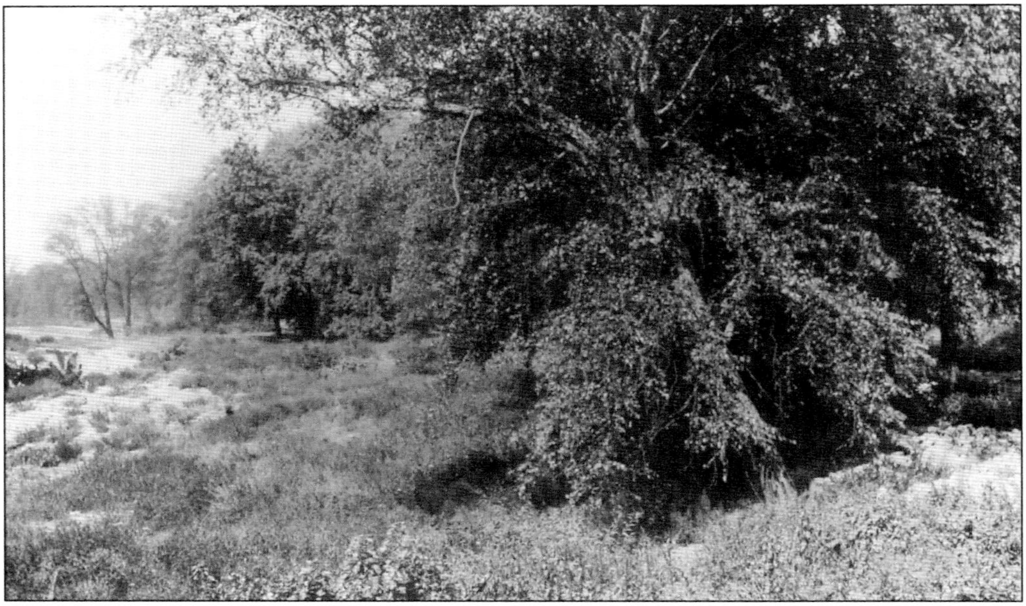

This photograph was taken from the north side of Aiken Street looking northeast on September 26, 1912, at 10:27 am. (AT)

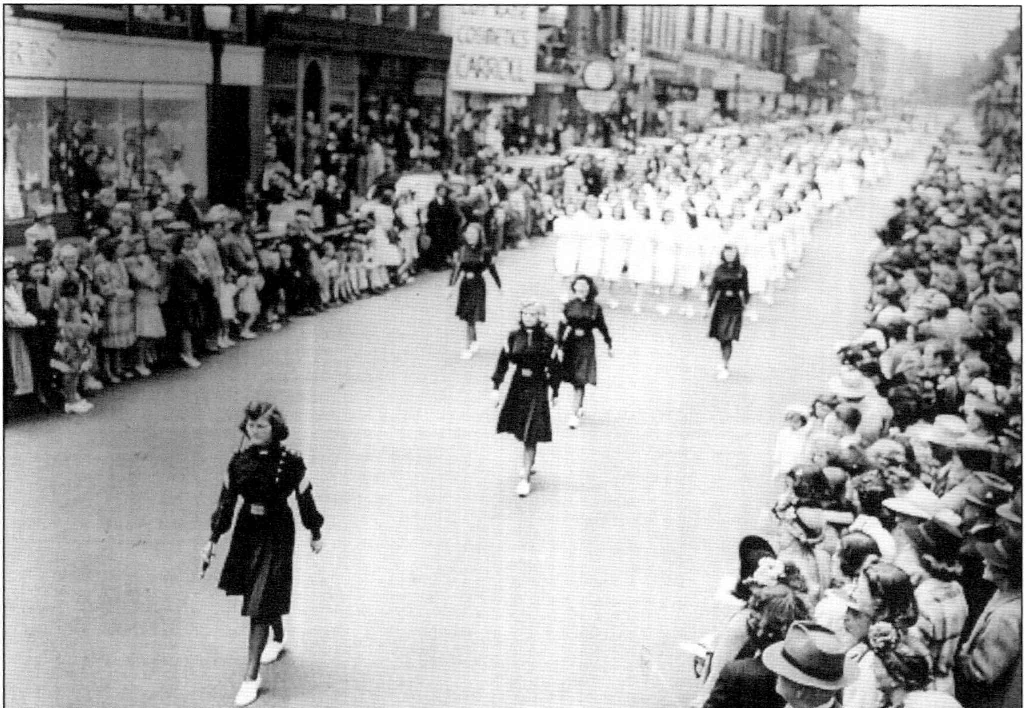

Girl officers from Lowell High School march down Merrimack Street en route to May Day exercises at the South Common. (PF)

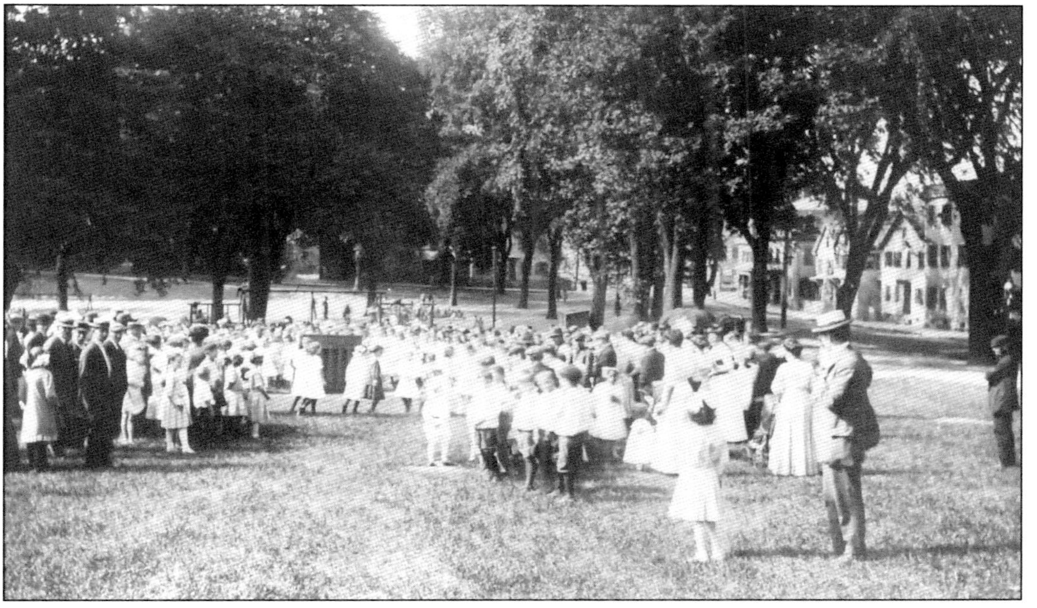

Girls are dancing on the South Common in this 1912 photograph. Notice the piano brought out to the field for the occasion. (AT)

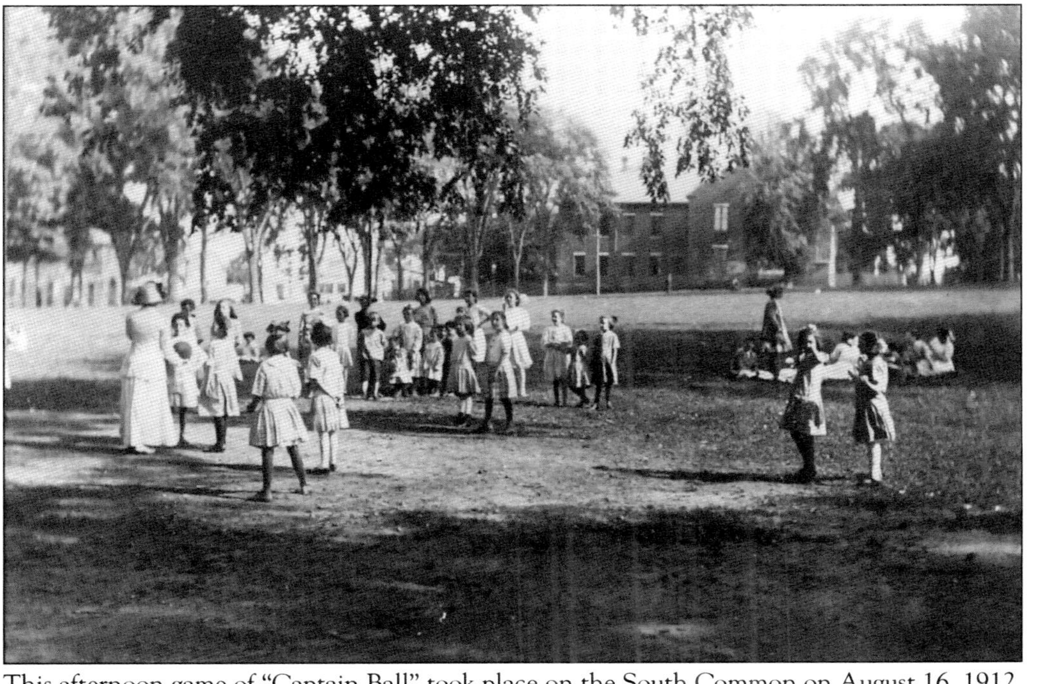

This afternoon game of "Captain Ball" took place on the South Common on August 16, 1912, at 3:21 pm. (AT)

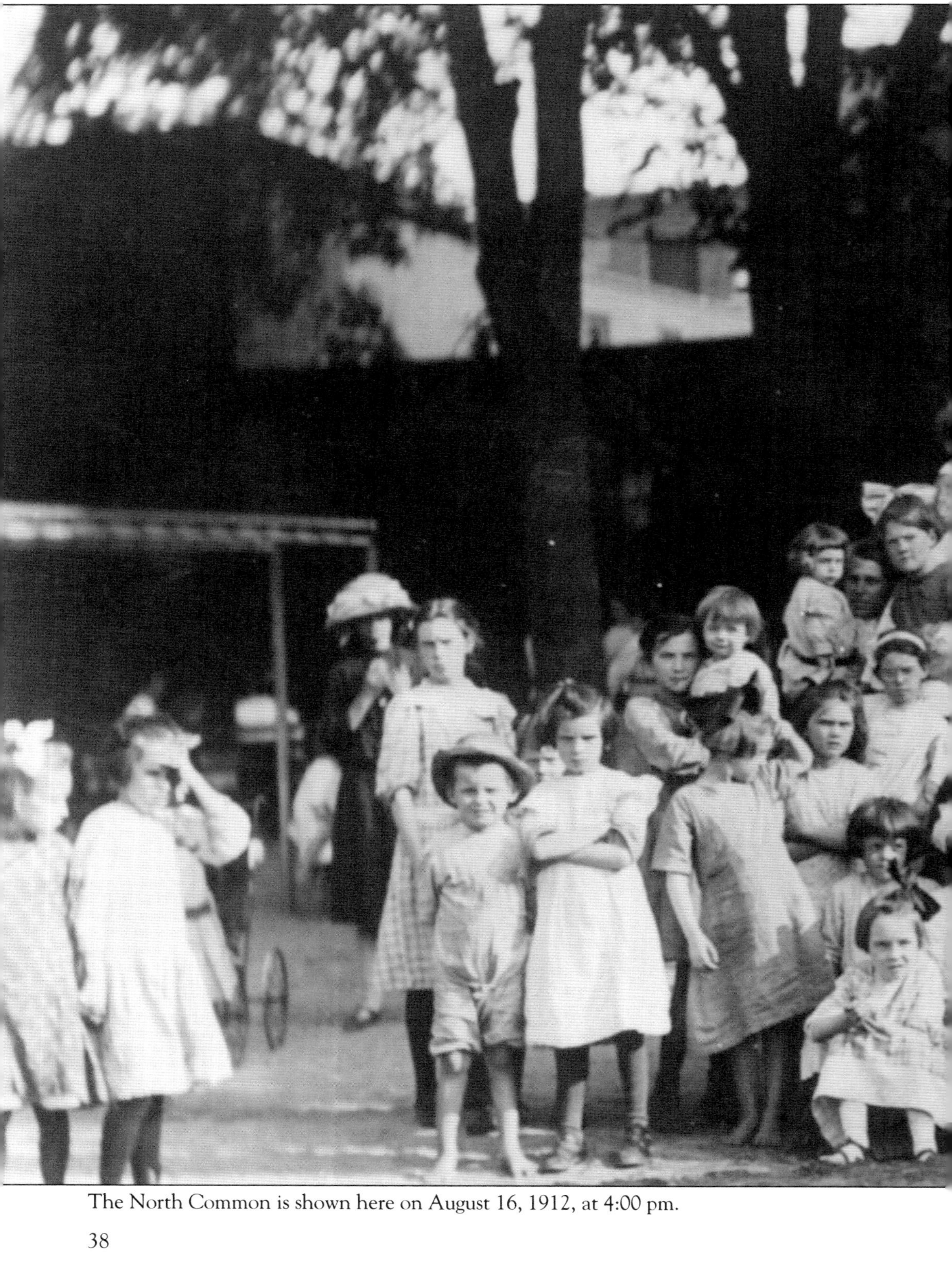

The North Common is shown here on August 16, 1912, at 4:00 pm.

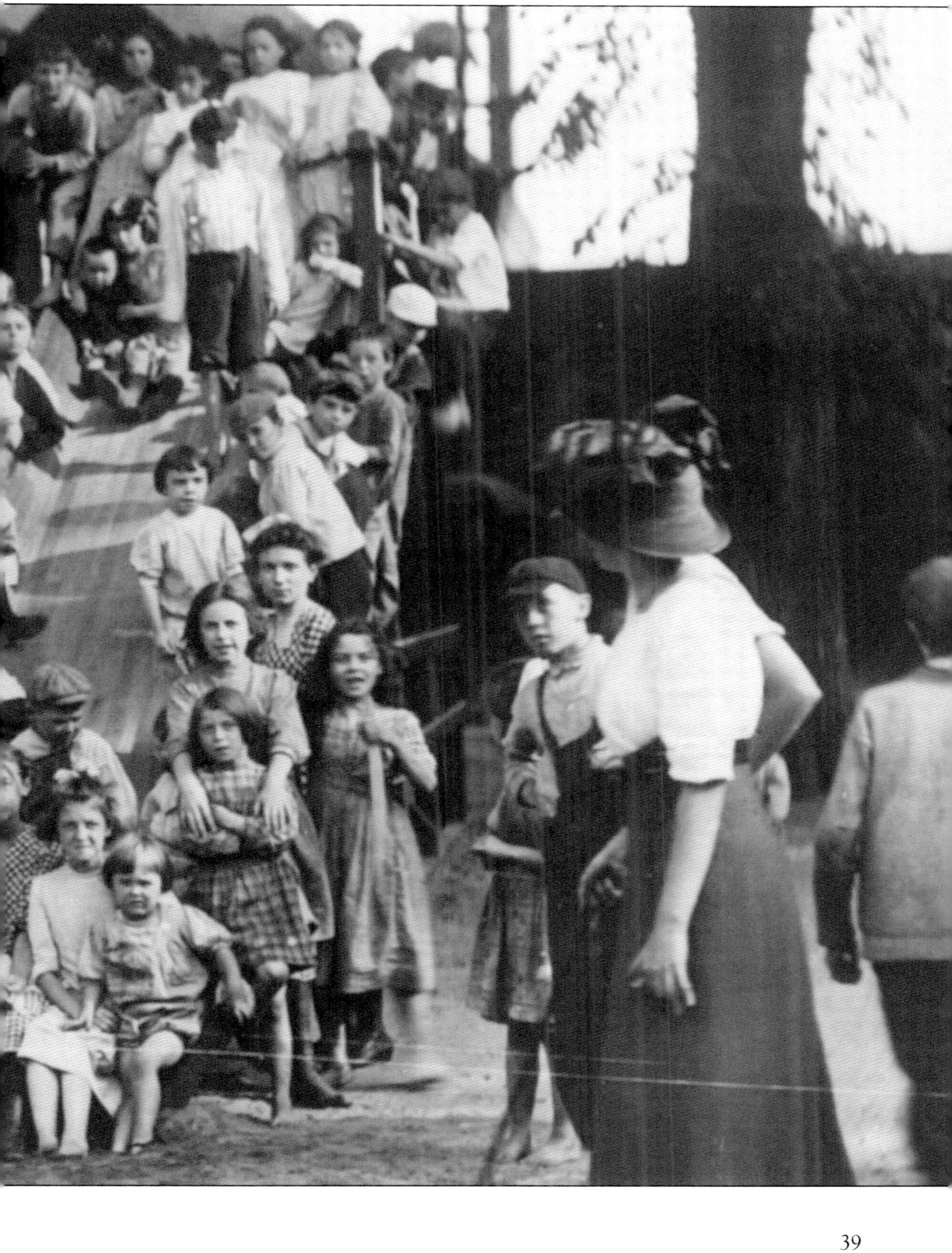

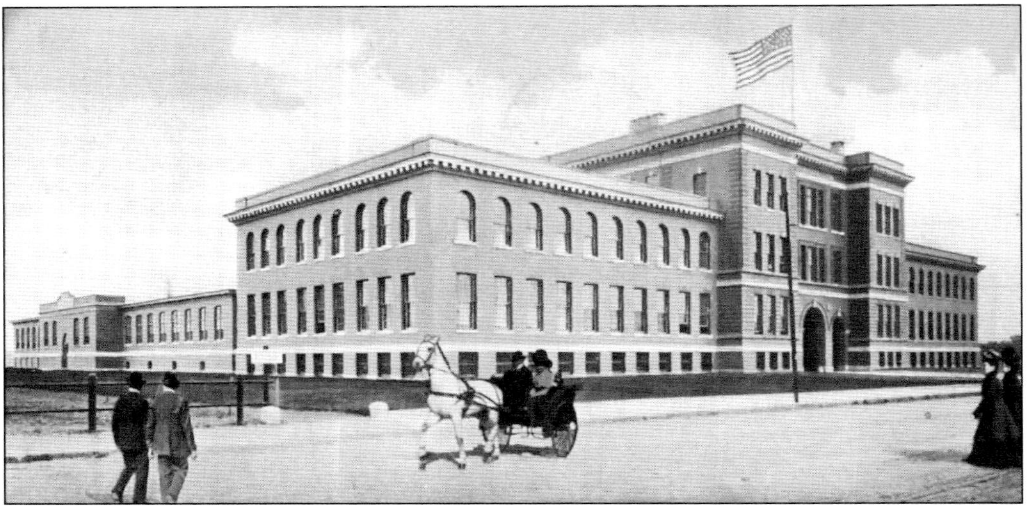

UMass Lowell, originally the Lowell Textile School, was founded in 1896. Southwick Hall, which faces the roadway, was named for a Quaker family killed by Puritans in the late 1600s. This postcard view was taken in 1916. (CP)

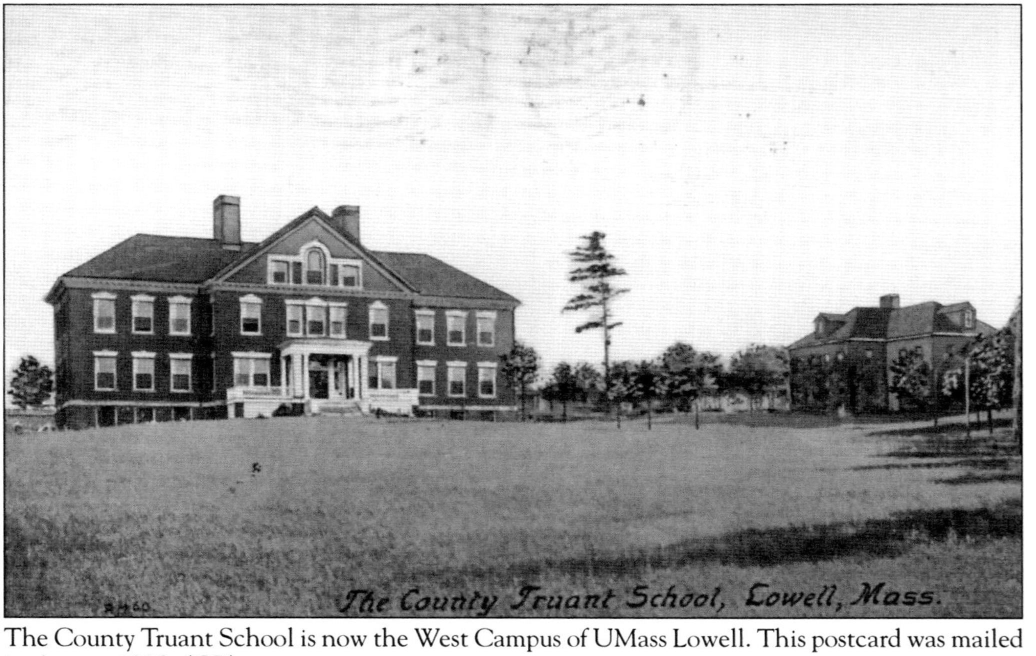

The County Truant School is now the West Campus of UMass Lowell. This postcard was mailed in August 1913. (CP)

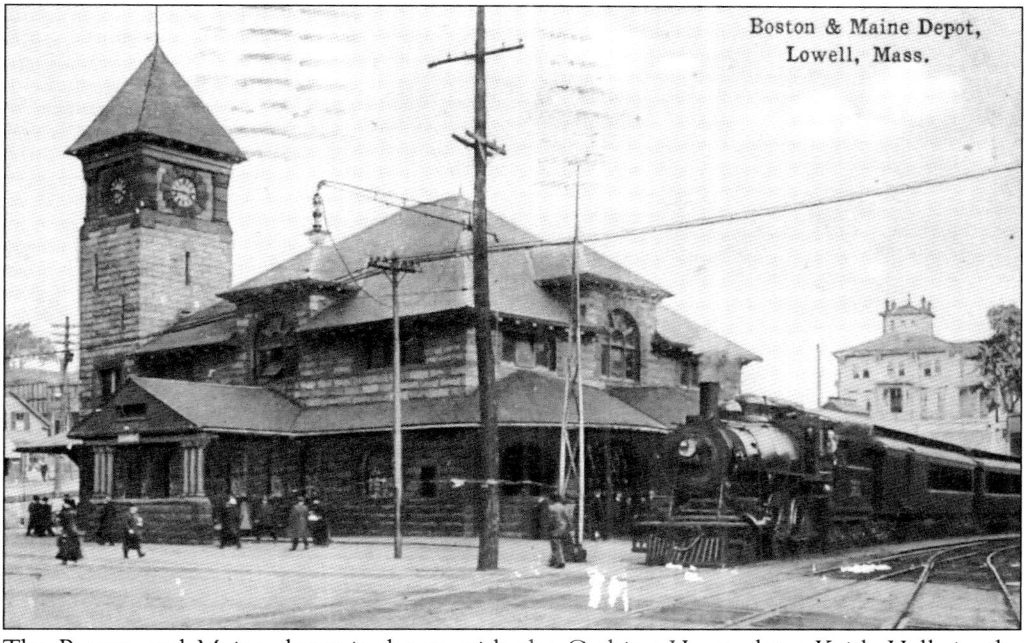

The Boston and Maine depot is shown with the Cushing House, later Keith Hall, in the background of this postcard. (CP)

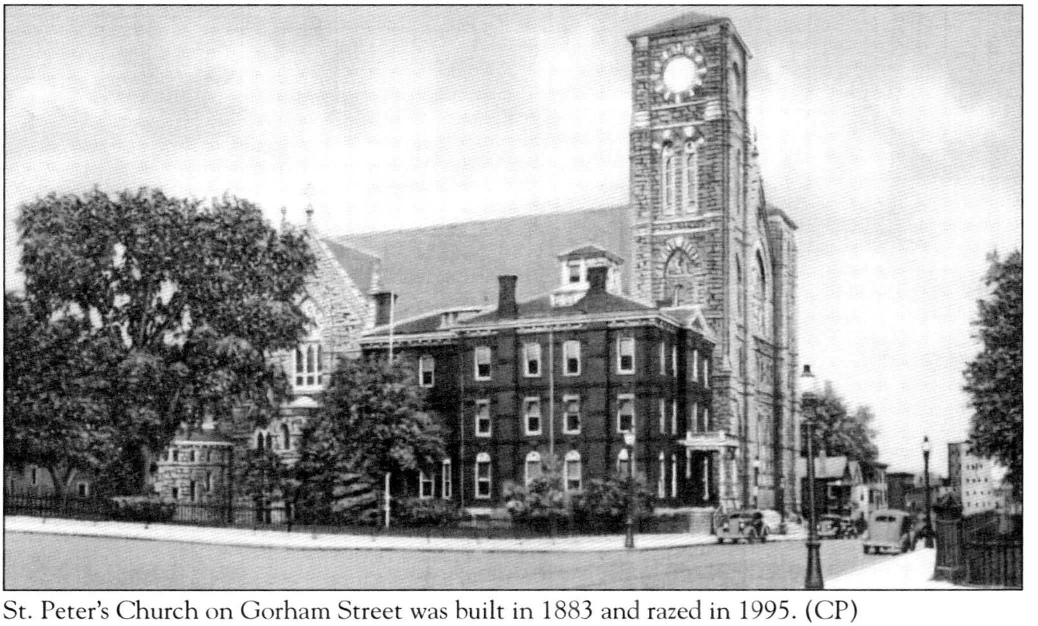

St. Peter's Church on Gorham Street was built in 1883 and razed in 1995. (CP)

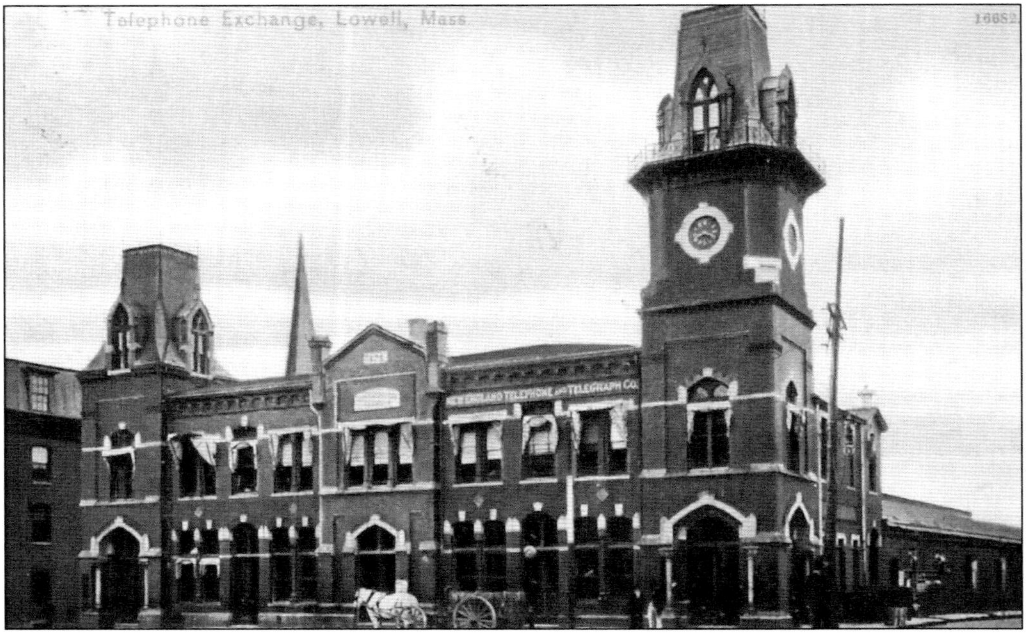

The Lowell Telephone Exchange, formerly the Boston and Maine Railway depot, is shown here in 1909. Built in 1876, it is presently being restored. (DHS)

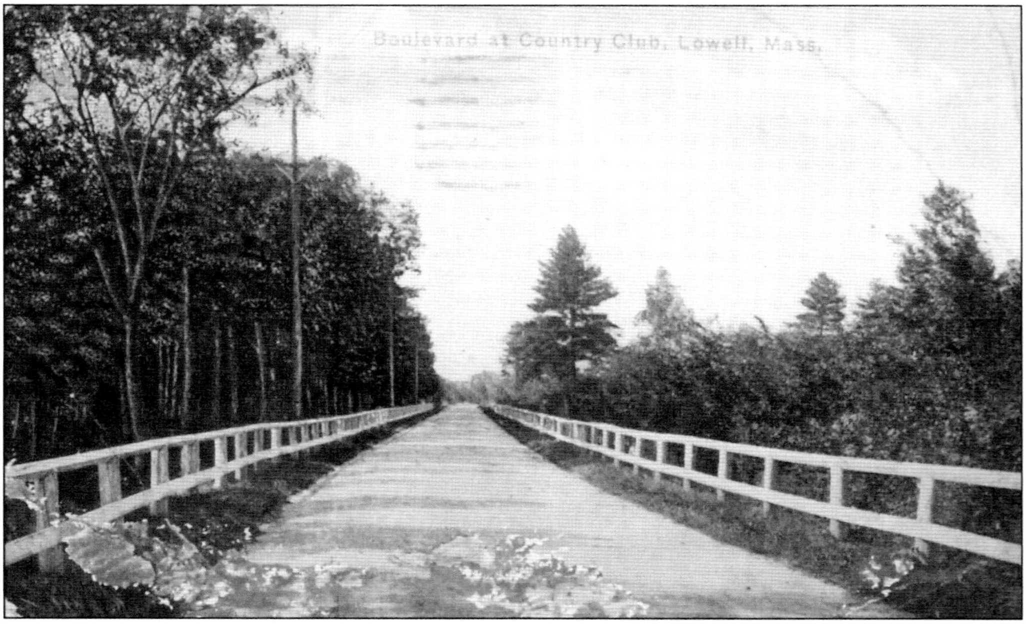

This view looks north up the Pawtucket Boulevard in 1911. (CP)

An exterior view of St. Peter's Church is depicted in this 1920 postcard. (CP)

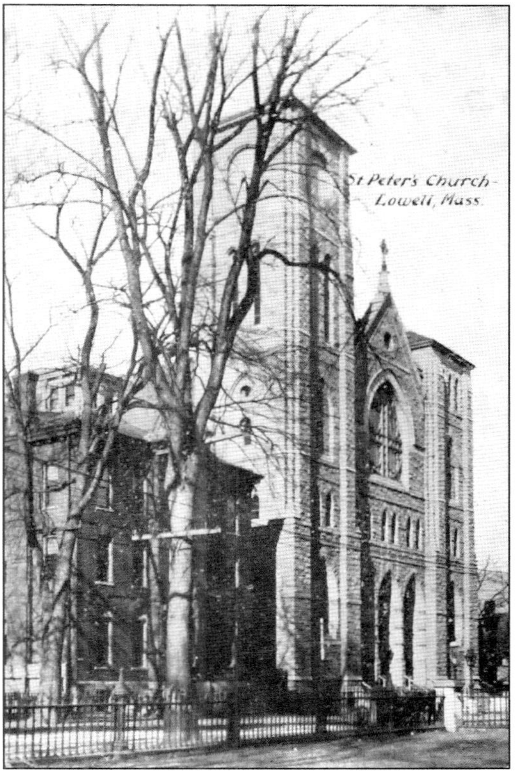

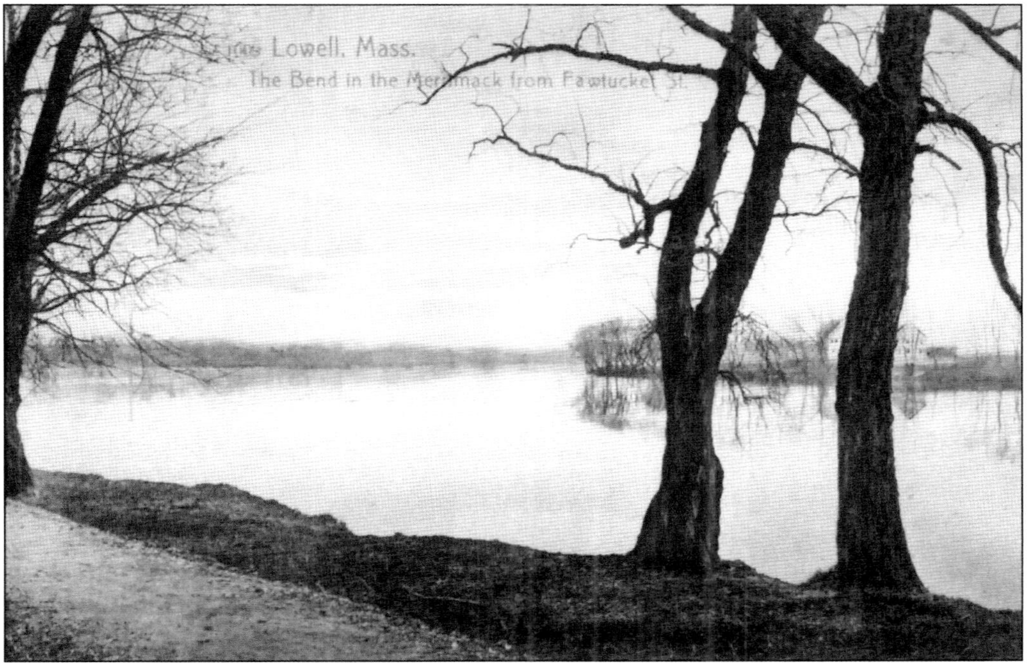

The bend in the Merrimac is seen looking northerly from Pawtucket Street at the present location of Sheehy Park. (CP)

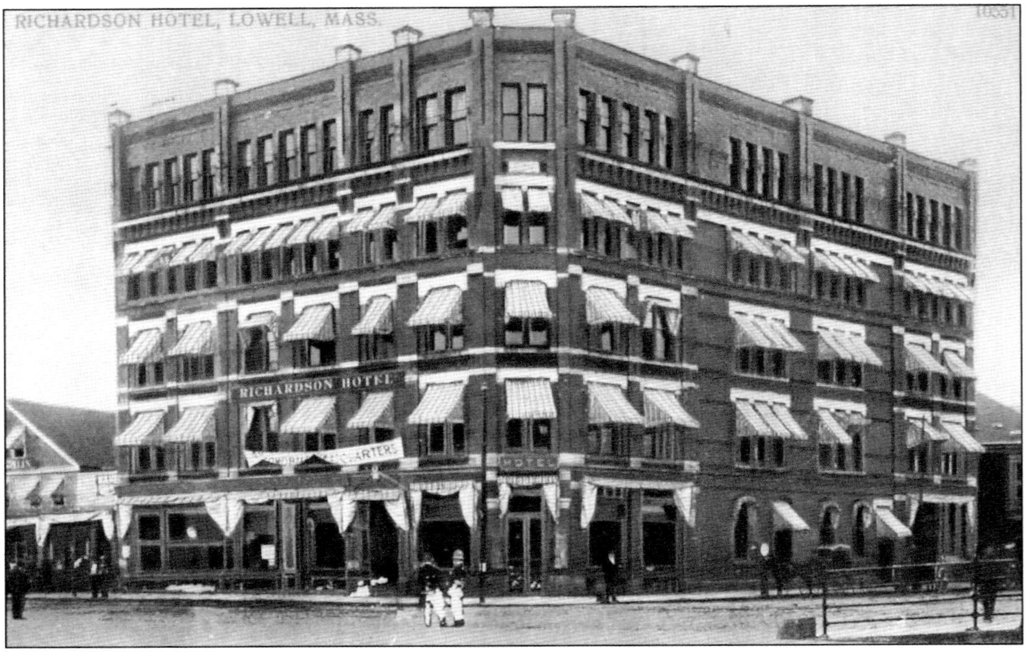

The Richardson Hotel, built in 1879, was across from the depot on Middlesex and Thorndike Streets and is pictured here in 1909. It was later known as the Merrimac Hotel. The Mirror Lounge was a well-known feature of the hotel. A photograph on page 117 depicts the hotel after a fire. (CP)

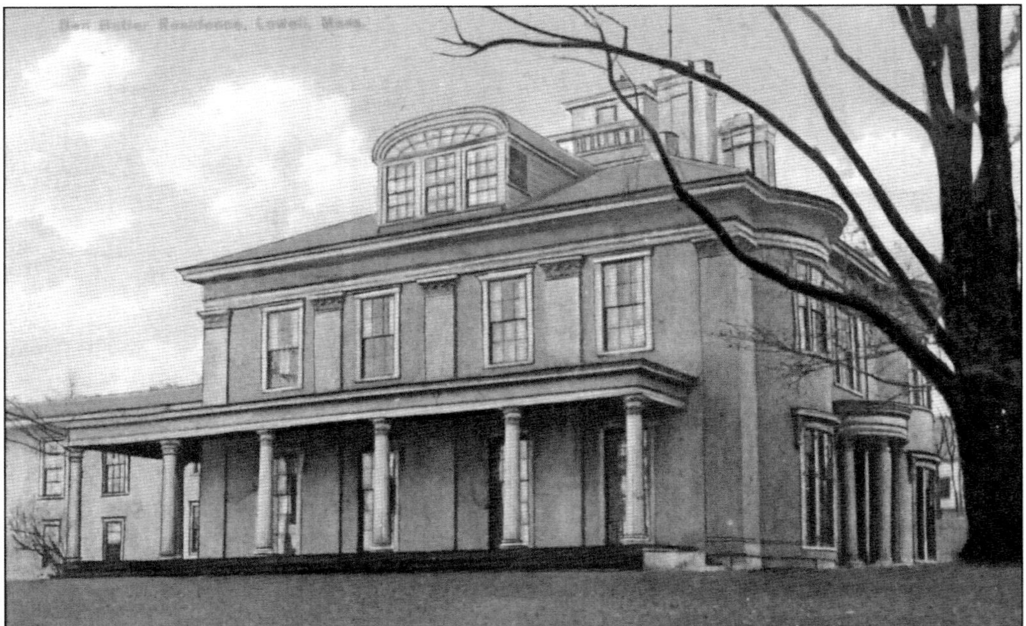

Benjamin Butler's stately home on Andover Street was razed in the late 1970s. (CP)

Fred's Country Store was located at 1717 Middlesex Street and is shown here in 1960. As advertised, it sold "Hot Bread—Homemade Pastries—delicatessen Varieties—Books and Magazines—Coca-Cola—and other soft drinks. Hard to find Kitchen/Pantry utensils. Unground Aromatic Coffee. Homemade pies are our specialty." (CP)

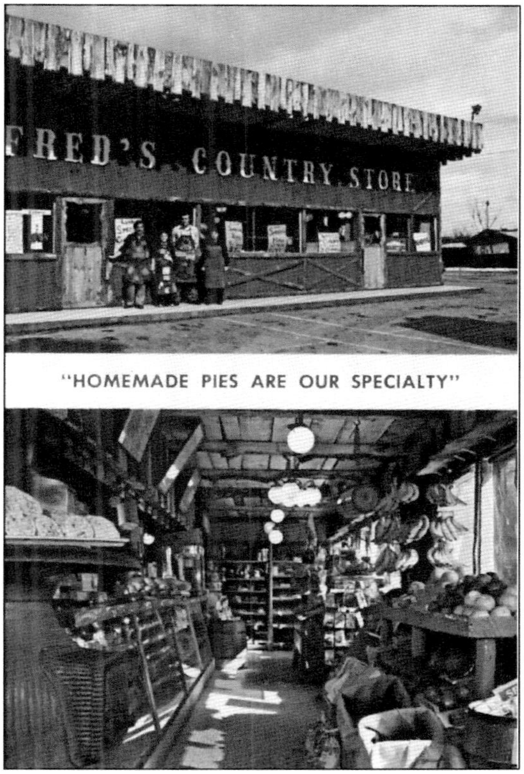

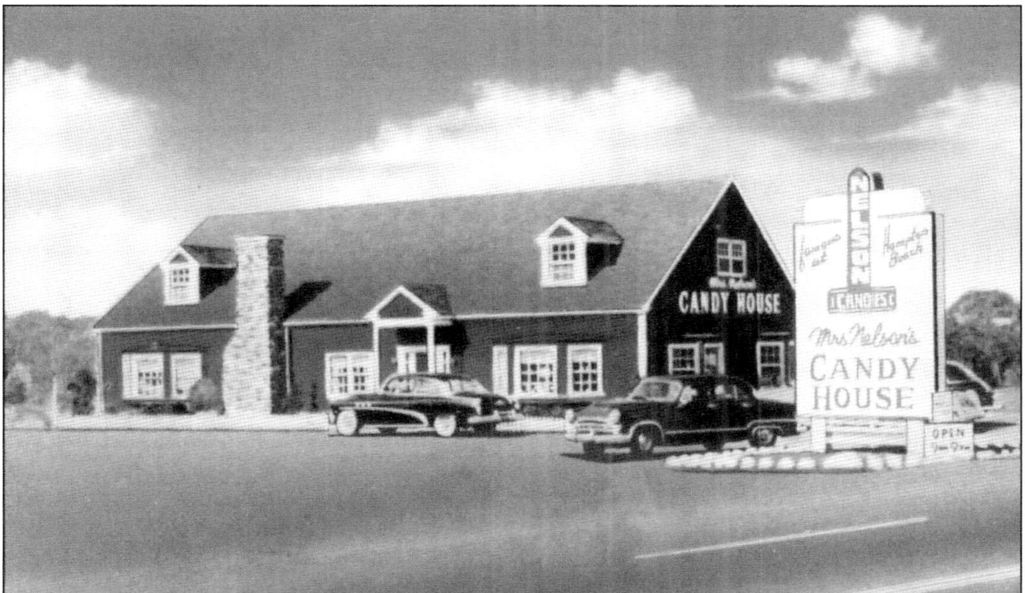

Mrs. Nelson's Candy House is located over the Chelmsford line a bit, but Lowellians know the spot well, as they do Skip's Restaurant, situated a short distance further up Chelmsford Street. (CP)

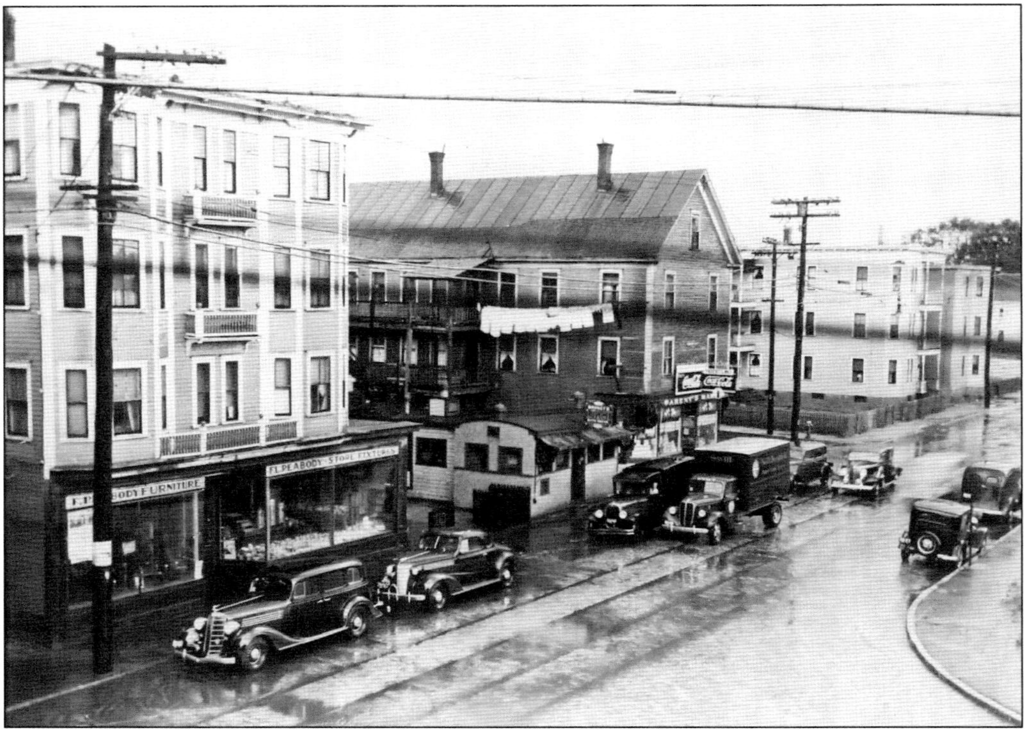

This 1938 image looks down on Brunet's Diner, later the Cameo Diner, on Lakeview Avenue between Ennell Street and Aiken Avenue. (DHS)

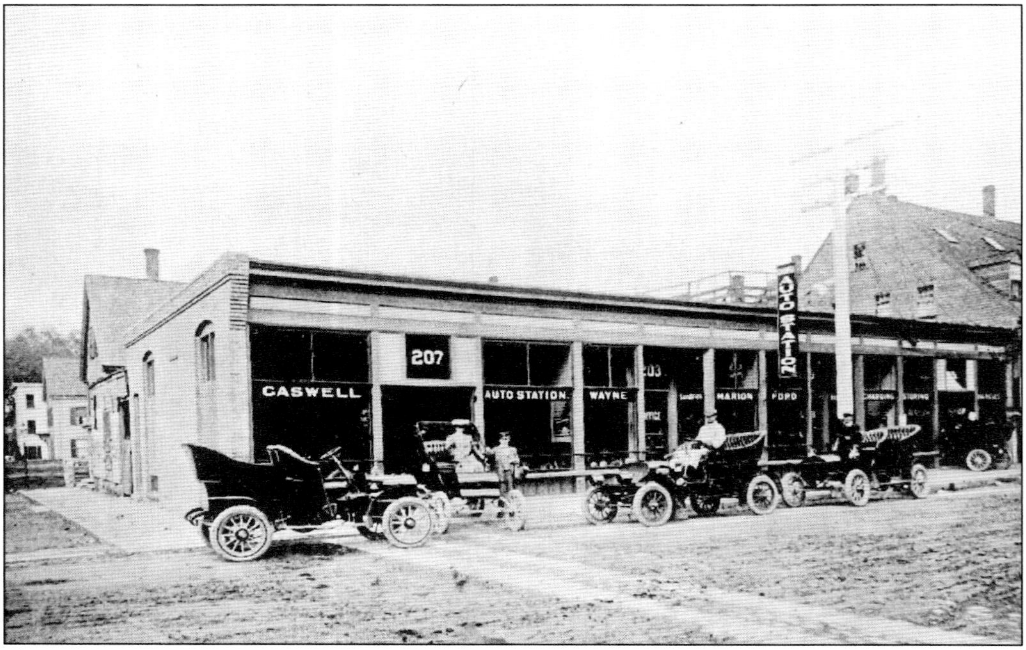

The Caswell Automotive Station was located on 207 Moody Street in 1905. (DHS)

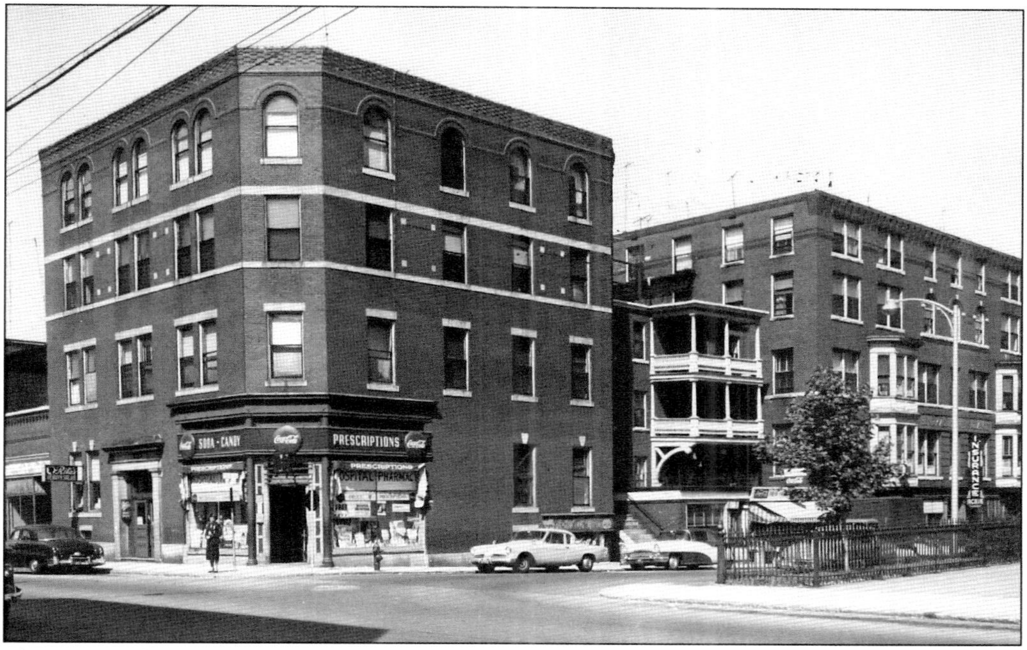

The Hospital Pharmacy was on the corner of Aiken and Merrimack Streets, and Rita's Beauty Salon was in the same building. In the Achin Building was Henry Achin's insurance company, and sandwiched in between was the Hand R Fruit Company. Across Aiken Street, the St. Jean d'Arc Church still stands (see page 73). This corner is now a parking lot. This photograph and the next were taken by George Poirier. (DHS)

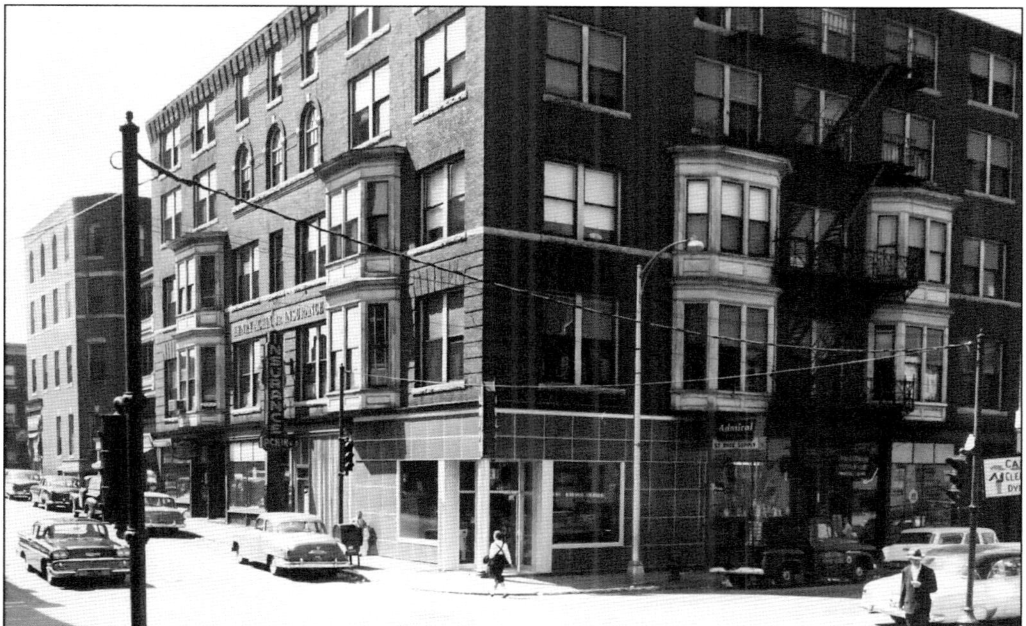

On the other end of the block at Aiken and Moody Streets was Charron's Drug Store. Both of these photographs date back to 1961. (DHS)

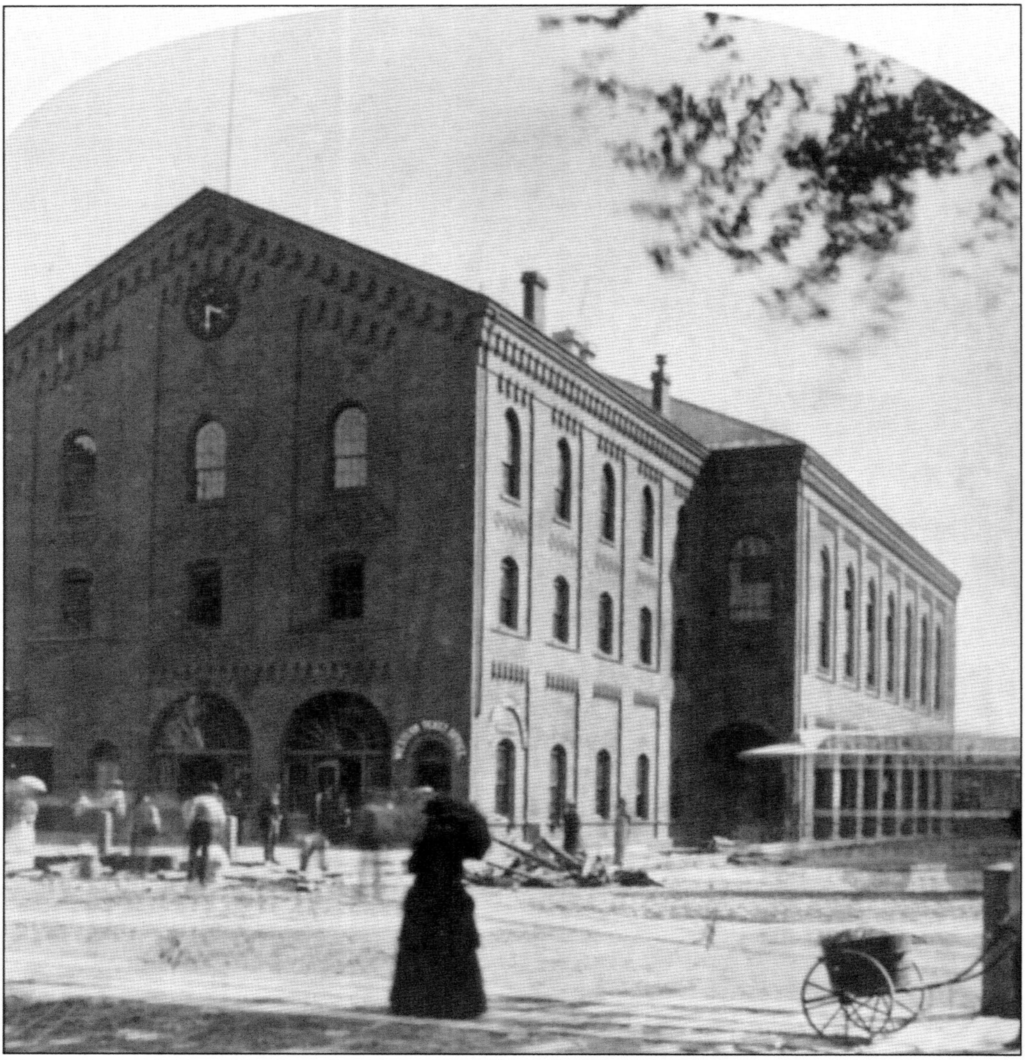

Huntington Hall on the corner of Merrimack and Dutton Streets was named for Dr. Elisha Huntington, Lowell's frequent mayor (elected in 1839, 1844, 1852, 1858, and 1859). The funeral ceremonies for Luther Ladd and Addison Whitney, the first Lowell victims of the Civil War, were held in Huntington Hall (shown here *c.* 1875). The 6th regiment, Ben Butler's brigade, was the first to reach Baltimore and the first to experience any resistance. When they arrived, the brigade had to pull the railroad cars with horses to the Washington depot on the other side of the city. Riots and shooting ensued and the two boys were killed. Until these two boys (age seventeen and twenty-six years old) were killed, Lowell had remained relatively pro-slavery because of its cotton interests. Following word of their deaths, the city became extremely anti-South. Today, on Merrimack Street, a single brick wall with three arches similar to the ones in the photo are in its place.(PF)

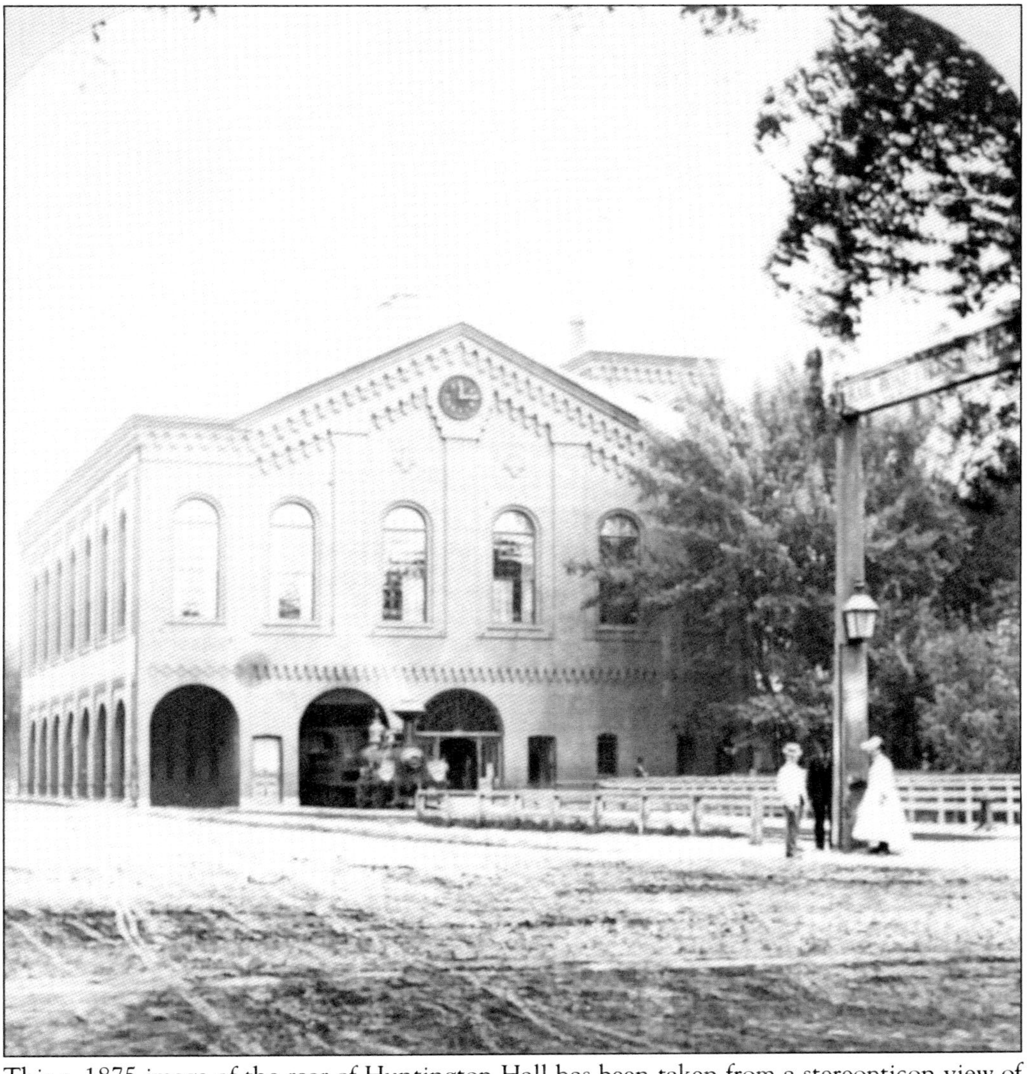

This c. 1875 image of the rear of Huntington Hall has been taken from a stereopticon view of Dutton Street looking towards Merrimack. The building burned to the ground in 1904. (PF)

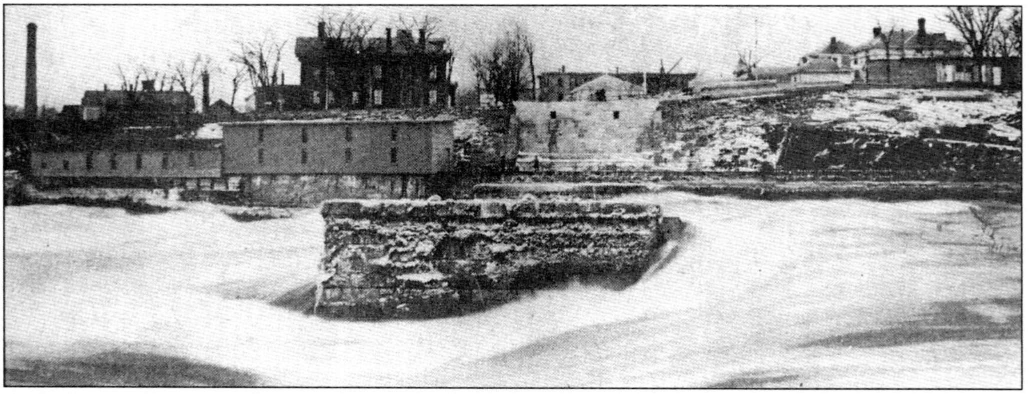

A freshet rushes past the construction of the Moody Street Bridge on March 19, 1897. The bridge opened to traffic later that year. (DHS)

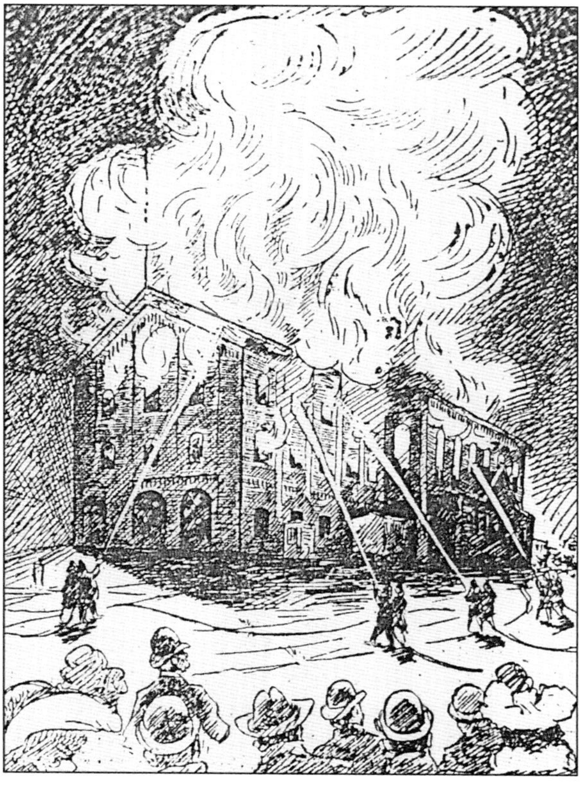

This newspaper drawing depicts the fire that gutted Huntington Hall on November 7, 1904. (DHS)

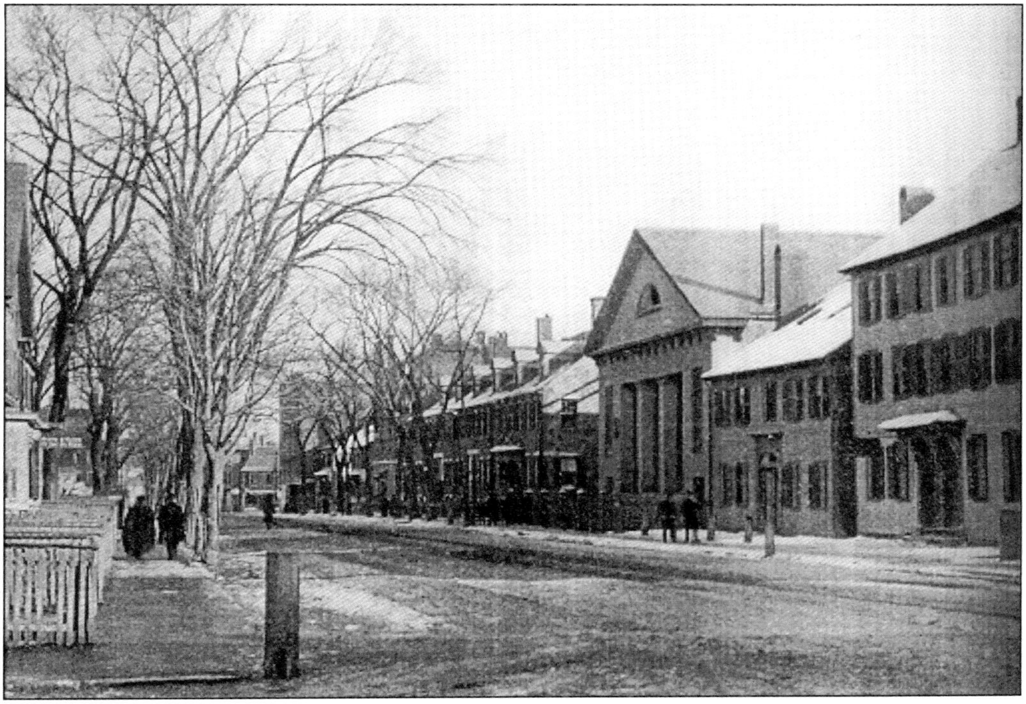

Appleton Street, in the 1880s, was far more residential than in later years. (SP)

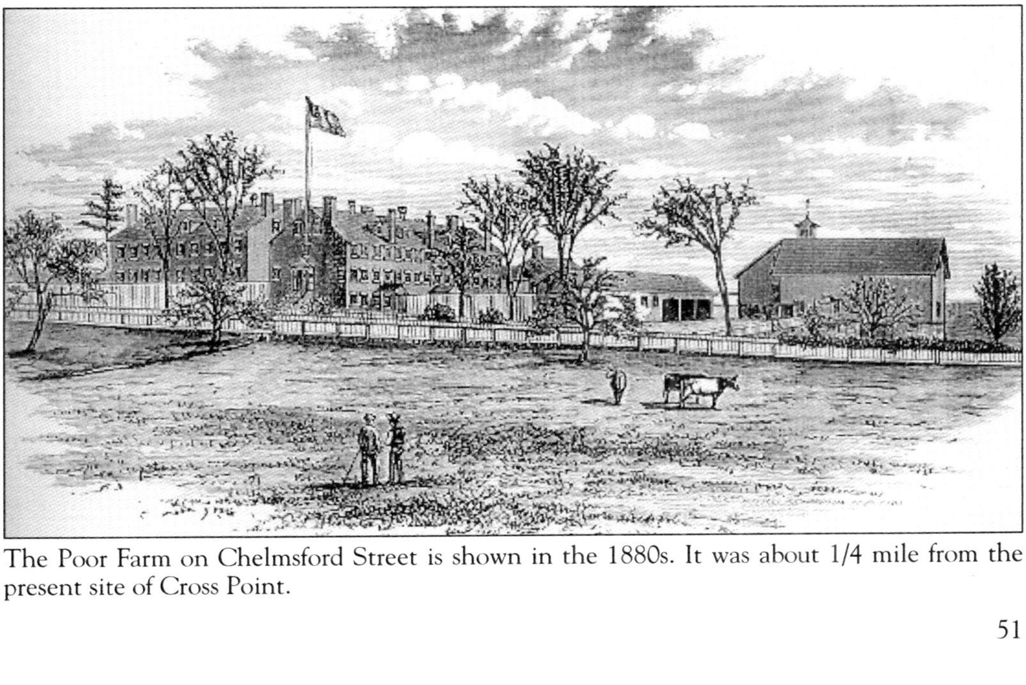

The Poor Farm on Chelmsford Street is shown in the 1880s. It was about 1/4 mile from the present site of Cross Point.

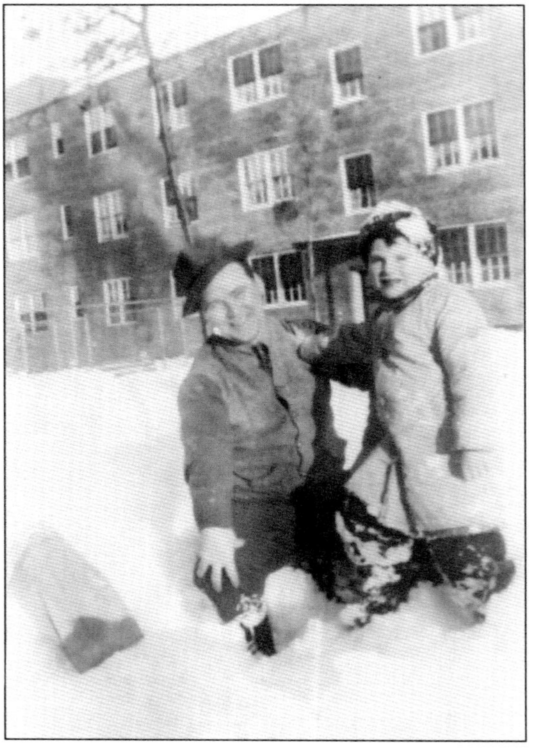

The author and his father are pictured at the Lowell Housing Project on Market Street in 1943. (JP)

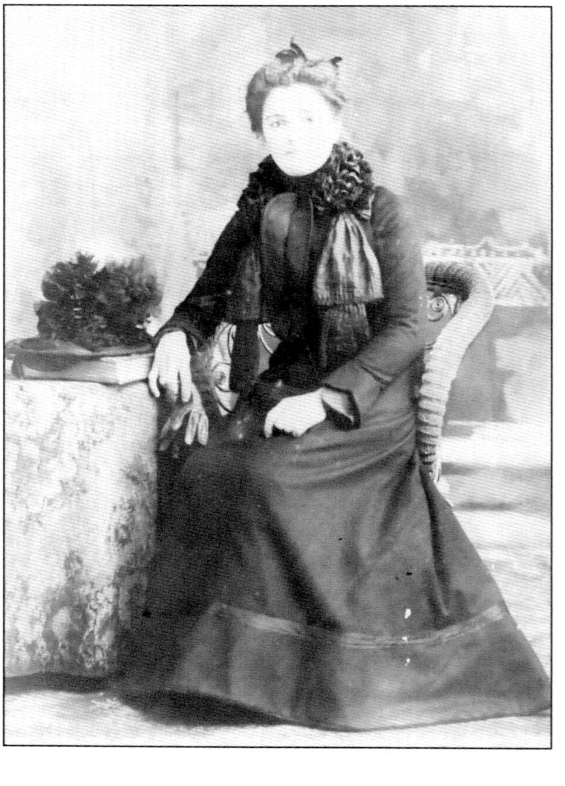

This photograph was taken at Duclos studios in Lowell before the turn of the century. (JP)

The residence depicted in the 1850s photograph on page 21 belonged to this early resident of Lowell. Joshua Merrill became a schoolteacher in "a neat little building at the corner of Middlesex and Eliot Streets." This was the first schoolhouse in Lowell. He had seventy-five students, age three to twenty. In 1828, he earned $28 a month. He composed a large article about Lowell's school, which is recorded in the *Illustrated History of Lowell* (1894). (IHL)

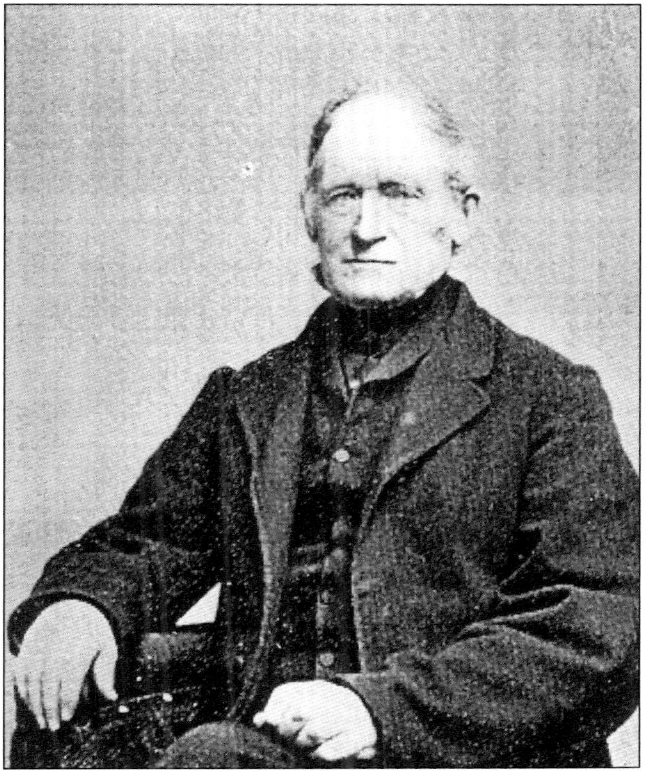

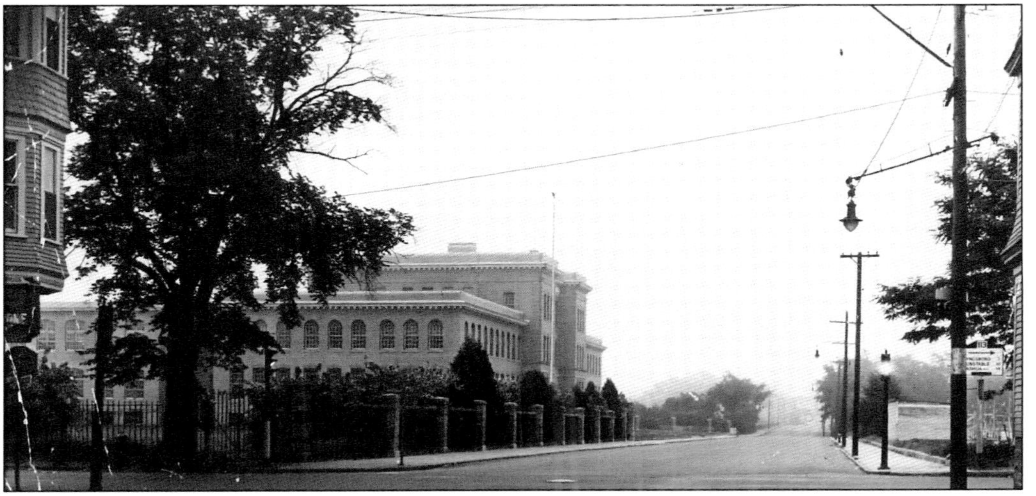

To see Textile Avenue, now University Avenue, fenced in without Cumnock Hall and the library is interesting, but the absence of traffic is remarkable. This photograph is from the 1920s. (DHS)

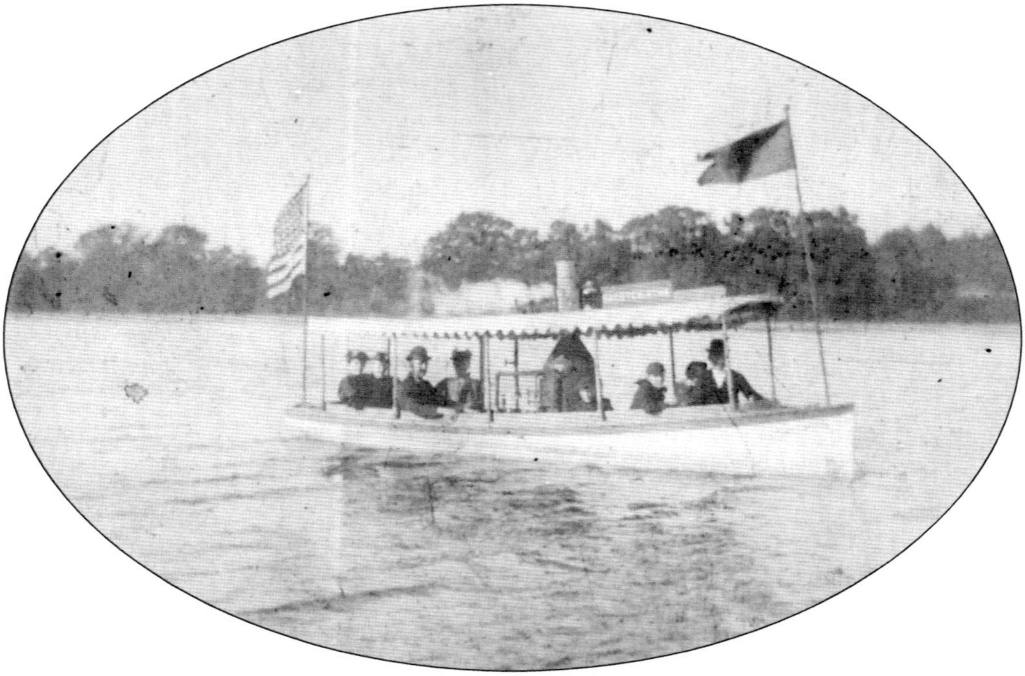

"Beyond Tyng's Island," is pictured here from September 28, 1895. (CP)

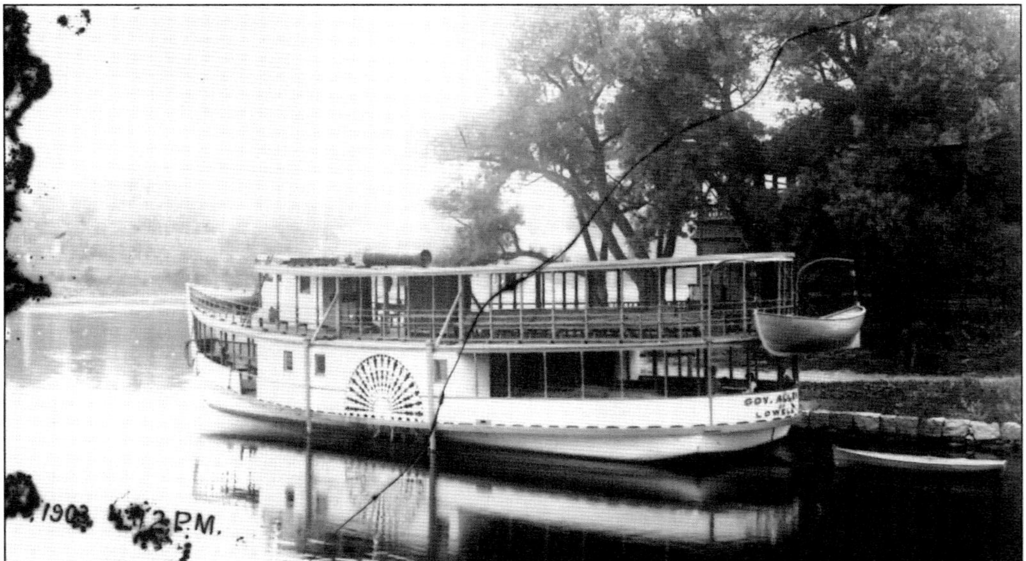

The *Governor Allen* traveled all the way to Nashua. It was named after the first governor of Puerto Rico, who made his residence a bit further upriver; interestingly, the governor lived here even during his office term. The mansion is now in an unused and decaying state on the grounds of UMass Lowell. The boat is docked at the Vesper Boat House (now an apartment building), at the point where the Pawtucket Canal enters the Merrimac. Note the large crack in this 1903 glass plate negative. (JP)

Three

Their River

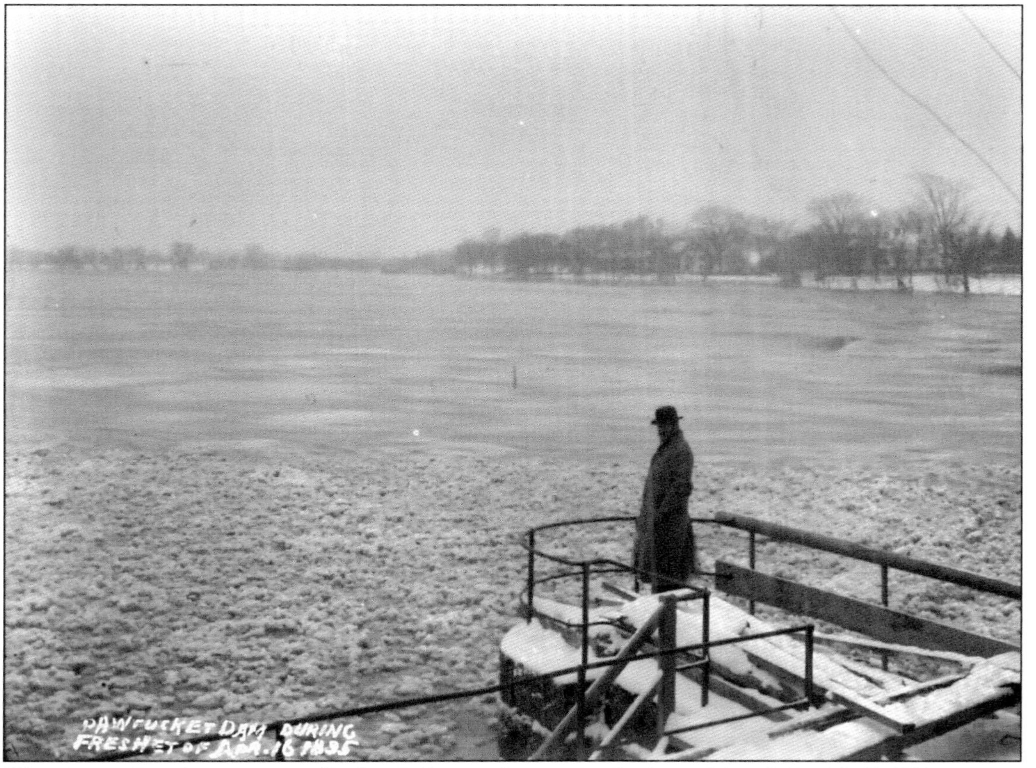

The Pawtucket Dam was totally flooded over during the freshet of April 18, 1895. (JP)

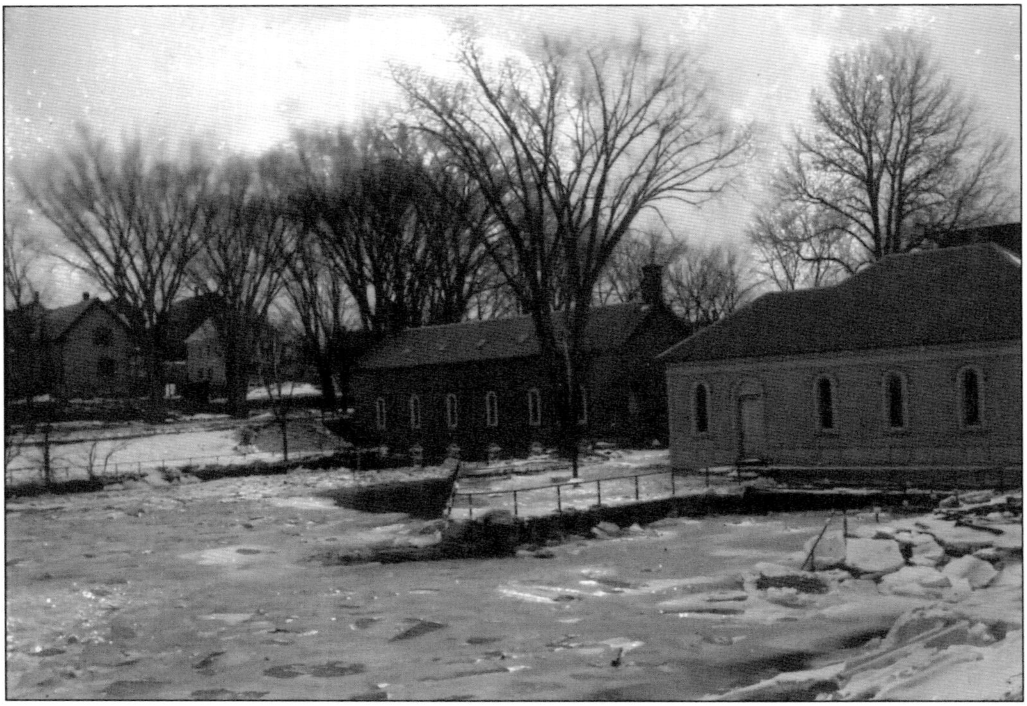

The waters are perilously high during this winter freshet at the Francis Gate. This print was made from an undated glass plate negative. (JP)

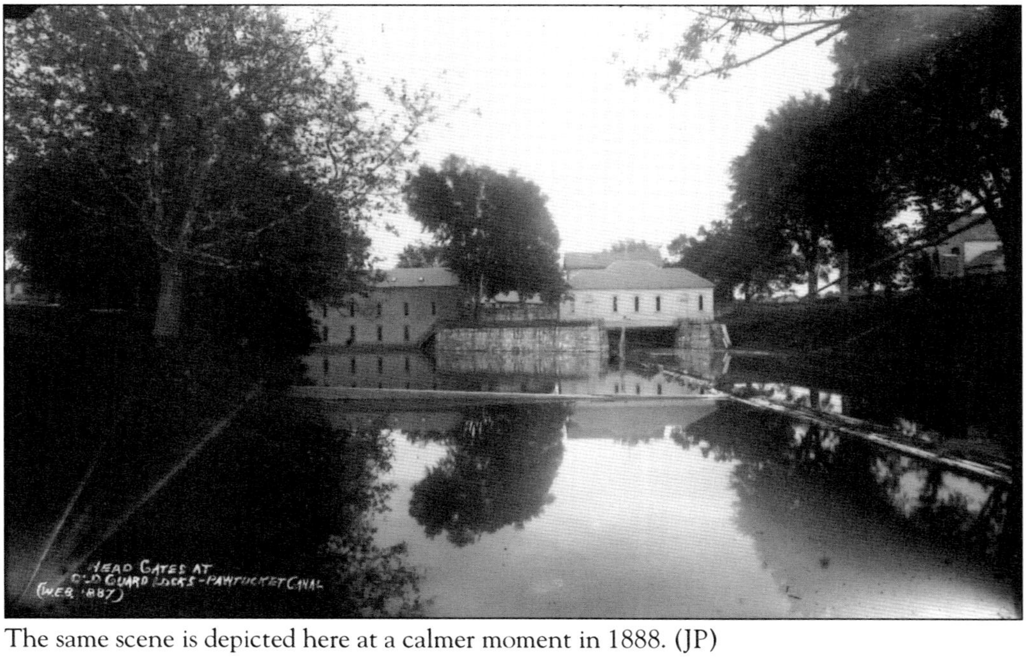

The same scene is depicted here at a calmer moment in 1888. (JP)

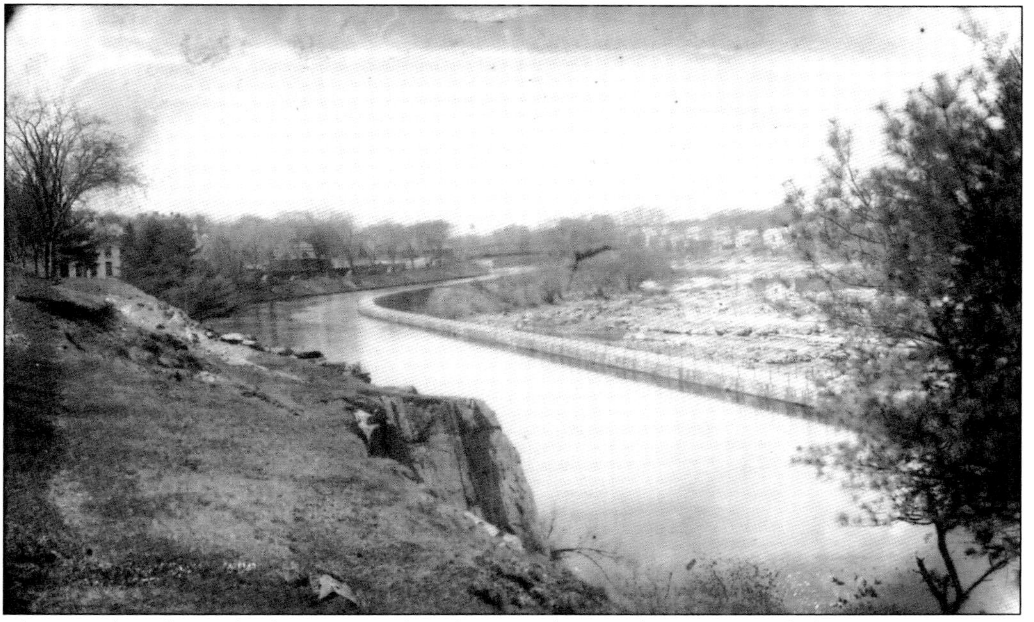

The Canal Walk was built in 1887. This photograph was taken in 1888. (JP)

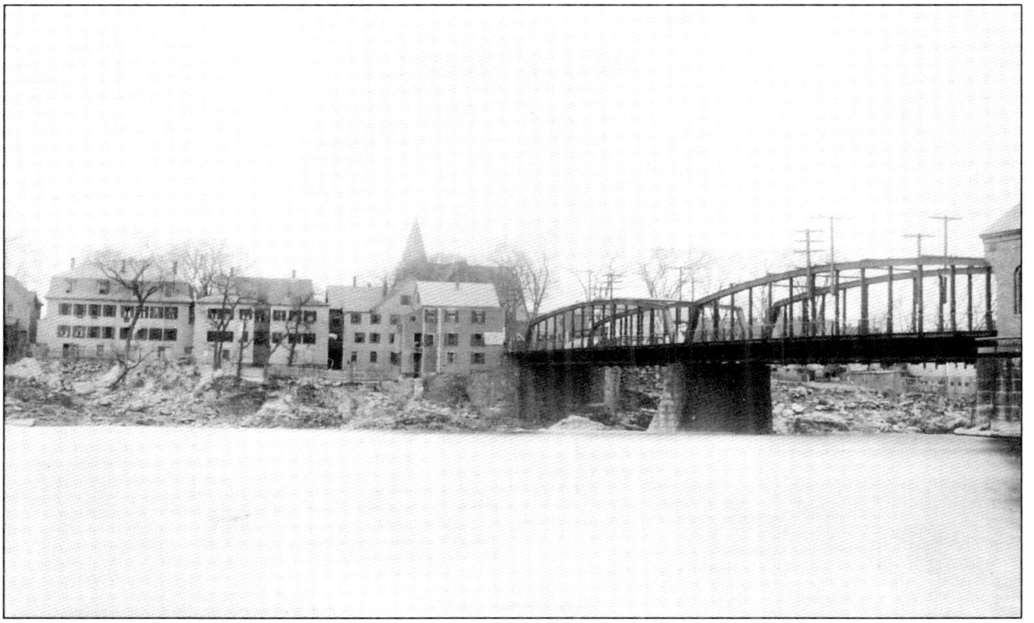

The Pawtucket Bridge, shown here in 1902, was the first bridge across the Merrimac. It was constructed of wood in 1792 by Dracut citizens, mostly under the supervision of Parker Varnum. A toll was charged to cross this bridge until the 1860s. The houses directly on the bank on the Pawtucketville side, long gone, are already in a state of disrepair in this May 3, 1902 photograph. The tower of the First Congressional Church—on the site where Passaconaway had his major domicile until about 1660—is visible in the near distance. (DHS)

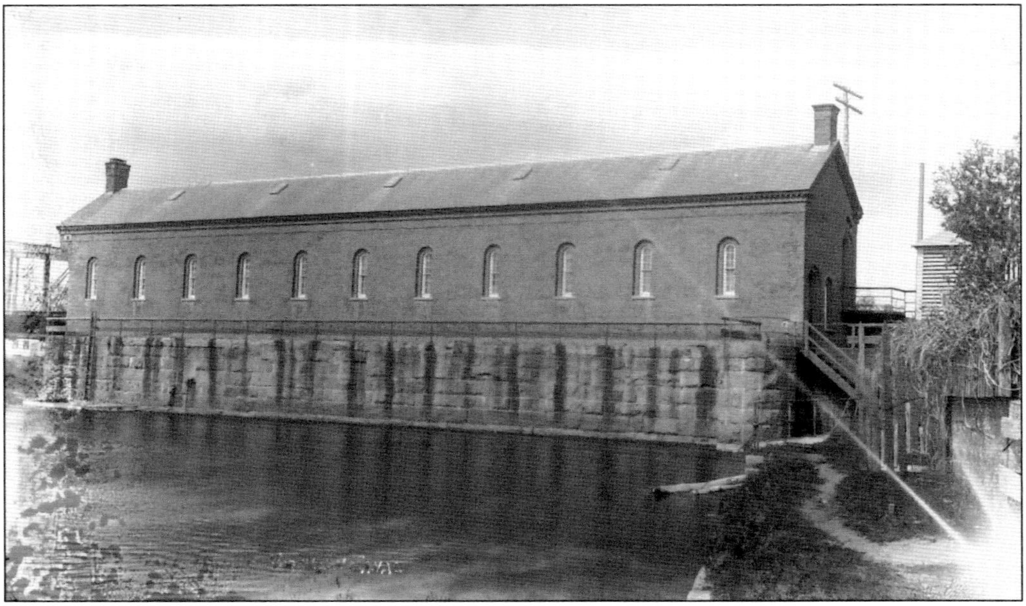

The gatehouse of the northern canal is pictured here *c.*1902. (JP)

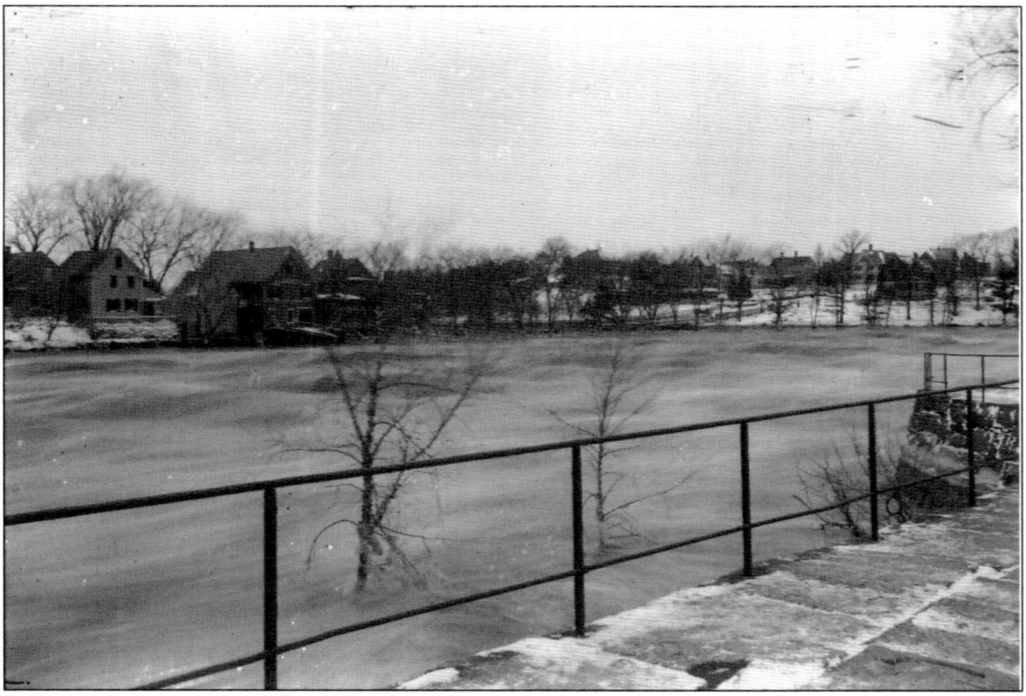

The freshet of April 1895 is shown from the Canal Walk. (JP)

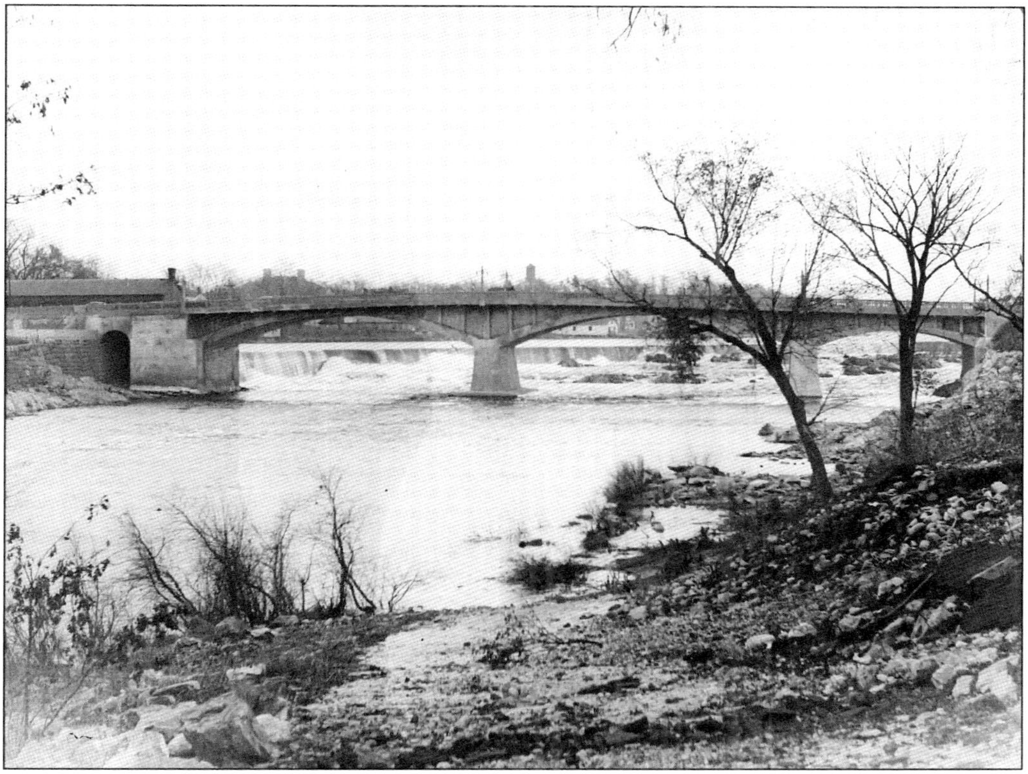

The Pawtucket Bridge and Falls appear here in the 1930s. (JP)

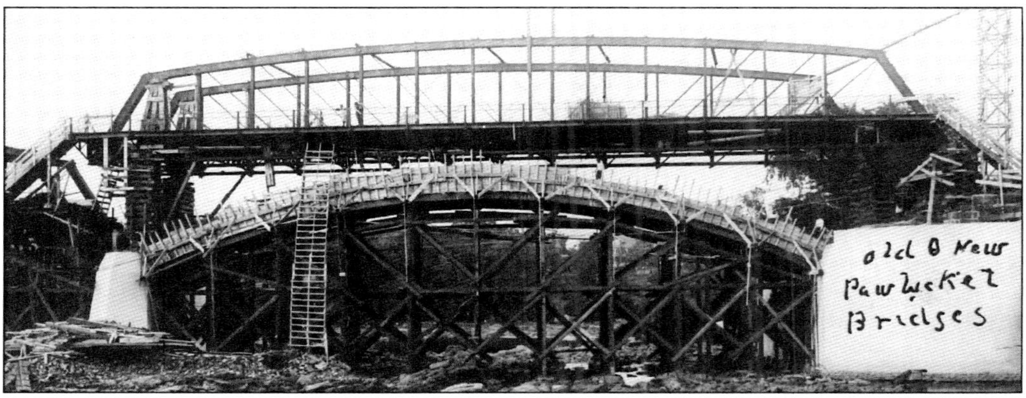

This view, looking downstream, shows both the old and new Pawtucket Bridges in July 1916. One is constructed as the other is dismantled. (DHS)

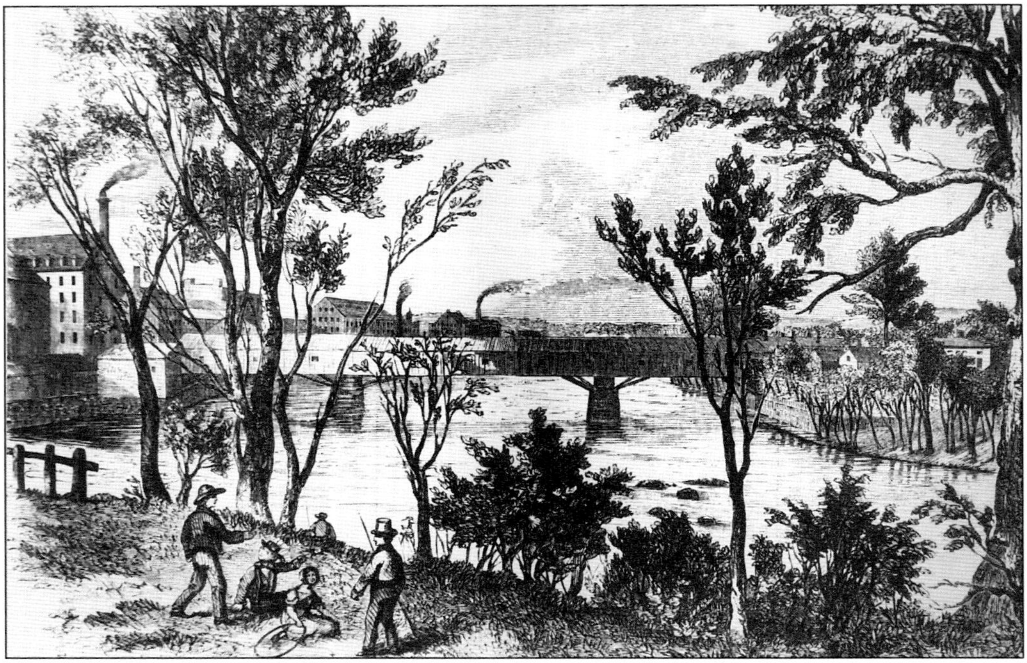

The Wilson Bridge, seen here in a 1965 depiction, was located at the junction of the Concord and Merrimac Rivers. At this location, before any bridge across the Merrimac was constructed in Lowell, a ferry was established in 1769 called Bradley's Ferry. The first bridge was opened in 1825 with tolls, and it was the first covered bridge across the Merrimac. (DHS)

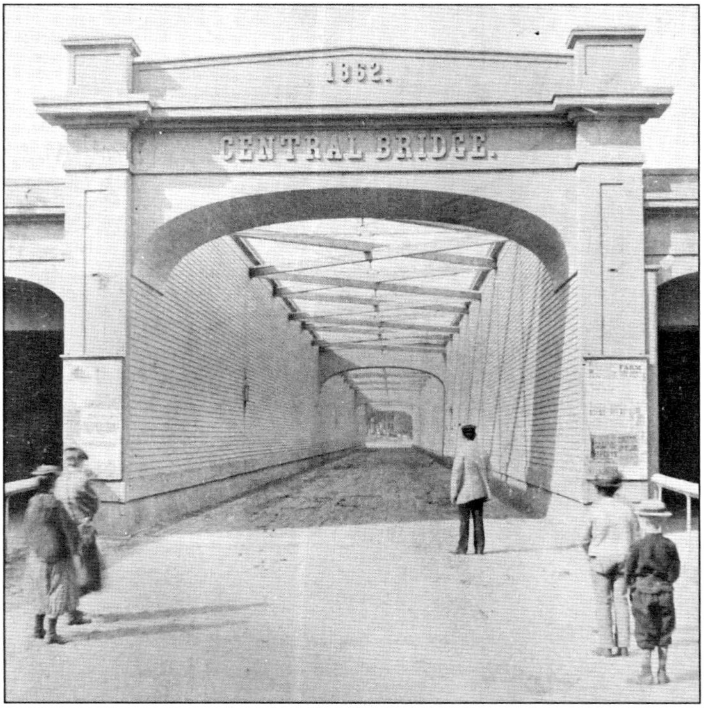

In 1862, the Central Bridge opened, replacing the old Wilson Bridge. This is known popularly today as the Bridge Street Bridge. (DHS)

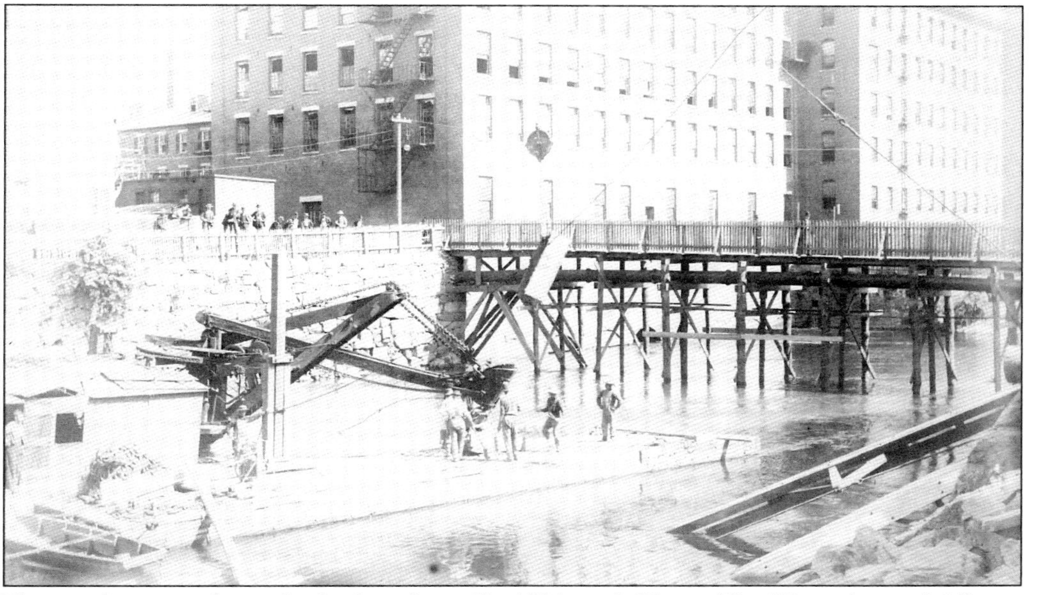

The northern canal was dredged on June 22, 1894, at 8:55 am. The Wannalancet Mills are visible in the background. (PP)

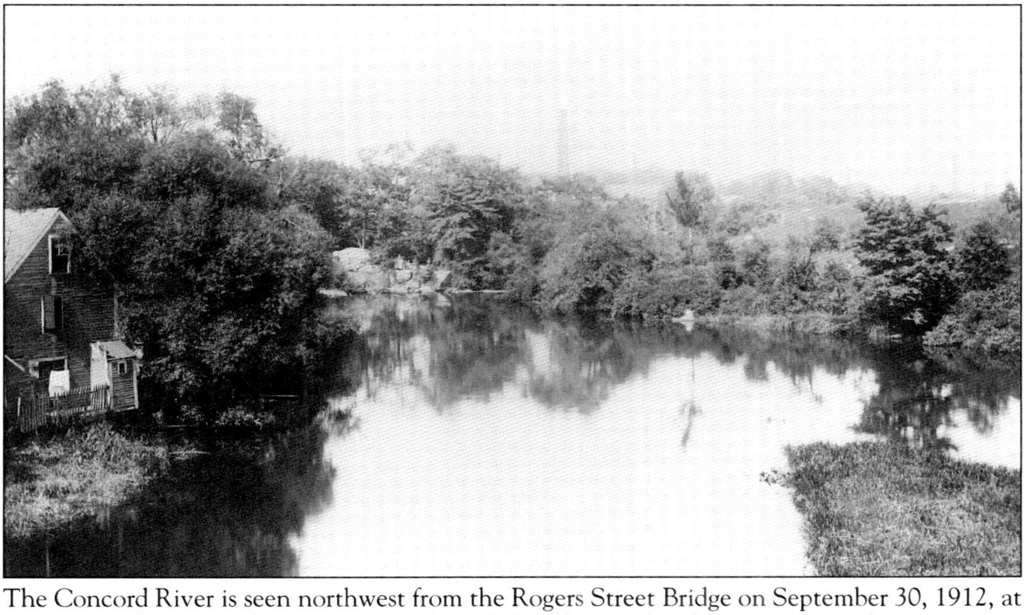

The Concord River is seen northwest from the Rogers Street Bridge on September 30, 1912, at 11:37 am. This particular area was a relatively highly-populated location in prehistoric times. Many Native American artifacts have been excavated here.(AT)

LIFE IN LOWELL

VOL. 1. No 21. LOWELL, SATURDAY, FEB. 17 1844. PRICE, THREE CENTS.

The man whose hardy spirit shall engage
To lash the vices of a guilty age,
At his first setting forward ought to know,
That every rogue he meets must be his foe;
That the rude breath of satire will provoke
All who feel, and more who fear the stroke.

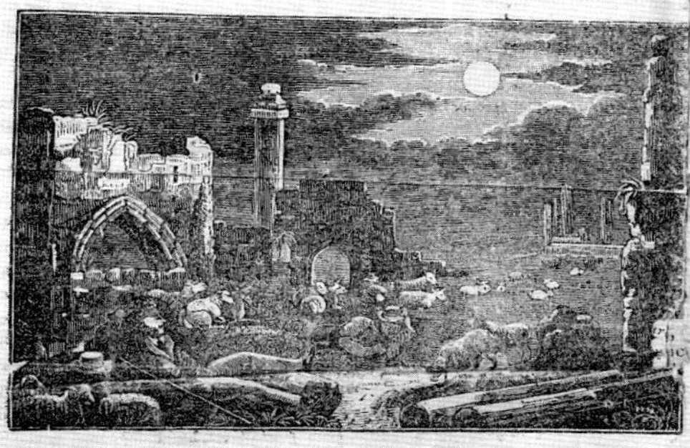

RUINS OF CARTHAGE.

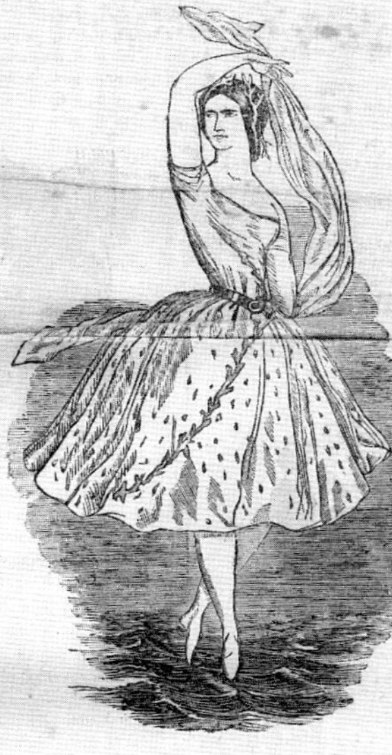

CERITO AS UNDINE.

LIFE IN LOWELL,
IS PUBLISHED EVERY
SATURDAY MORNING.
J. C. PALMER, Editor and Proprietor.
Terms—One Dollar a year, 25 cents for 3 months in advance. Single Copies, 3 cents. For sale at the News Rooms.

WHAT CONSTITUTES A GENTLEMAN. The Washington correspondent of a cotemporary says—

The colonization meeting last evening was very interesting. One of the speakers, with a view of showing the standard of morality among the African Princes, and their idea of what constitutes a gentleman, related the following anecdote:

A missionary, at an interview with one of the princes, incidentally spoke of certain gentlemen in the United States.

The prince said—'Ah—I wish I were a gentleman.'

'The missionary was surprised, and asked him if he had not great wealth and plenty of servants.

'Yes,' said the prince; 'but *that* does not make me a gentleman.'

'What does then,' replied the missionary, 'make a gentleman?'

'A proper number of wives,' said the prince.

'Why, how many wives have you?'

'Only two,' said the prince, 'but I must have *six* before I can be a gentleman.'

The idea of it requiring six wives to make a gentleman, created no little mirth among the female portion of the audience. There were some hard looks at the bachelors, as much as to say, 'What miserable creatures must you be then!'

LEGACY TO EDITORS BY AN EDITOR. The Rev. J. R. Breckenbridge has discontinued the 'Spirit of the Nineteenth Century,' and leaves this legacy to editors:

'Of all literary efforts, those connected with the periodical press are the most fruitless and evanescent.

'Of all kinds of influence, that exerted by it is the most doubtful and precarious.

'Of all cares, those imposed by its superintendence are the most wasting and ceaseless.

'Of all responsibilities, it inflicts that which is most comprehensive and embarrassing.

ALL ABOUT THE EYE.

What part of the eye is like a rainbow? The iris.

What part is like a schoolboy. The pupil.

What part is like the Globe? The ball.

What part is like the top of a chest? The lid.

What part is like a piece of a whip? The lash.

What past is like the summit of a hill. The brow.

BABIES. It strikes us that more fibs are told about babies than about any thing else in this world. We all say they are sweet, yet every body that can smell knows they are sour; we all say they are lovely, yet nine babies to ten have no more pretensions to beauty than a pug dog; we praise their expressive eyes, yet all babies squint; we call them little doves, though one of them makes more noise than a colony of screech owls; we vow they are no trouble, yet they have to be tended night and day; we insist they repay us for all our anxiety, though they take every opportunity of scratching our faces or poking their fingers in our eyes; in short, we make it our business to tell the most palpable falsehoods about them every hour of the day. Yet, strange to say, wedlock seems devoid without them; and those who have them, even while telling these self-evident untruths, look just as if they expected people to believe them!

BEAUTIFUL LITTLE ALLEGORY. A humming bird once met a butterfly, and being pleased with the beauty of its person and glory of its wings, made an offer of perpetual friendship.

'I cannot think of it,' was the reply, 'as you once spurned me, and called me a drawling dolt.'

'Impossible,' exclaimed the humming bird. 'I always entertained the highest respect for such beautiful creatures as you.'

'Perhaps you do now,' said the other, 'but when you insulted me, I was a caterpillar. So let me give you this advice. Never insult the humble, as they may one day become your superior.'

A GERANIUM AT THE WINDOW. It was the remark of Leigh Hunt, that it sweetens the air, rejoices the eye, links you with nature and innocence, and is something to love.

Life in Lowell was a weekly newspaper printed on Central Street. This particular edition is volume I, number 21 (February 17, 1844). (JP)

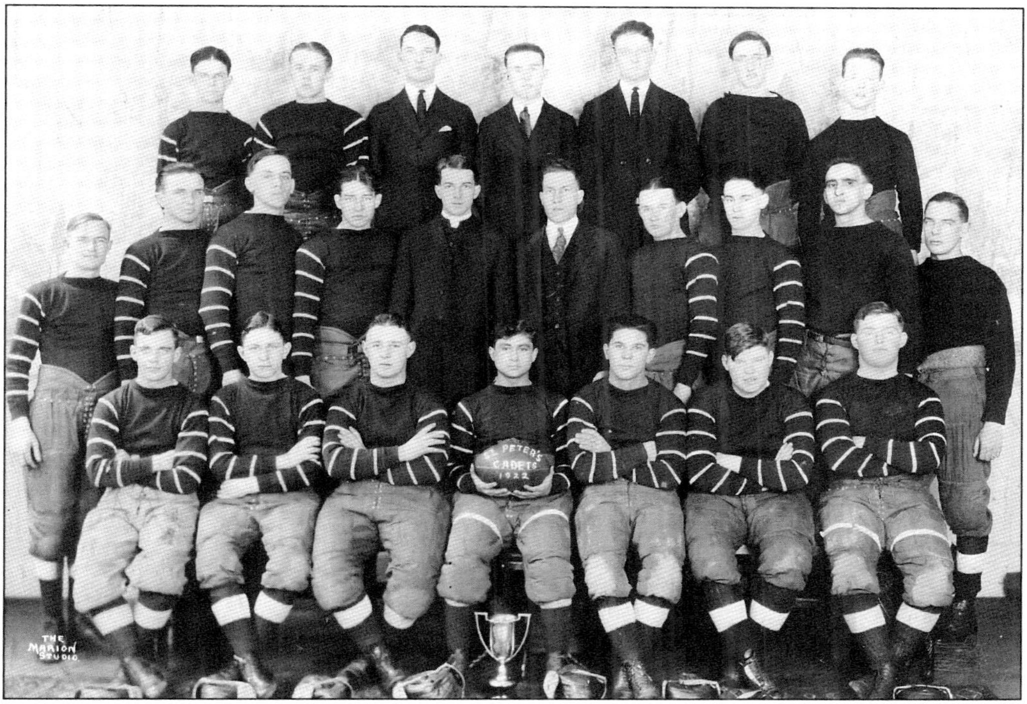

St. Peter's Cadets appear here in 1922.

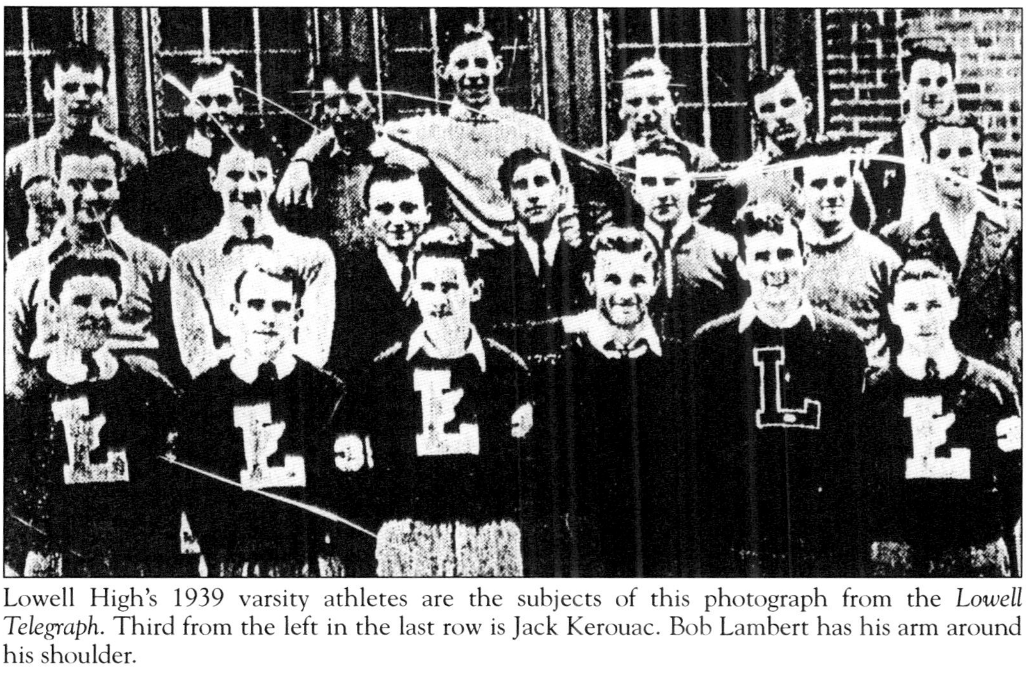
Lowell High's 1939 varsity athletes are the subjects of this photograph from the *Lowell Telegraph*. Third from the left in the last row is Jack Kerouac. Bob Lambert has his arm around his shoulder.

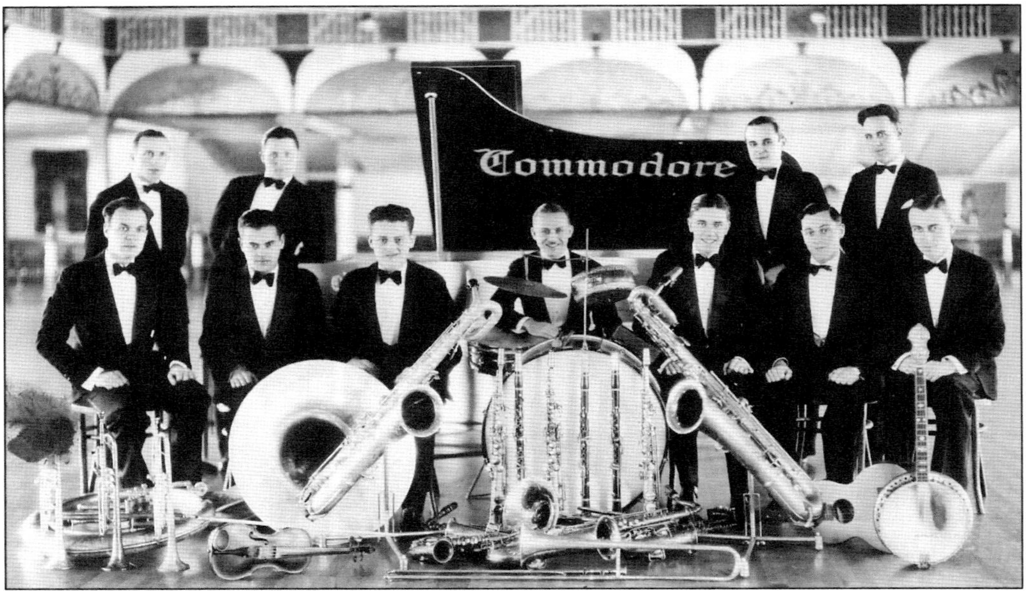

Whitey Meisky's Orchestra had two baritone saxes when the group played the Commodore Ballroom in the 1920s.

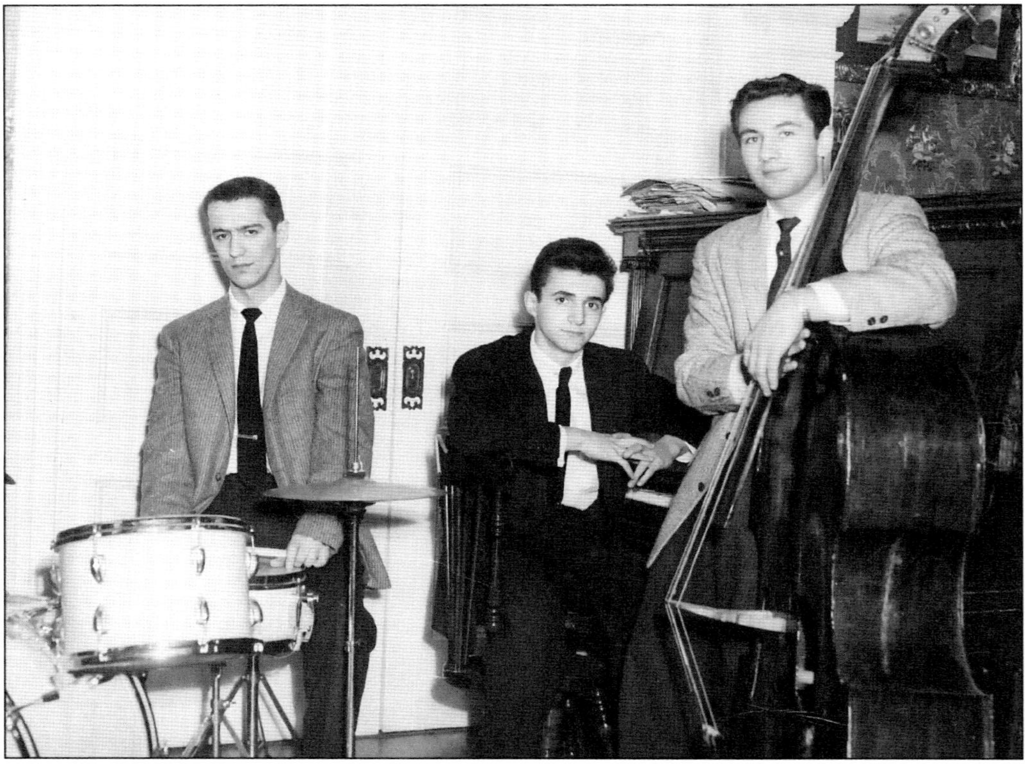

Don Bacon (drums), Charles Panagiotakos (piano), and Roger Marchard (bass) rehearsed on Branch Street in 1957. Don Bacon, a longtime resident of Carolyn Street in Lowell, died on March 20, 1997. He was a highly respected jazz critic and scholar. (CP)

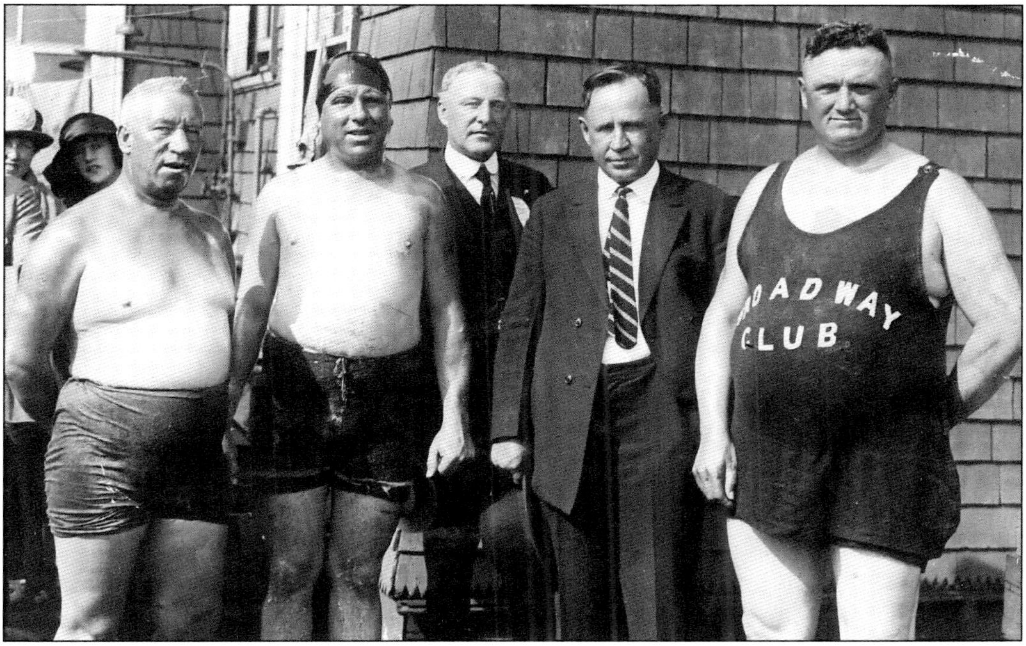

Rickey Keefe (second from the left) and Mike Rynne (far left) were champion swimmers in the twenties and thirties in the Merrimac despite their girths. Keefe swam from Nantasket Beach to the Boston lighthouse and back. This photograph was taken *c.* 1935.

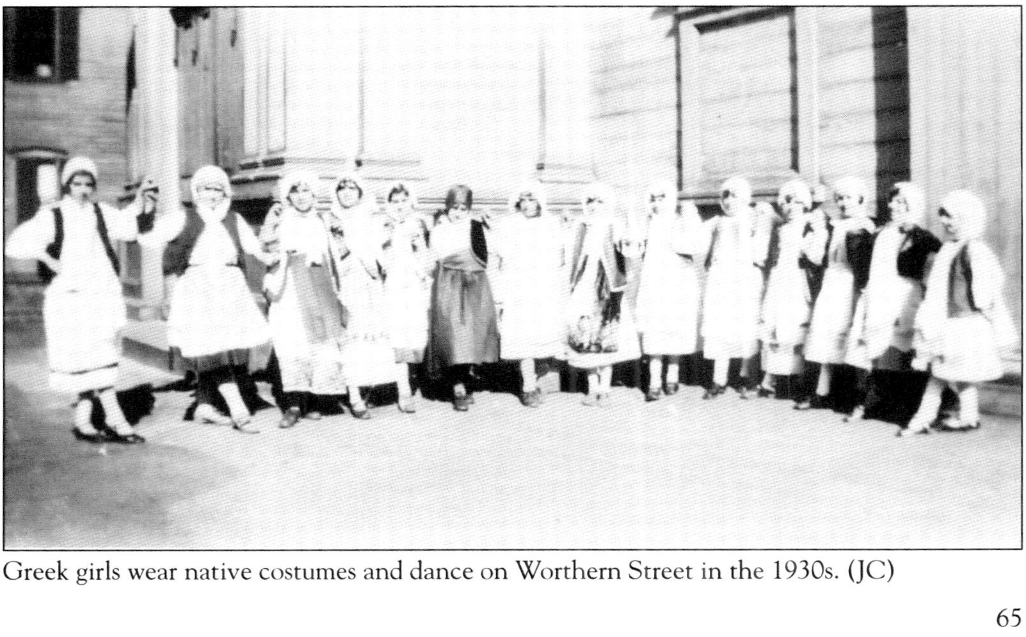

Greek girls wear native costumes and dance on Worthern Street in the 1930s. (JC)

PROGRAMME

—OF THE—

CELEBRATION OF ST. PATRICK'S DAY

AT LOWELL,

THURSDAY, MARCH 17, 1887.

HIGH MASS WILL BE CELEBRATED AT ALL THE CHURCHES AT 9 A. M.

PROCESSION WILL FORM AT MONUMENT SQUARE,

AT 12 O'CLOCK.

In the Afternoon and Evening the Following Entertainments will be Given for the benefit of

ST. JOHN'S HOSPITAL:

AT 2 O'CLOCK

Entertainment in Huntington Hall for Children.

AT HUNTINGTON HALL IN THE EVENING

"DUFFY DARLIN"

Will be presented by members of the Christian Doctrine Society of the Immaculate Conception Church.

AT MUSIC HALL,

Mr. Sullivan's New Drama

"WHEN MY SHIP COMES HOME"

Will be given by members of the Mathew Dramatic Company.

AT JACKSON HALL,

AT 7.30 O'CLOCK,

A GRAND COFFEE PARTY AND SUPPER

WILL BE GIVEN.

St. Patrick's Day was a citywide affair in 1887. (JP)

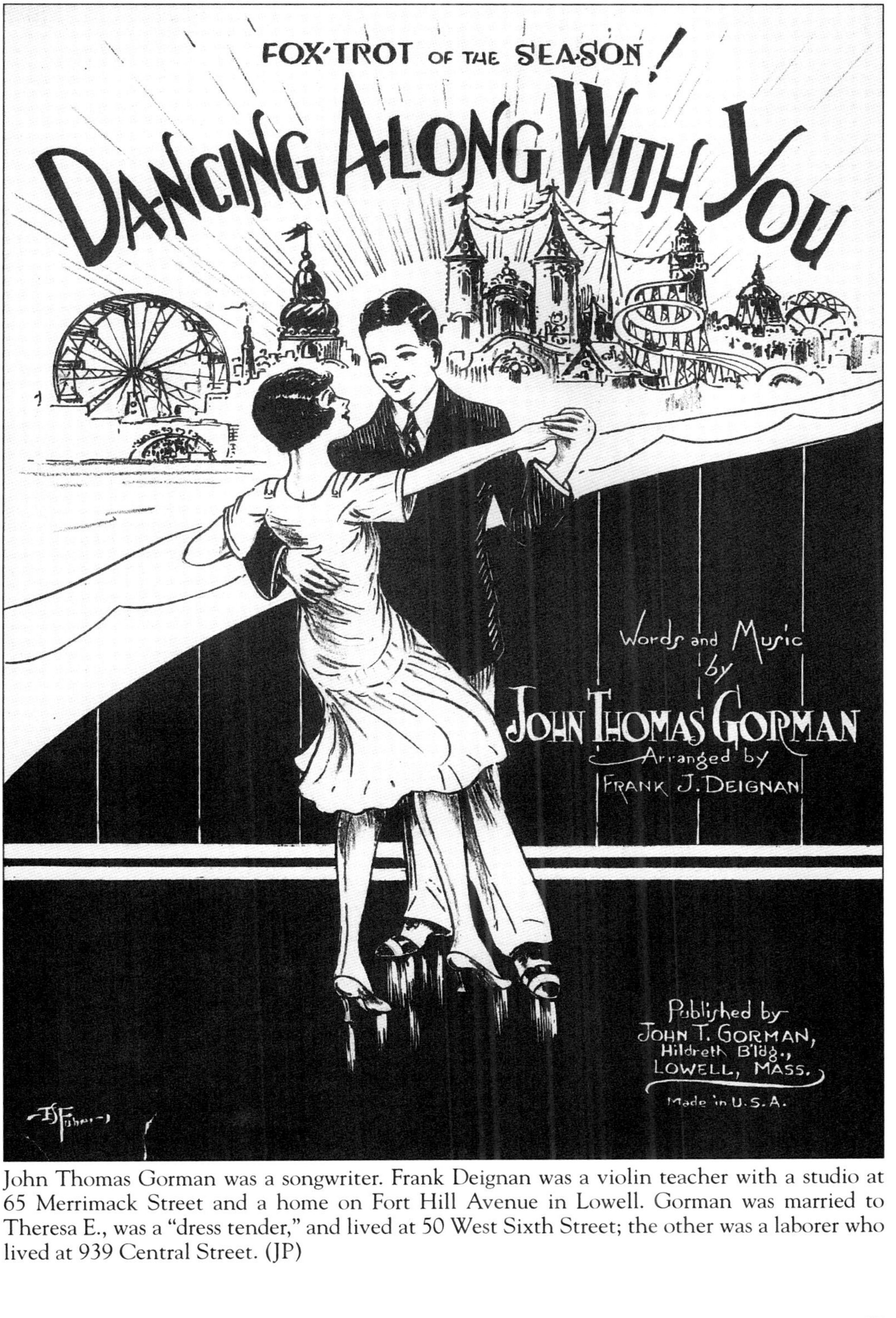

John Thomas Gorman was a songwriter. Frank Deignan was a violin teacher with a studio at 65 Merrimack Street and a home on Fort Hill Avenue in Lowell. Gorman was married to Theresa E., was a "dress tender," and lived at 50 West Sixth Street; the other was a laborer who lived at 939 Central Street. (JP)

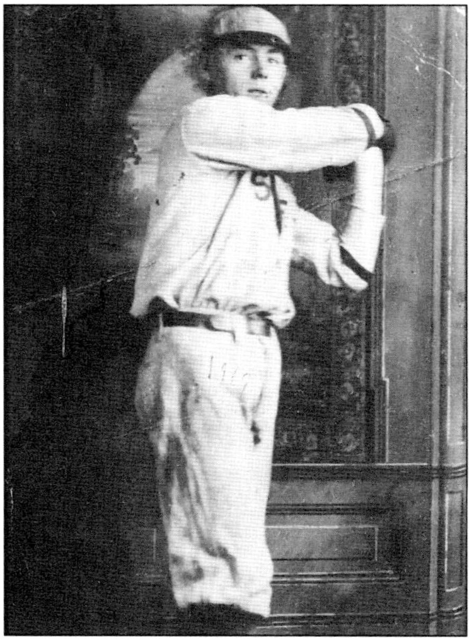

Hank Garrity was a sure starter for St. Peter's in 1919. (HG)

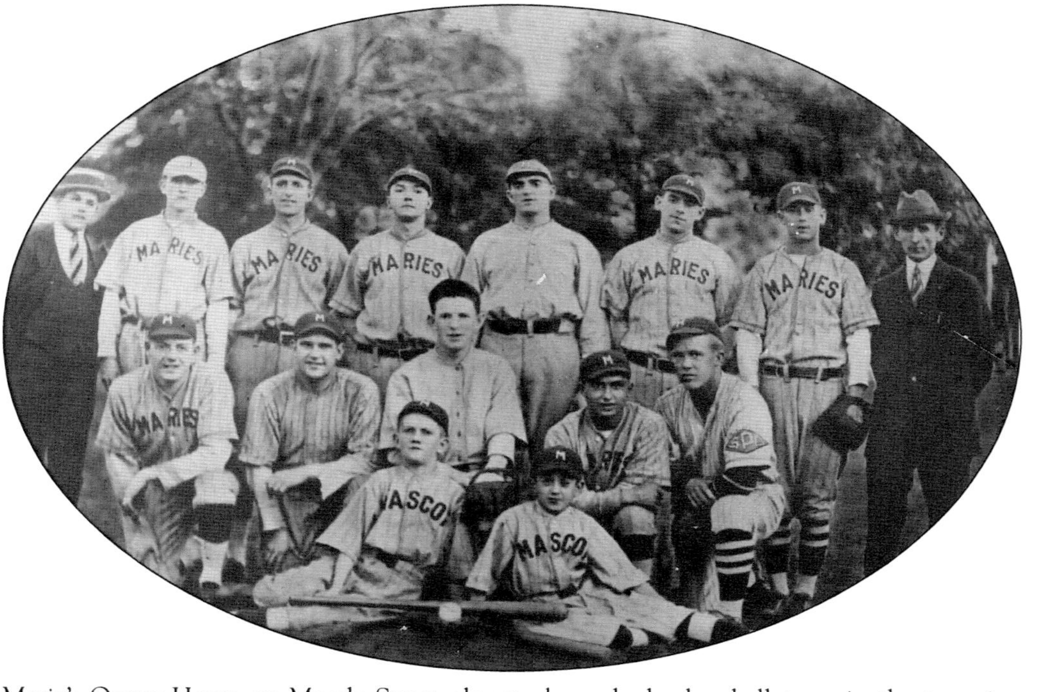

Marie's Oyster House on Moody Street almost always had a baseball team in the twenties. This 1925 team won the city championship. From left to right are: (front row) Hank Garrity (pitcher), Harold Dillon (catcher), Ed Gath (second base), Dick Onnie (outfield), and Frank Regan (pitcher); (back row) Buckey Freeman (pitcher), Joseph Smith (shortstop), Bill Harrington (outfield), Tom Breen (third base), Ralph Jenkins (first base), Bill Ryan (outfield), Jinks Barrold (infield), and John Pertus (manager). The mascots were recorded only as Didley and Nole. (HG)

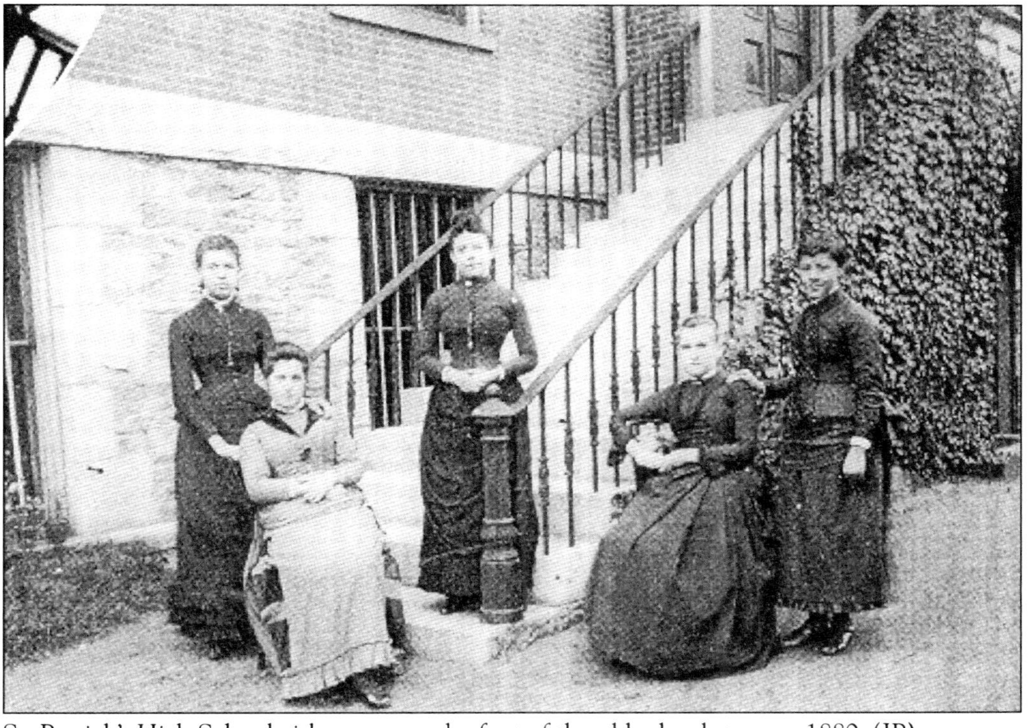
St. Patrick's High School girls appear at the foot of the old school steps, *c.* 1880. (JP)

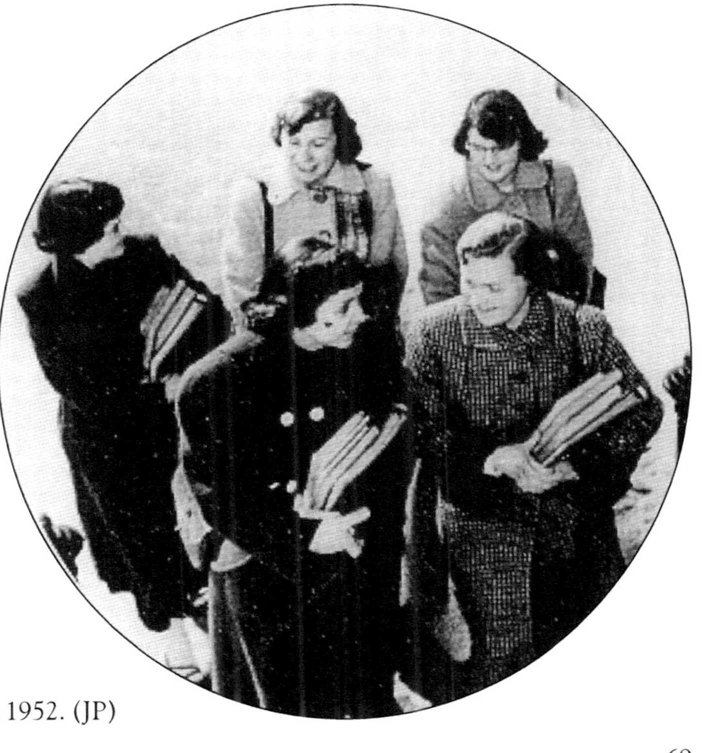
St. Patrick's girls pose again in 1952. (JP)

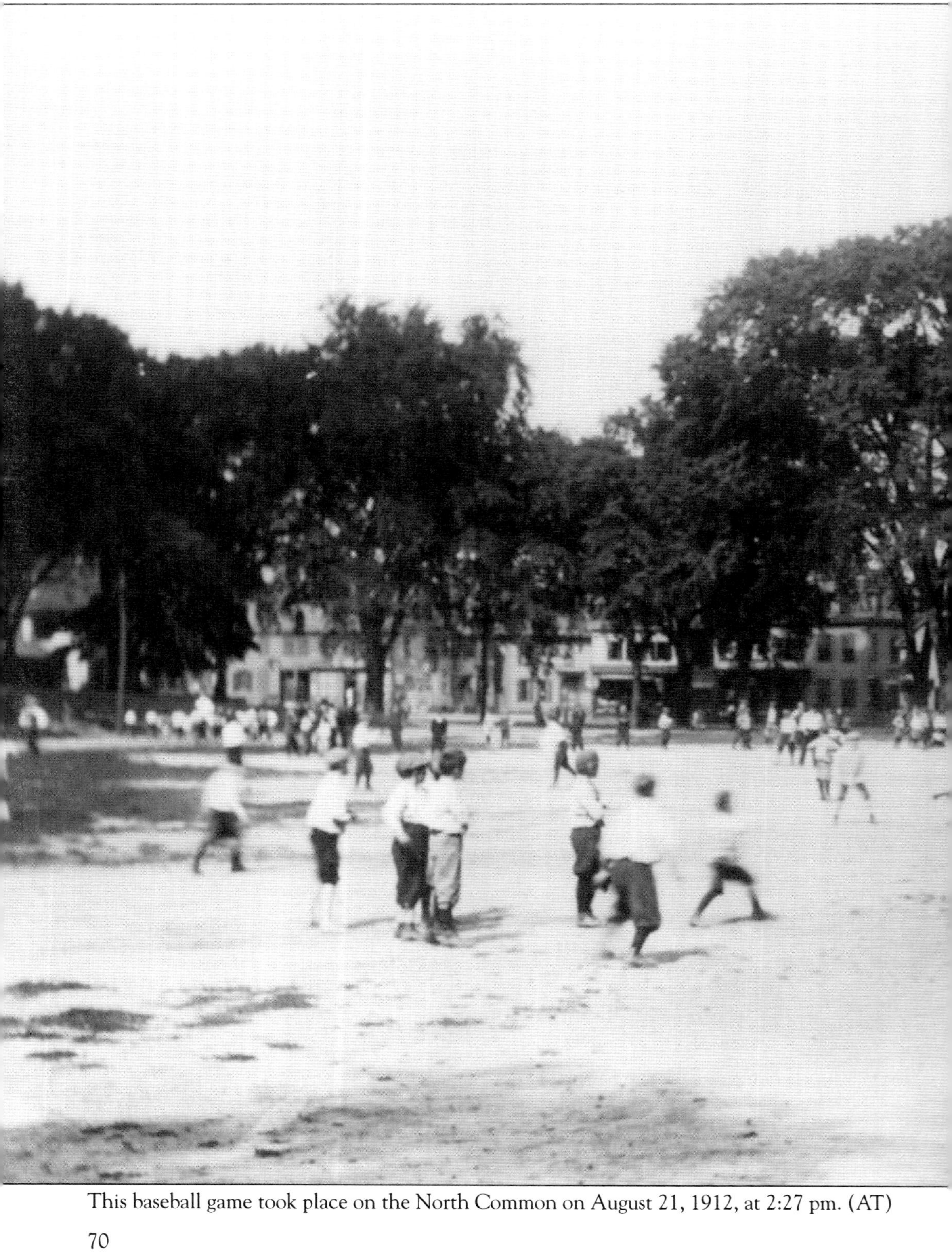

This baseball game took place on the North Common on August 21, 1912, at 2:27 pm. (AT)

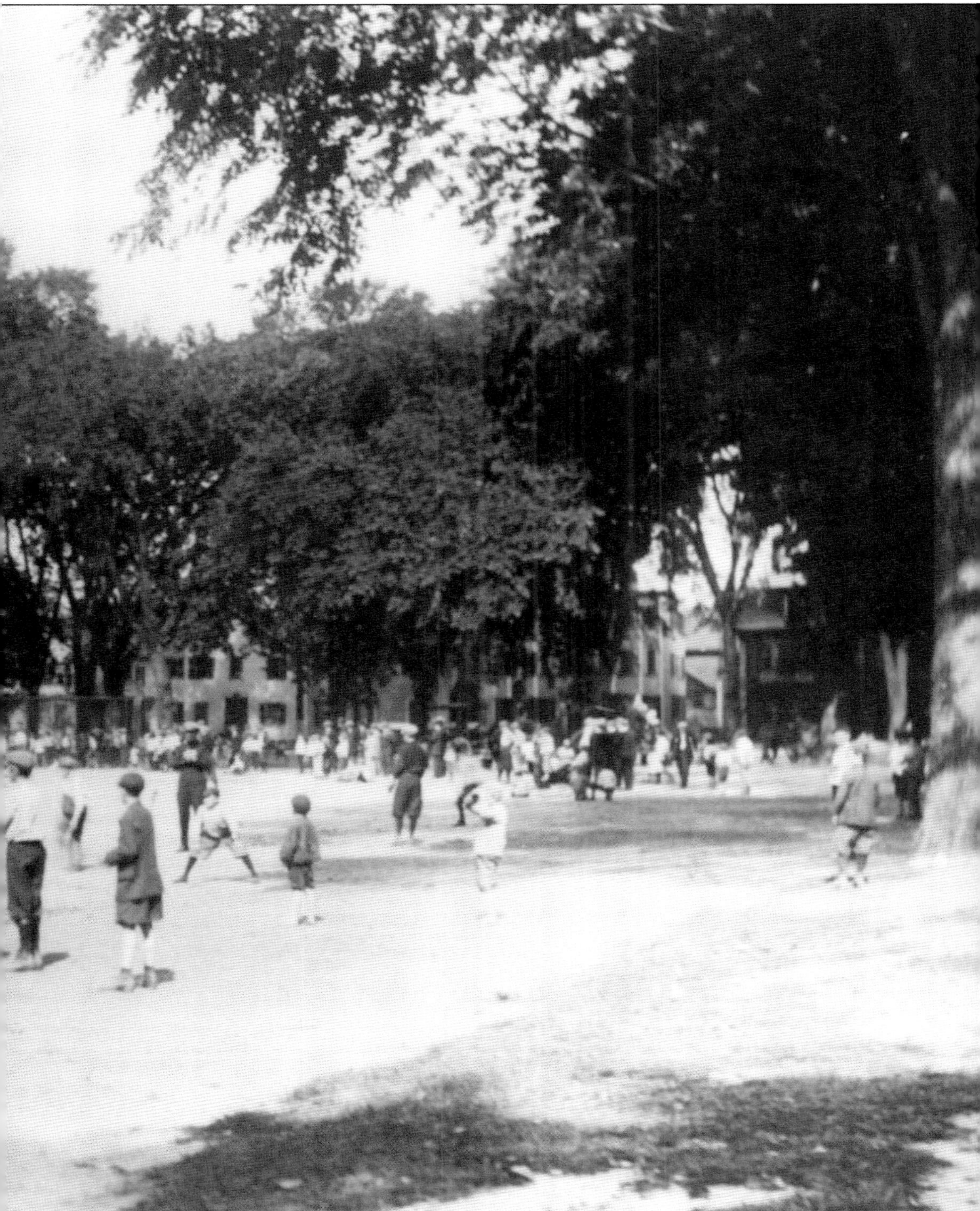

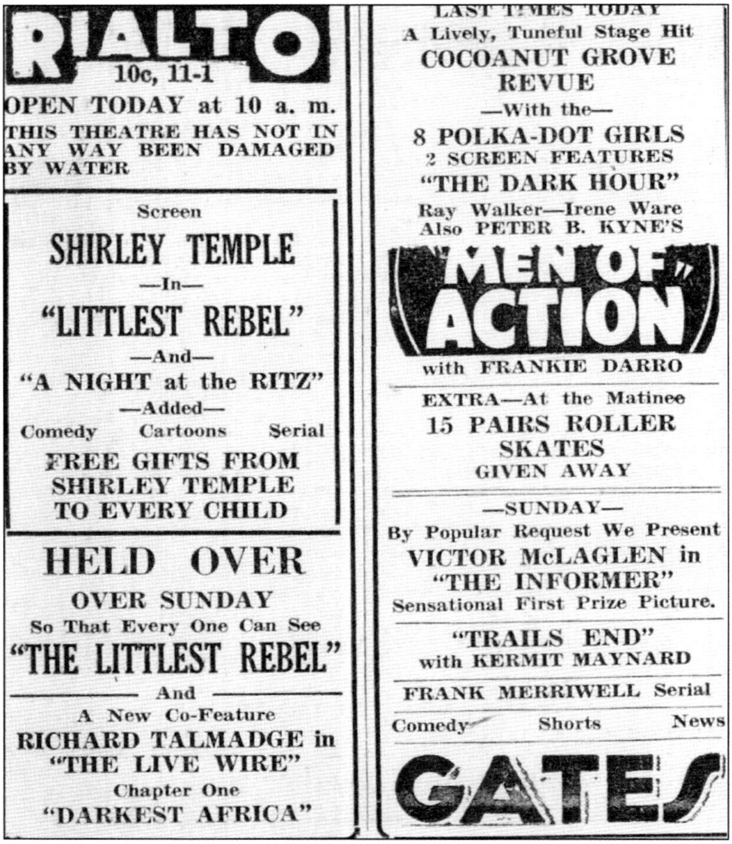

This variety of movie theater advertisements was taken from 1939 issues of the *Lowell Sun*. (JP)

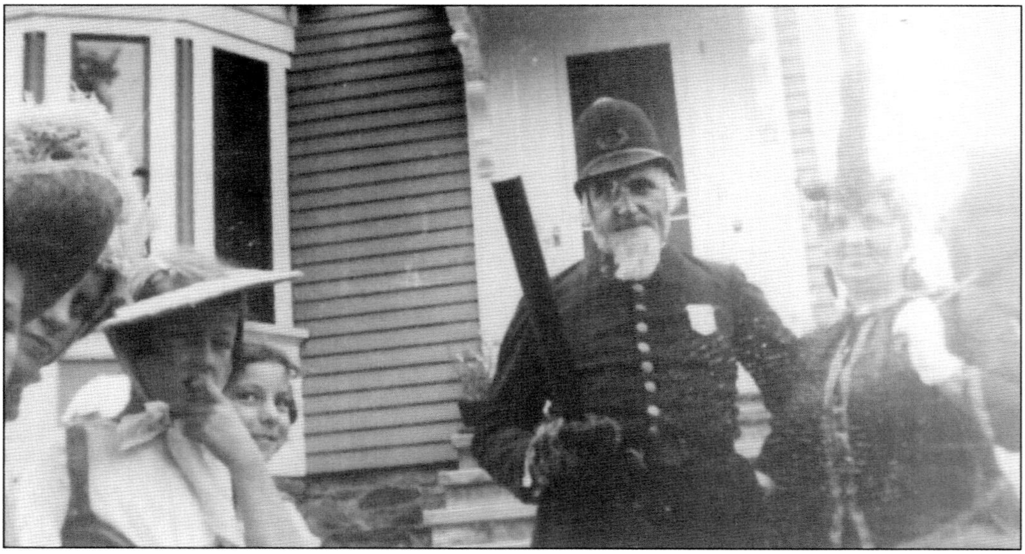

John and Margaret Hogan lived at 123 West Sixth Street in Centralville. He was a driver for the Eastern Mass. public transit and came to Lowell from Ireland. (JP)

Four

Their Work and Play

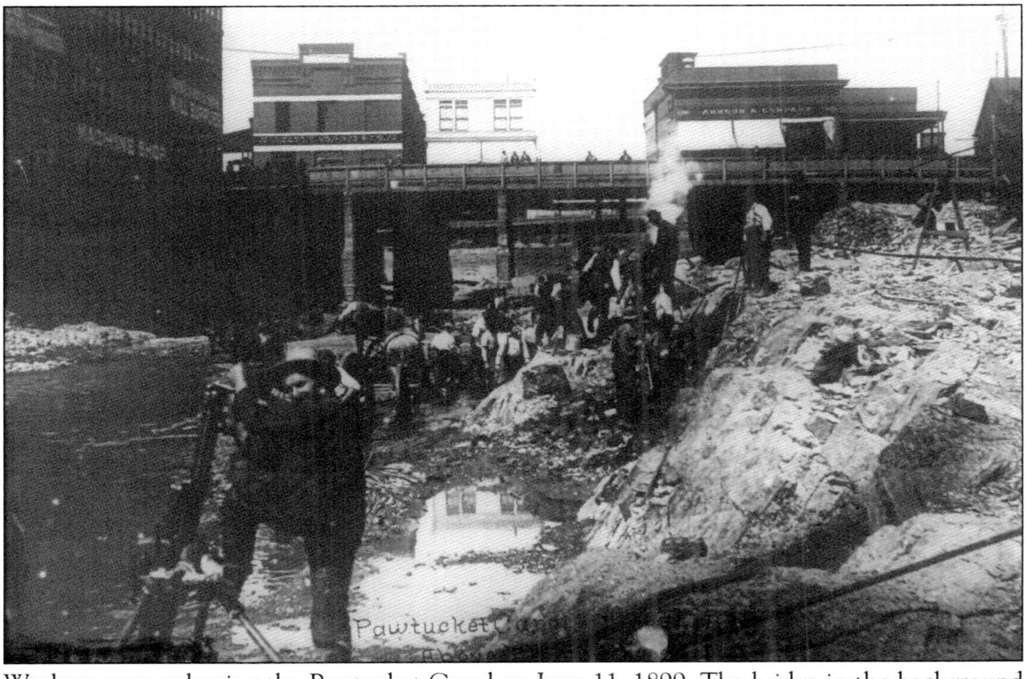

Workers were enlarging the Pawtucket Canal on June 11, 1899. The bridge in the background spans Thorndike Street. (PP)

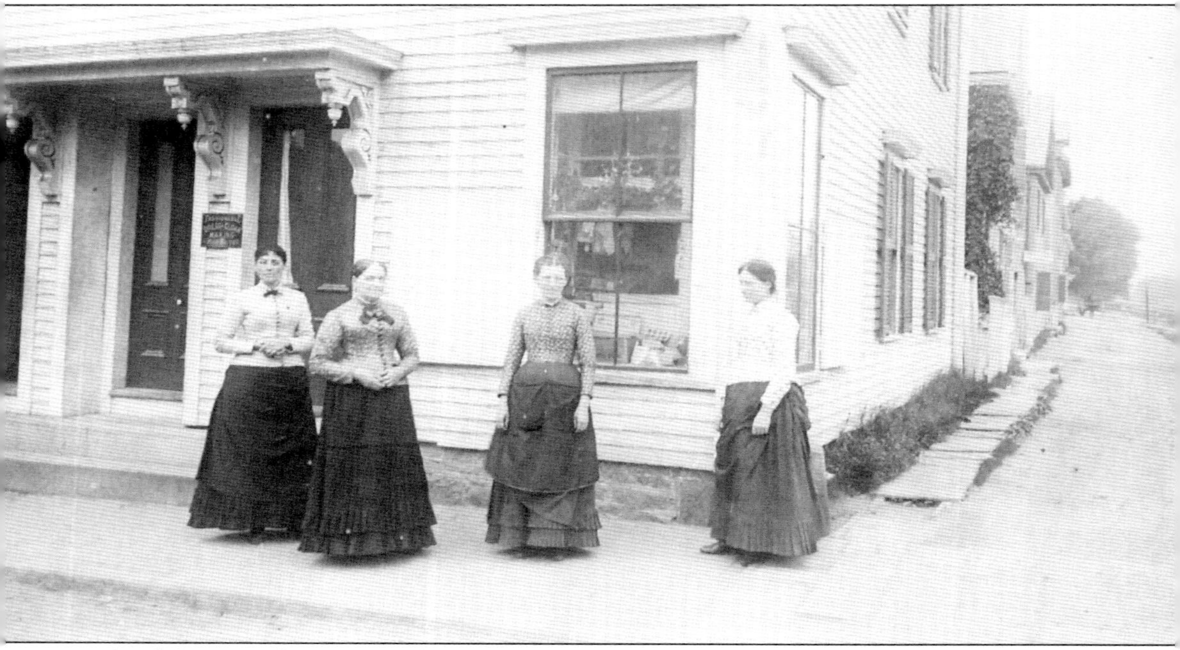

Sarah Barnett Sherman stands at the corner, and Persis Barnett is in front of the window of her dressmaking shop at the corner of Suffolk and Downing Streets. The sign reads, "Fashionable Dress and Cloakmaking." The two other women were probably seamstresses. This picture dates to about 1880. In 1897, Persis Barnett Sherman moved her business to Dracut Centre.

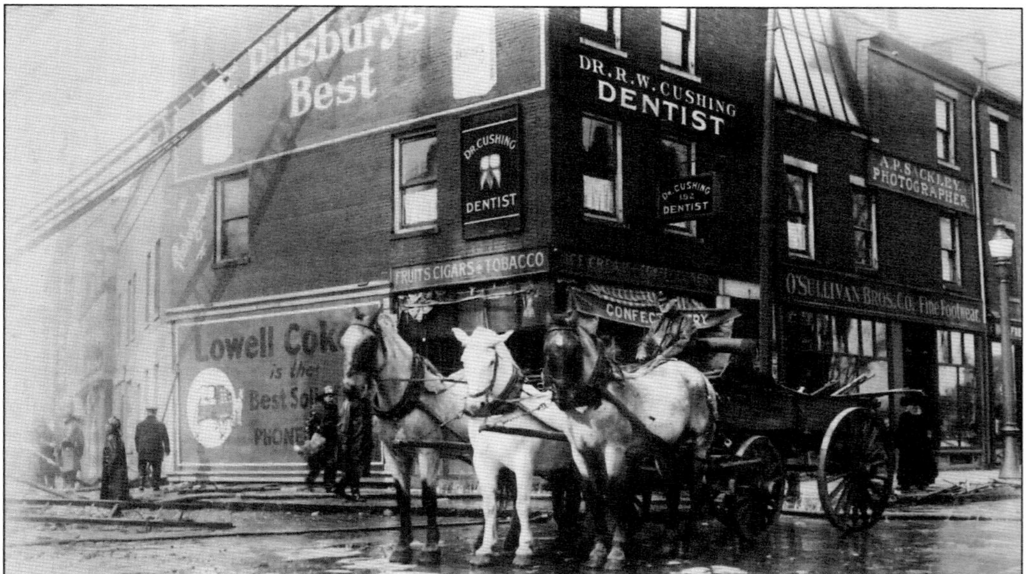

A horse wagon is stopped at the corners of Worthen and Merrimack Streets. They face the flames of the Associates Building Fire of April 1924. Turcotte's Package Store was on this corner for many years afterwards. Note Humphrey O'Sullivan's "Fine Footwear." O'Sullivan was the inventor of the rubber heel and a well-known Lowell personality.

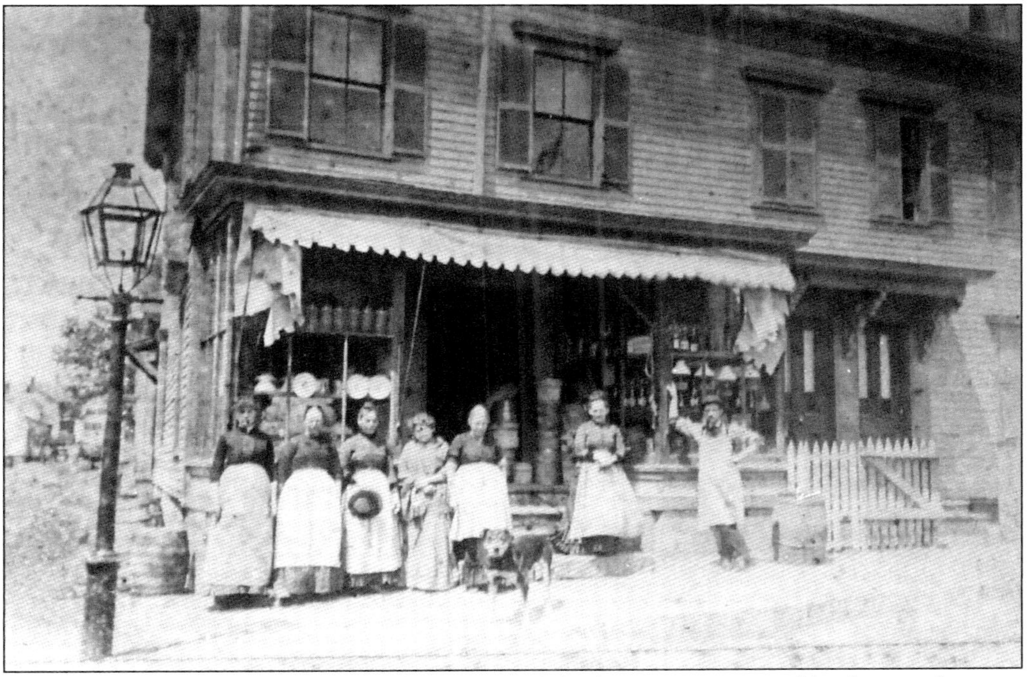

Cassidy's Store was located on Chapel Street *c.* 1875. This store was owned by the grandparents of Dracut educator George Englesby.

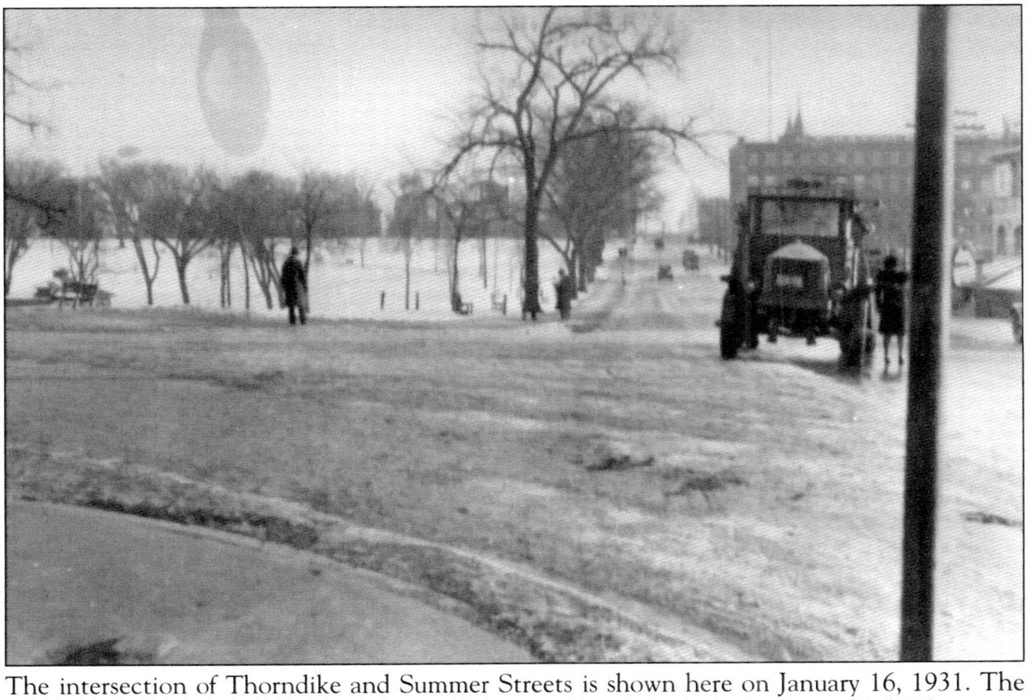

The intersection of Thorndike and Summer Streets is shown here on January 16, 1931. The South Common and C.I. Hood's Patent Medicine Factory are in the background. (BK)

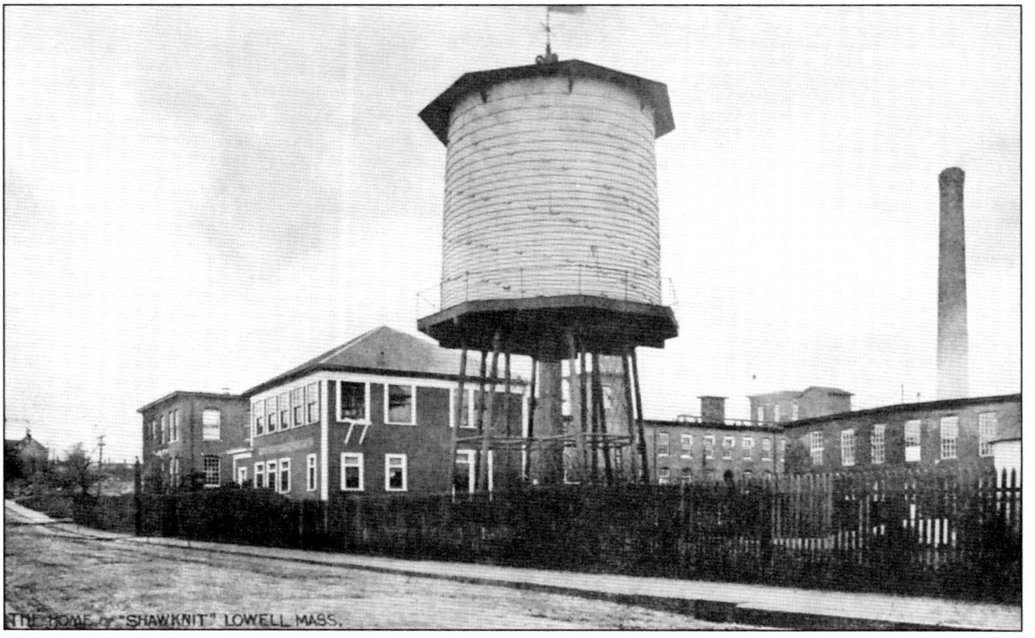

This is the Shawknit Hosiery Factory in November 1907. (JP)

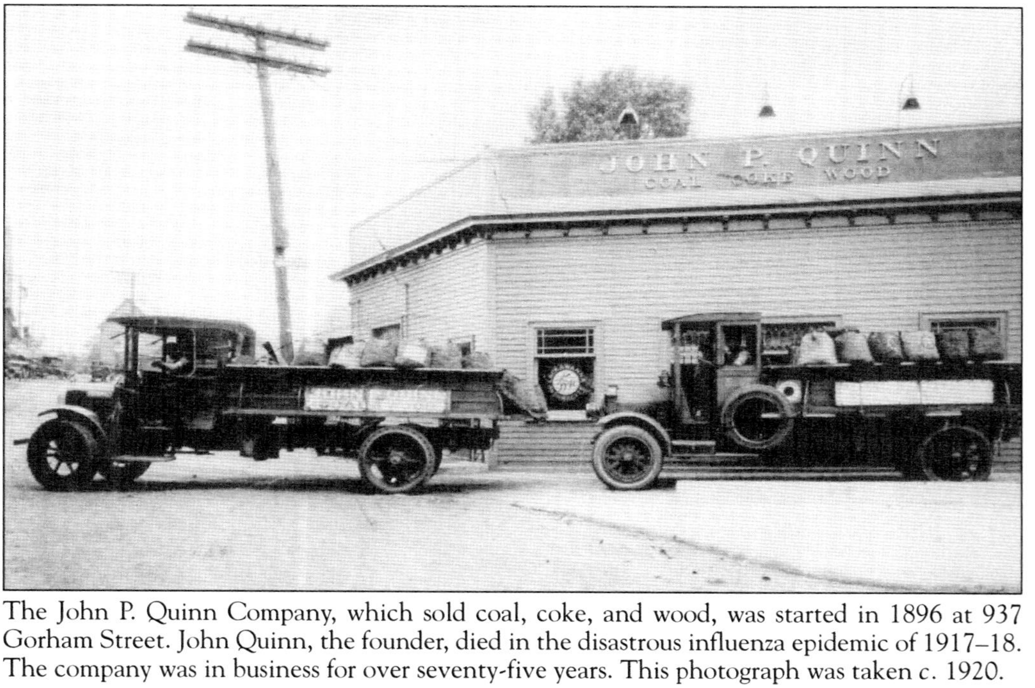

The John P. Quinn Company, which sold coal, coke, and wood, was started in 1896 at 937 Gorham Street. John Quinn, the founder, died in the disastrous influenza epidemic of 1917–18. The company was in business for over seventy-five years. This photograph was taken c. 1920.

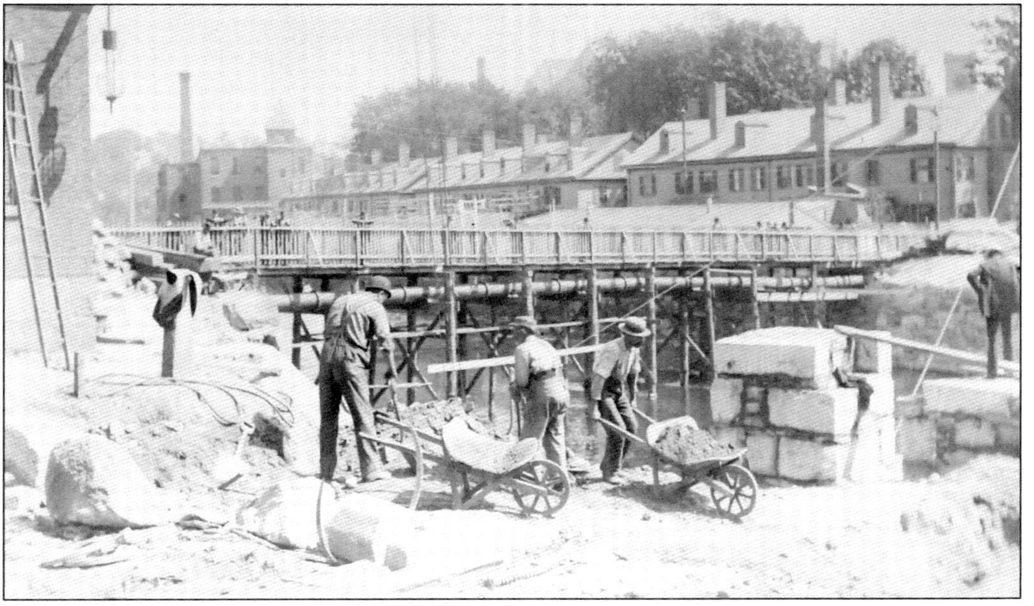

This temporary footbridge was constructed during the enlargement of the northern canal on September 6, 1894. People crossing this bridge are depicted on the cover of the first volume of the *Images of America: Lowell.*(PD)

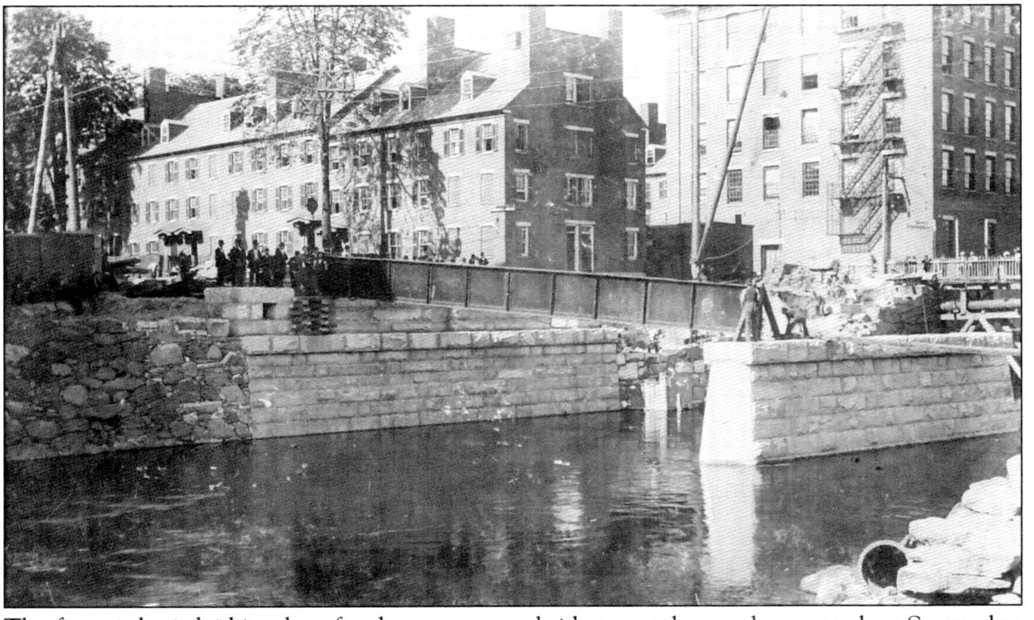

The first girder is laid in place for the permanent bridge over the northern canal on September 13, 1894, at 1:52 pm. (PD)

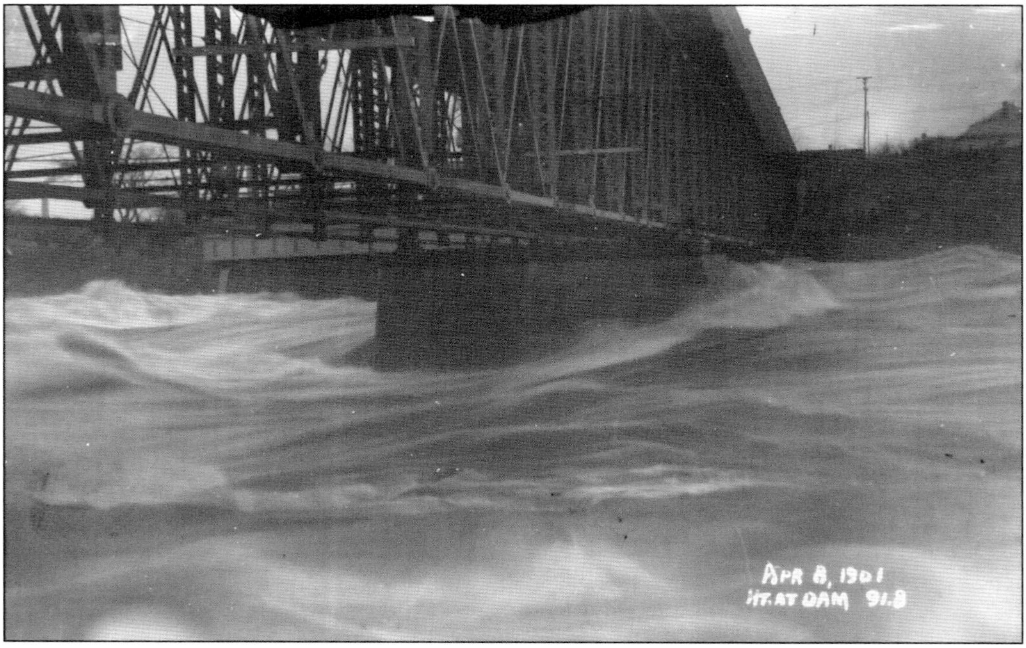

Water rushes furiously under the Moody Street Bridge during the spring freshet of April 8, 1901. (JP)

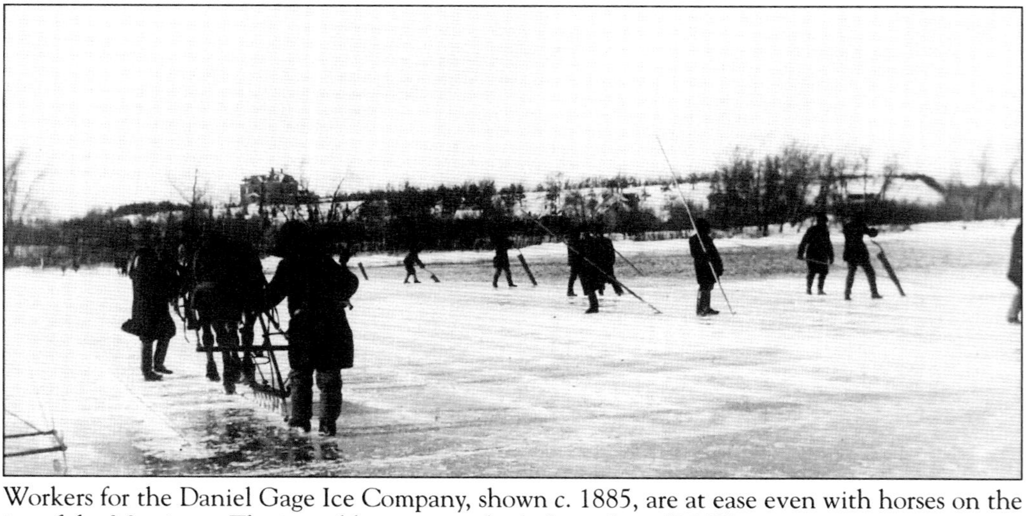

Workers for the Daniel Gage Ice Company, shown *c.* 1885, are at ease even with horses on the ice of the Merrimac. The ice seldom gets so thick these days. (DHS)

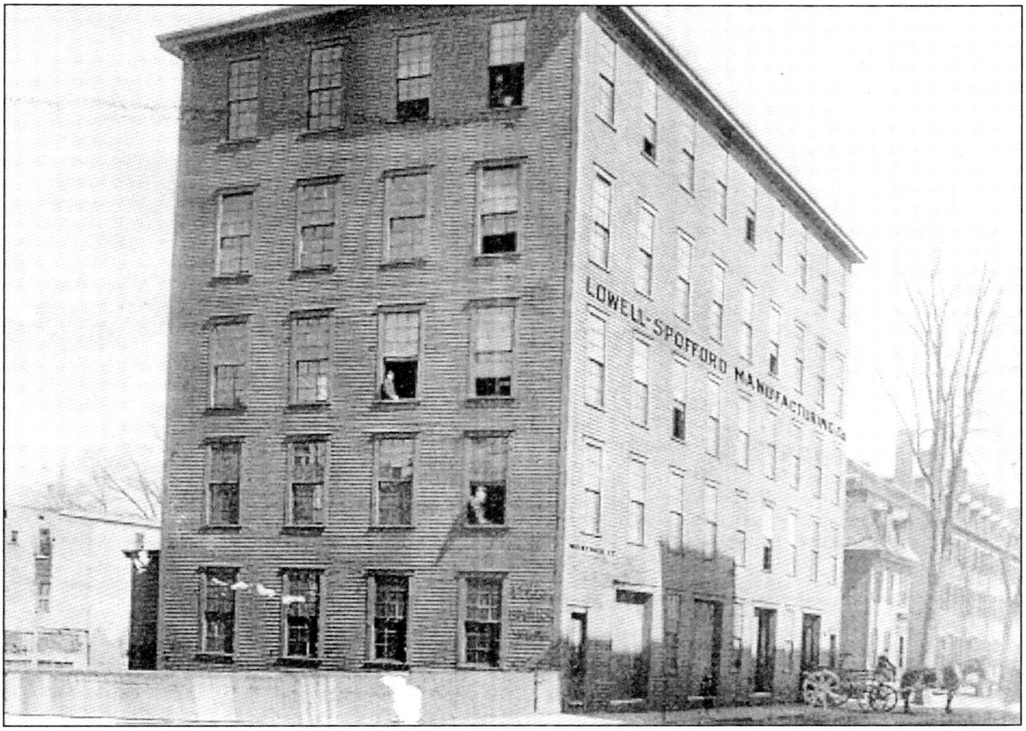

The Lowell Strafford Manufacturing Company was on Worthern Street. The company manufactured windmills and was very successful. Dudley Page wrote of his windmill, "The only fault I have to find is that it empties my well." Daniel Wills of Middlesex Village in Lowell wrote, "the 'Lowell' Windmill has given perfect satisfaction." (JP)

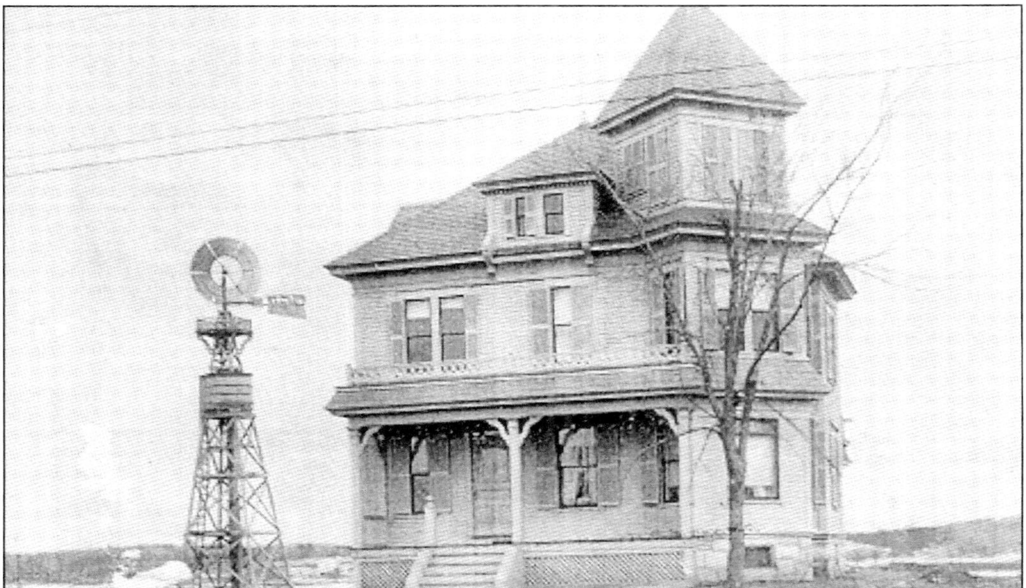

Daniel Wills' house in Middlesex Village is shown with his Lowell-Strafford windmill c. 1893.

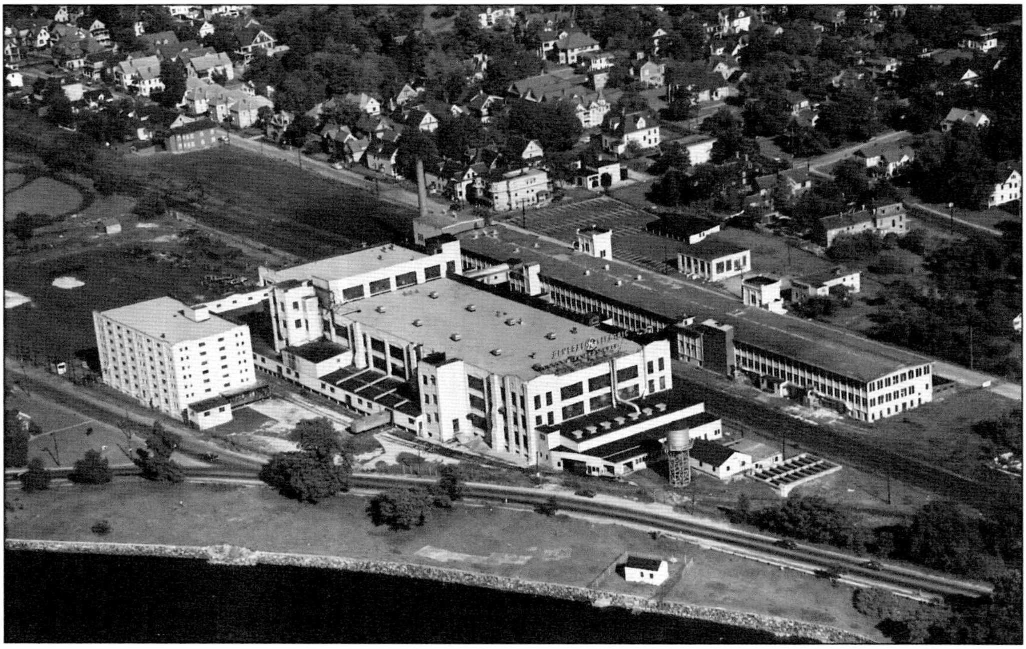

The General Electric Building on Broadway Street was photographed by George Poirier *c.* 1957 and razed in 1997 as this book goes to print. (GP)

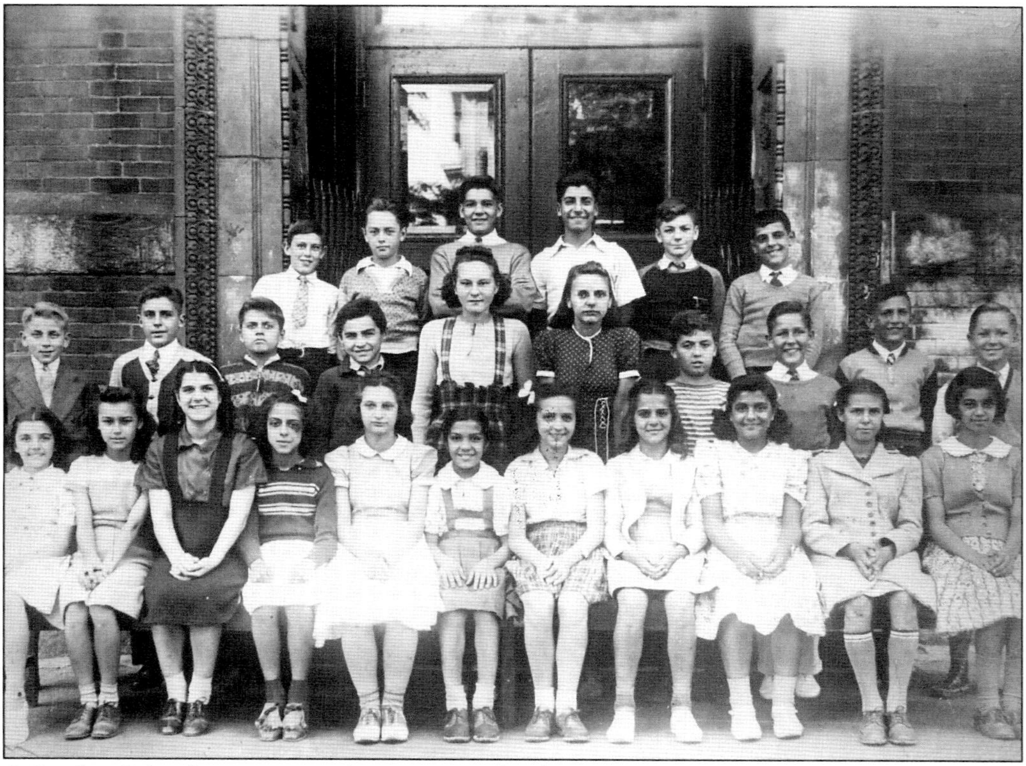

A Bartlett School group is seen here *c.* 1937. (GP)

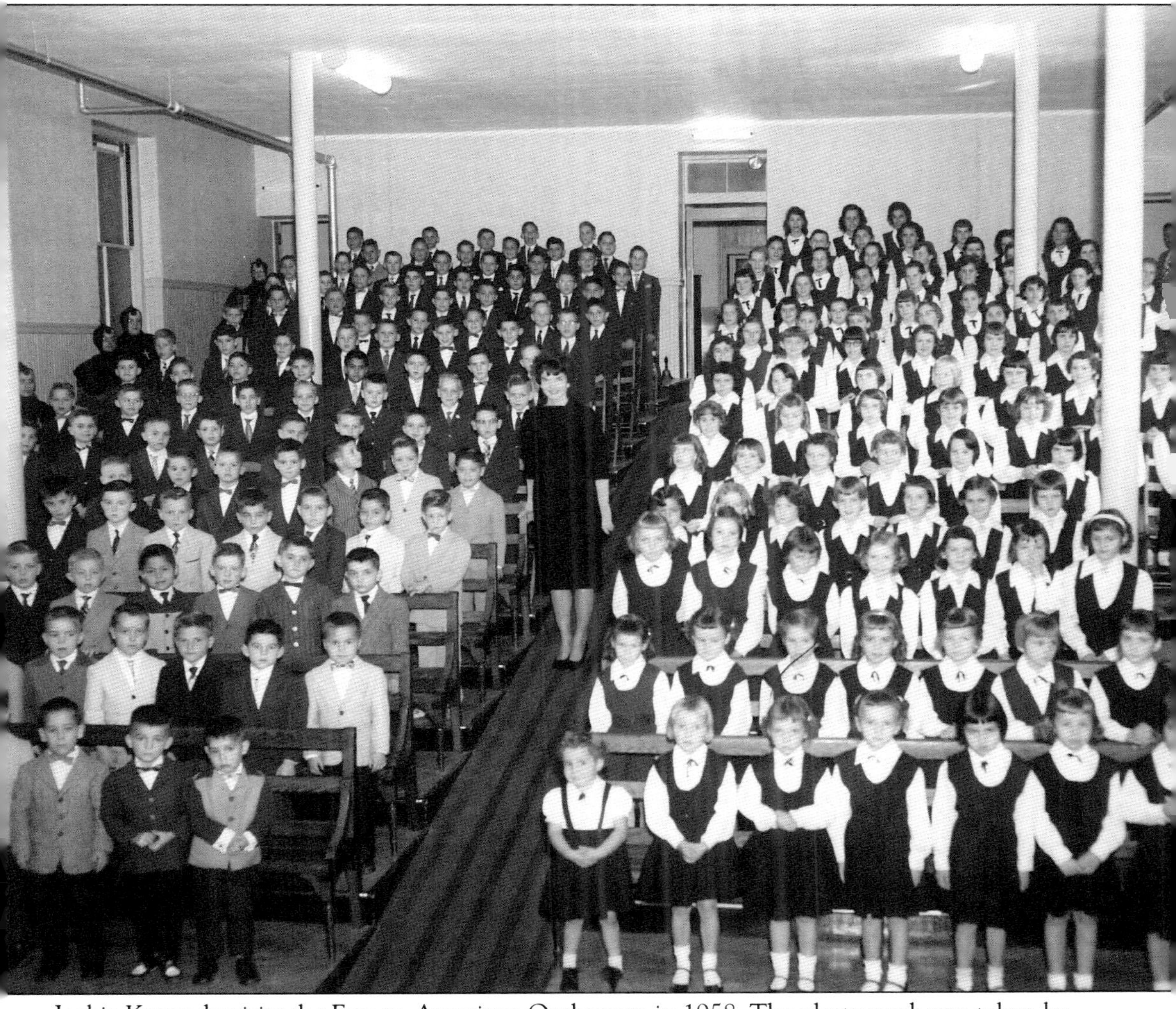

Jackie Kennedy visits the Franco-American Orphanage in 1958. The photograph was taken by George Poirier.

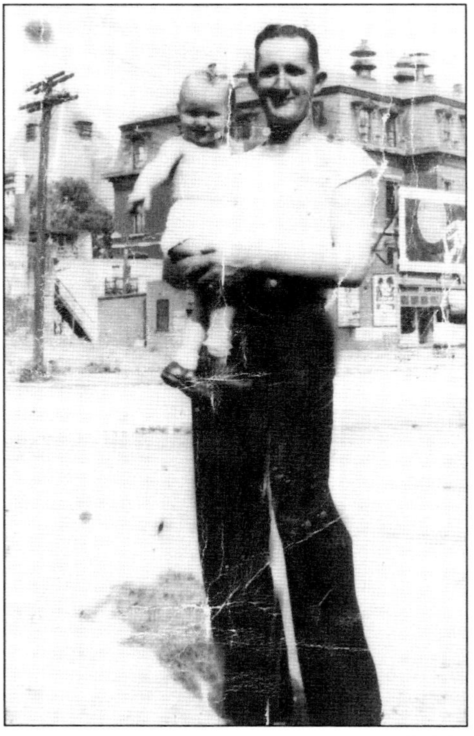

Richard Corcoran became a deacon at St. Patrick's Church. The *c.* 1942 photograph was taken from Conlon Terrace; the Green School is in the background. (GP)

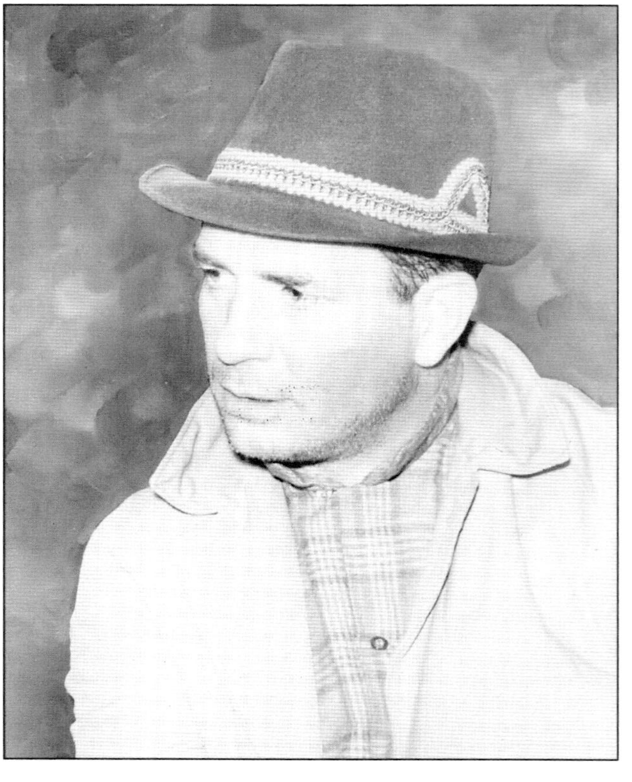

Jack Kerouac was photographed by George Poirier in 1968. (GP)

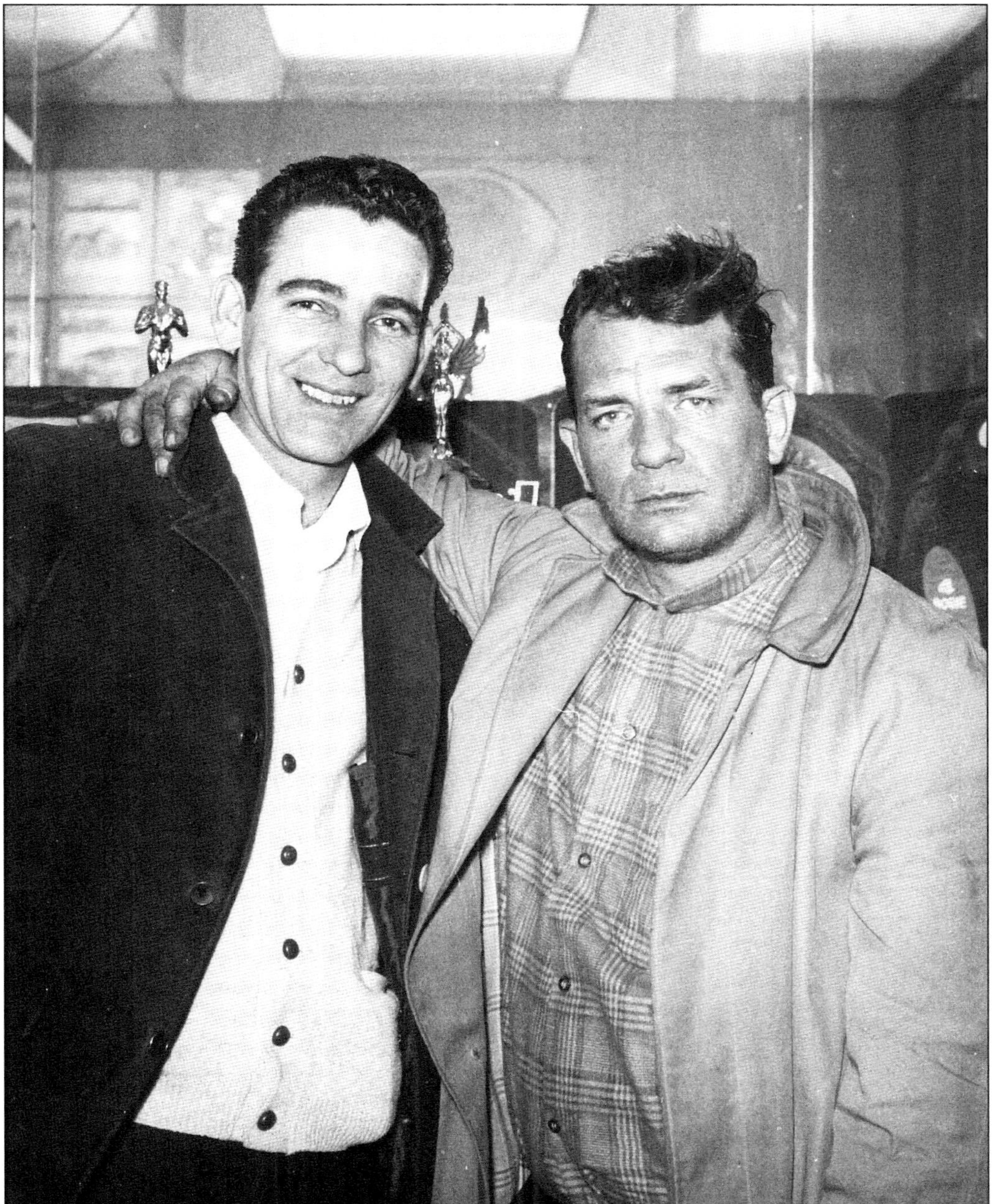

George Poirier, Lowell's most active photographer, appears with Jack Kerouac at the Celebrity Lounge. This photograph was taken by lounge owner Manny Bello on March 28, 1964. Legend has it that Johnny Depp, of *Edward Scissorhands*, etc. fame, purchased the raincoat for $58,000. (GP)

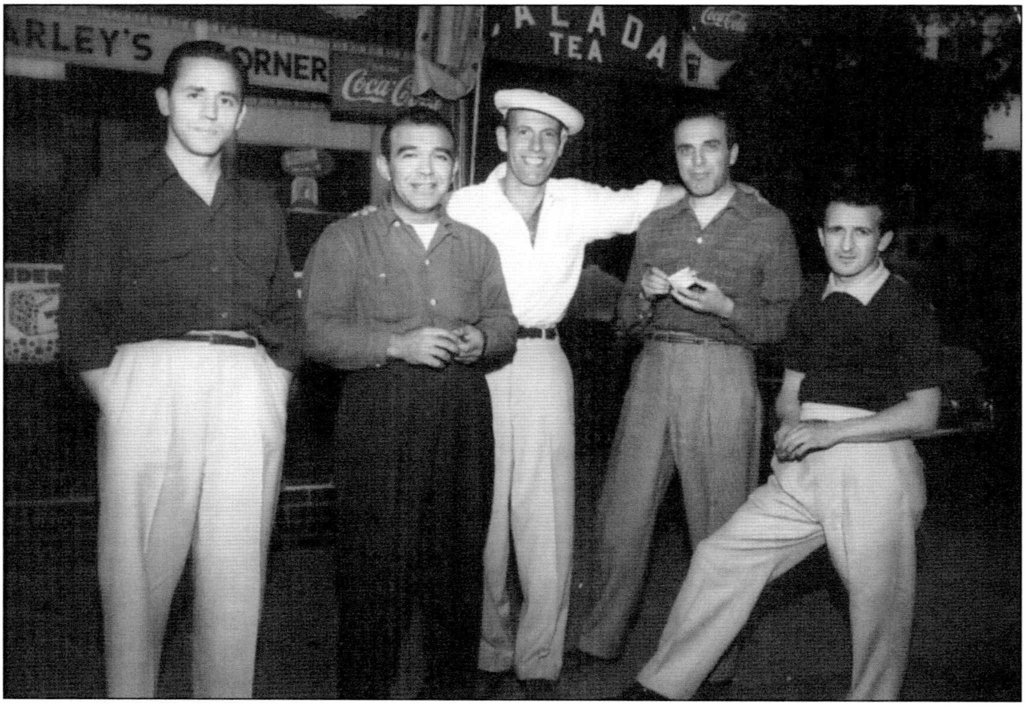

Outside Charley's Corner, night owls (from left to right) Chris "Pappy" Apostolakos, Chris "Keto" Christakos, Jim "Flash" Fletchers, William "Akie" Metilinos, and Bill Koumantzelis pass some time together in 1948. (BC)

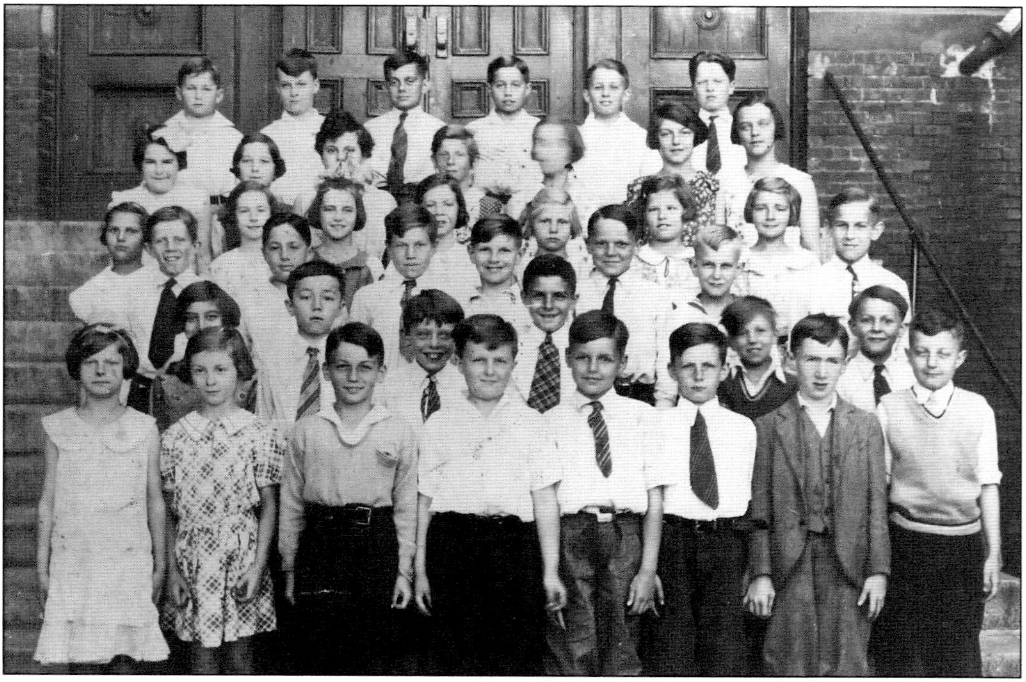

These students were photographed on the front steps of the Morey School, *c.* 1930. (GP)

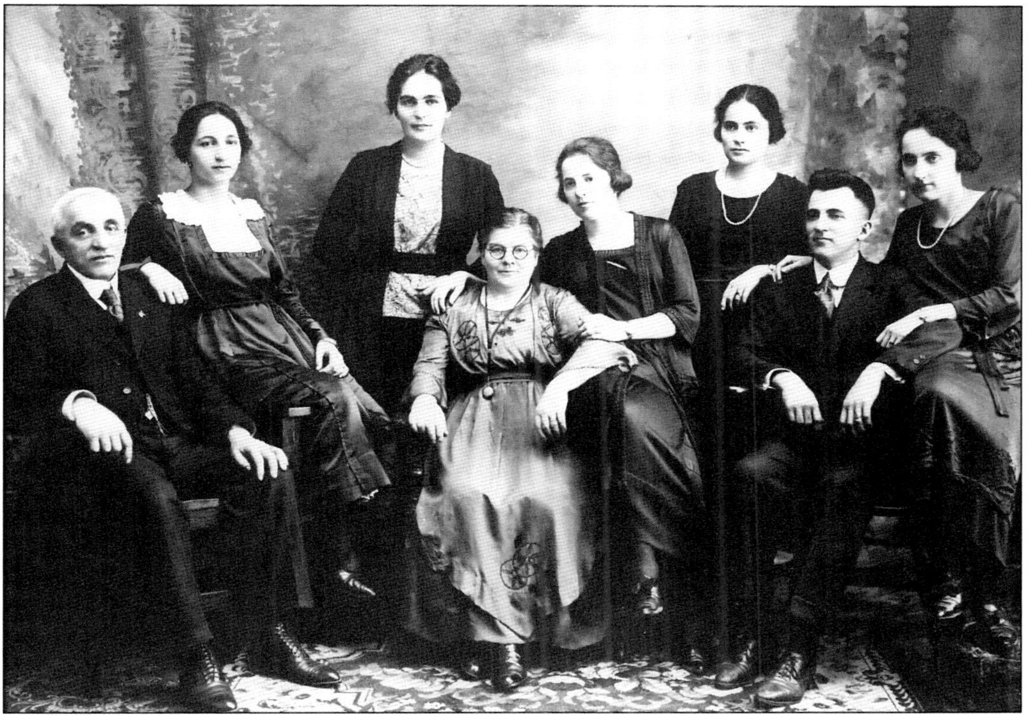

The Allard family, comprised of Mr. and Mrs. Allard, their six daughters, and one son, lived at 135 White Street, *c.* 1921. (GP)

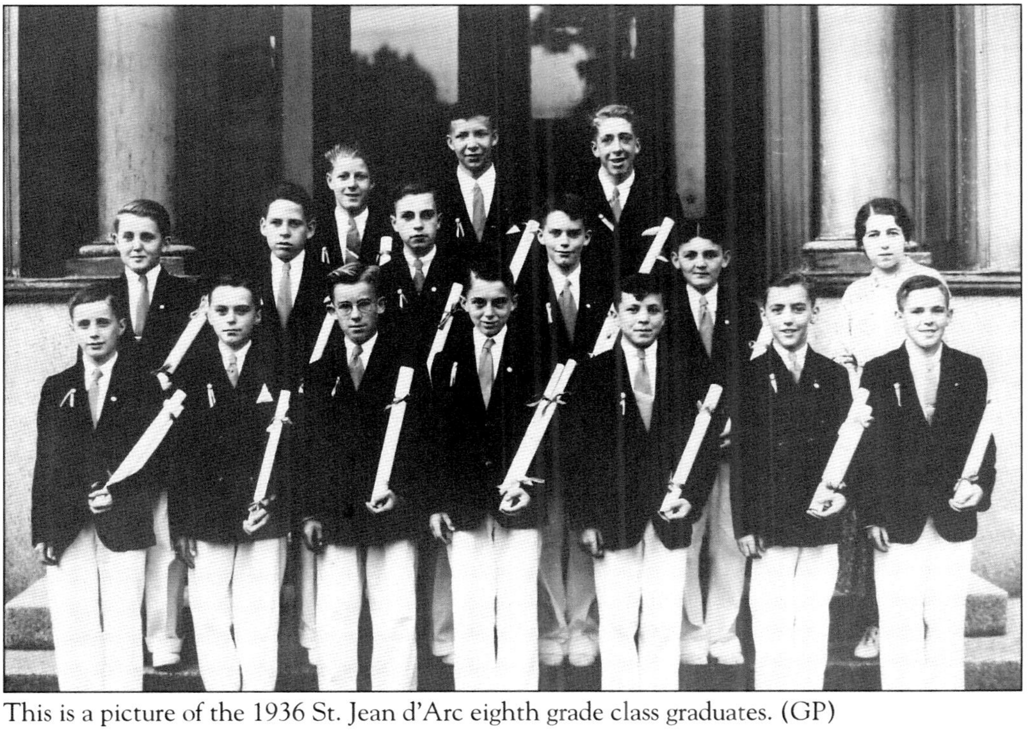

This is a picture of the 1936 St. Jean d'Arc eighth grade class graduates. (GP)

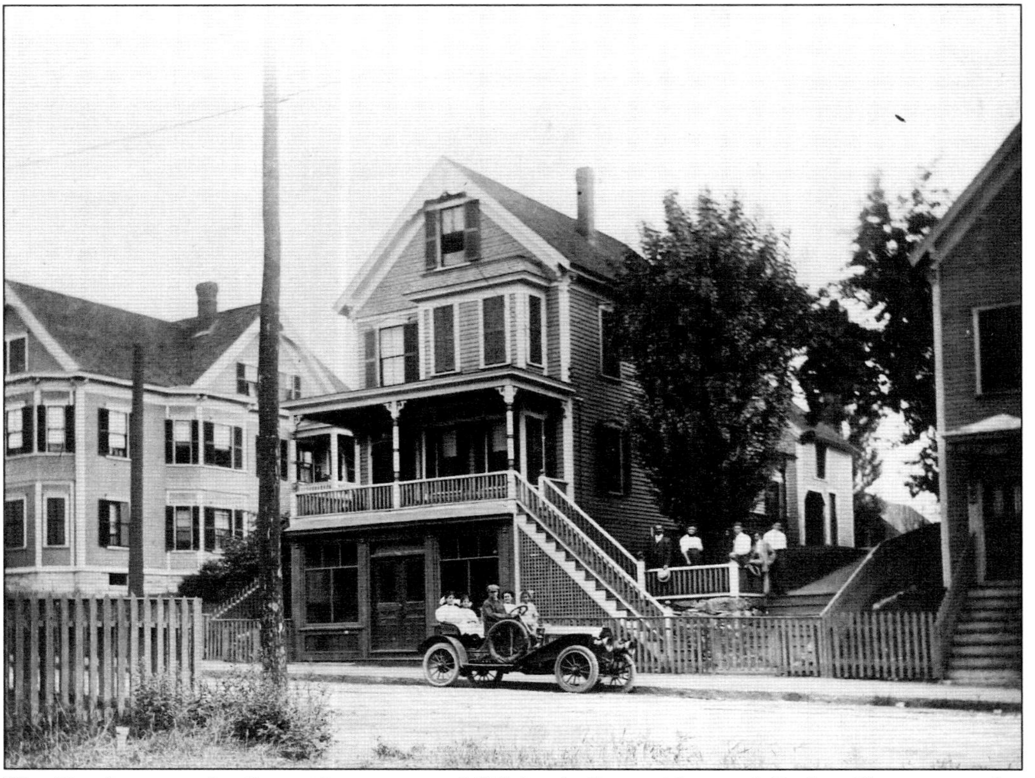

The Descheneaux family residence was at 767 Moody Street. Norman's Barber Shop was in the storefront below. (GP)

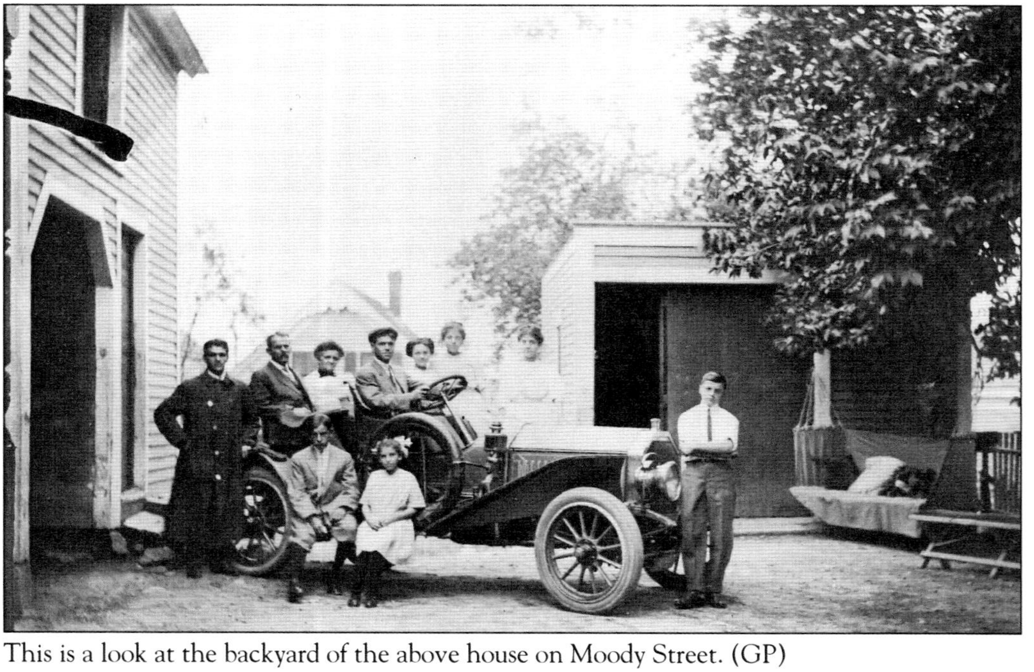

This is a look at the backyard of the above house on Moody Street. (GP)

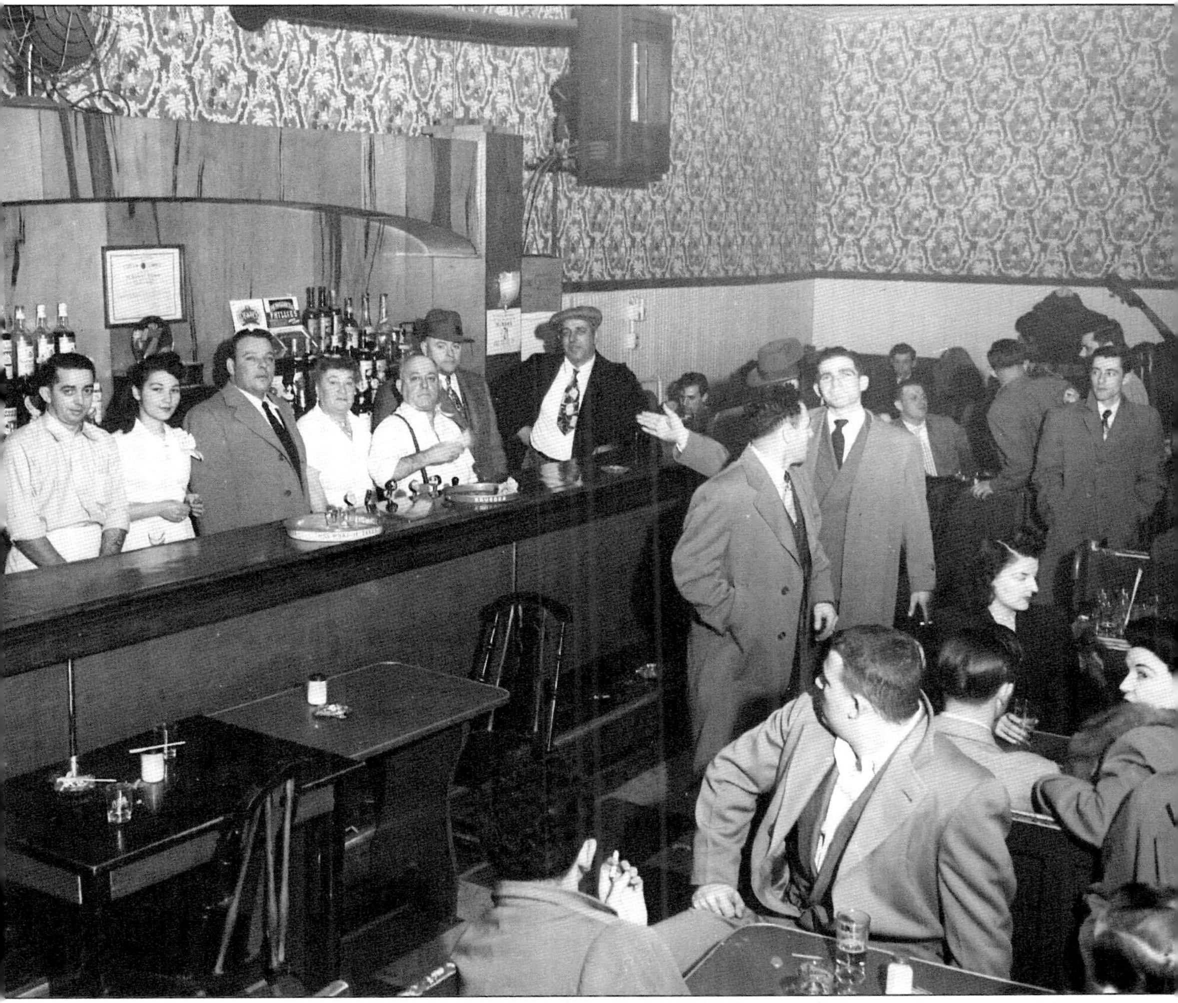

George Poirier took this shot of the Moody Gardens on Moody Street while standing on a table on New Year's Eve in 1951. Mary Lippe stands next to the central figure of Gene Berube, owner of the bar. Del Beland, owner of Del's Café, on Merrimack Street, near the corner of Cabot Street, is at the far end of the bar.

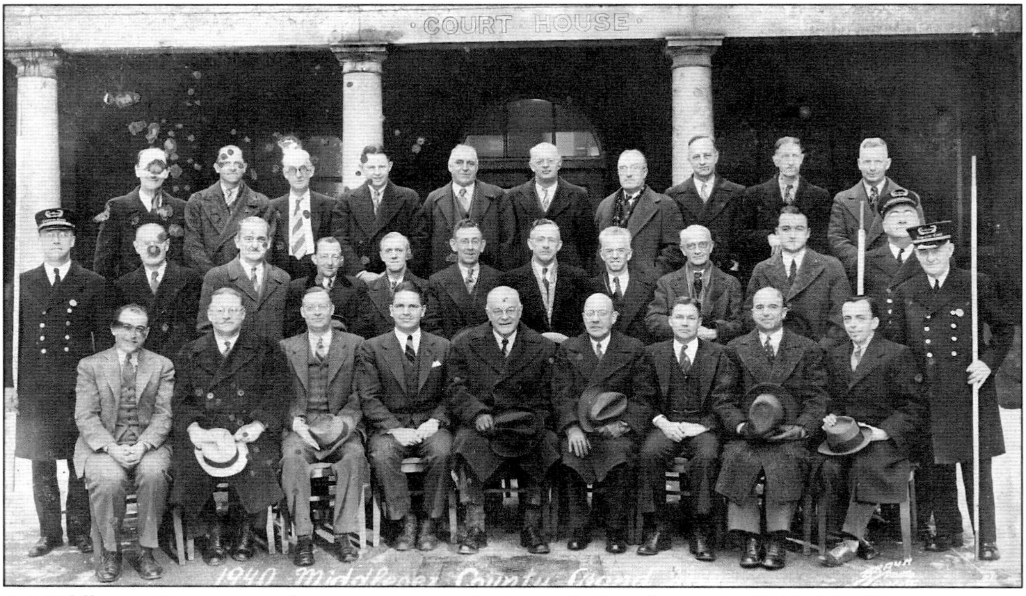

A Middlesex County grand jury appears at the Lowell Courthouse in 1940. (DHS)

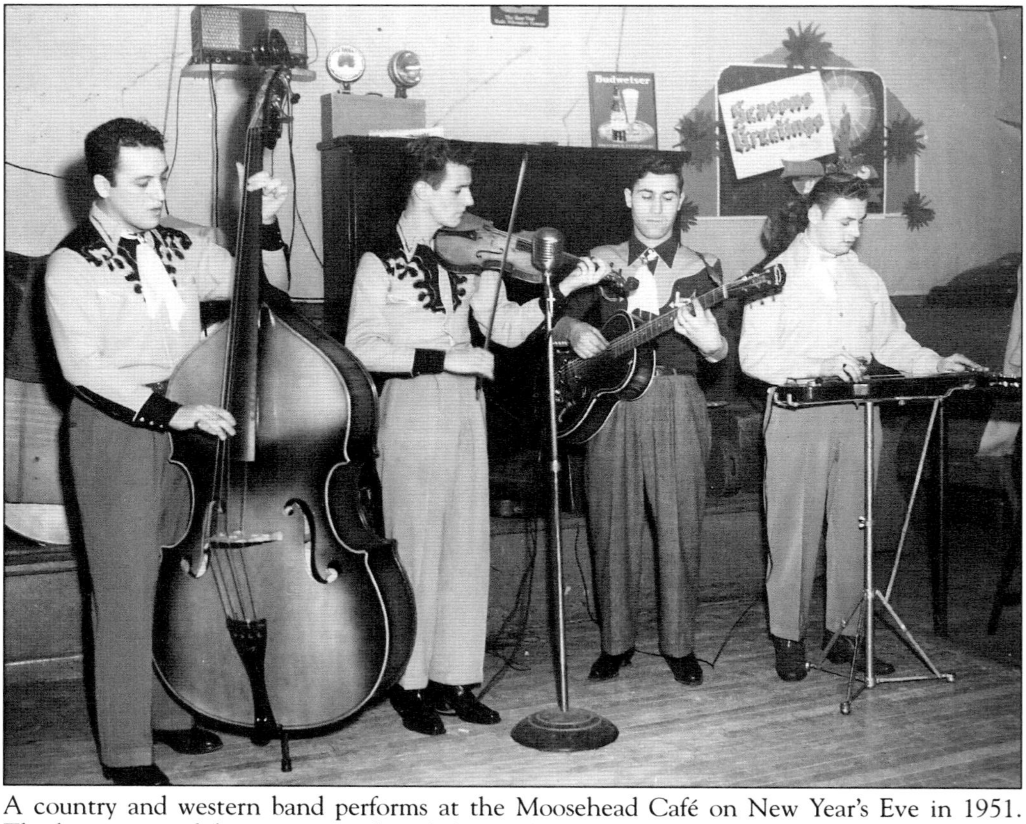

A country and western band performs at the Moosehead Café on New Year's Eve in 1951. The last names of the musicians, from left to right, are St. George, Arsenault, Damboise, and Desmarais. Vic Damboise is still playing Hawaiian guitar today. (GP)

Five

Some Streets

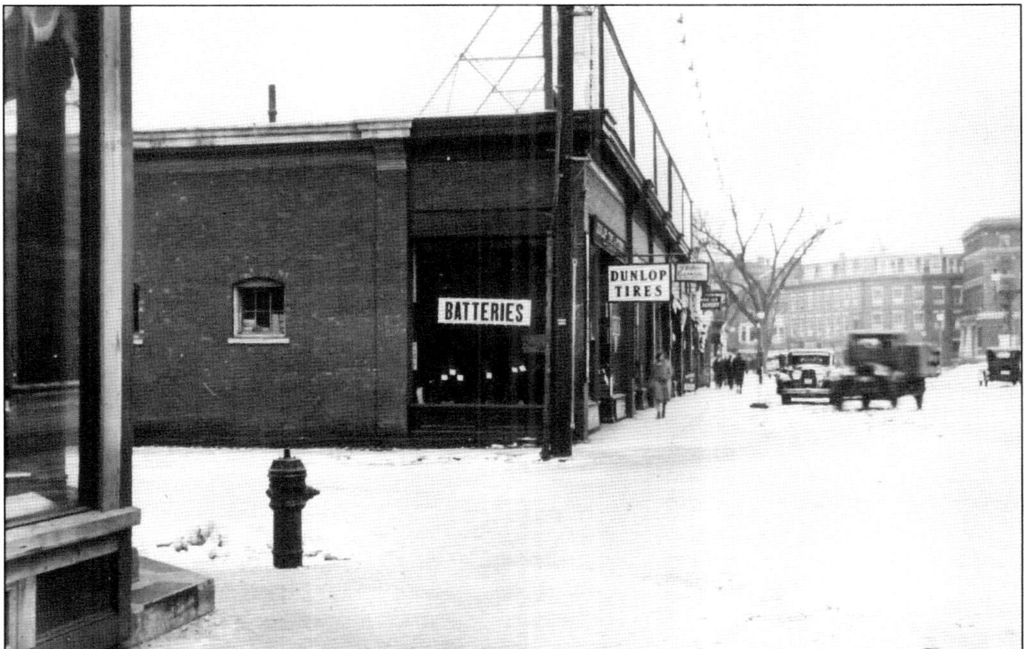

This January 13, 1931 image depicts Moody Street at Prince Street. (BK)

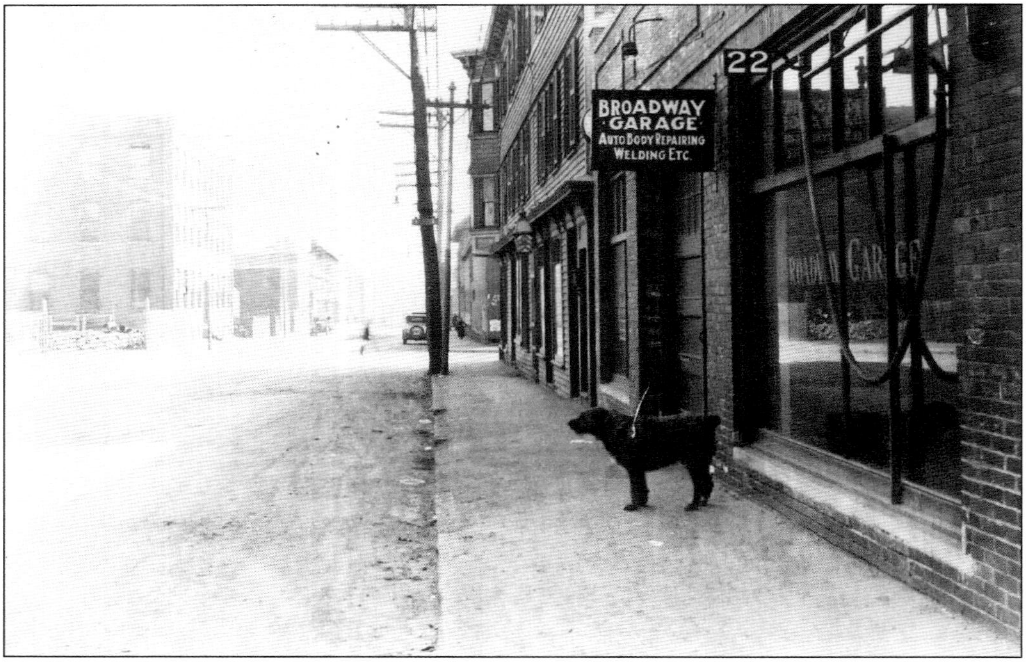

A solitary dog stands guard at the Broadway Garage at 22 Broadway Street on November 17, 1927. (BK)

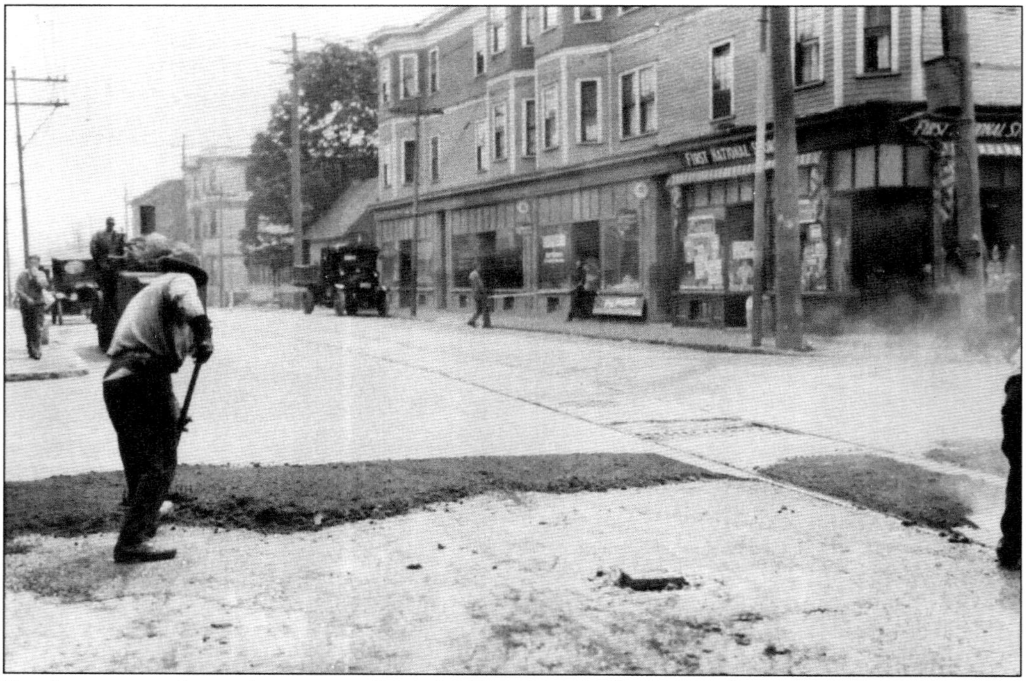

Road repair is taking place across from the First National Store at the corner of Broadway and School Streets on November 23, 1938. (BK)

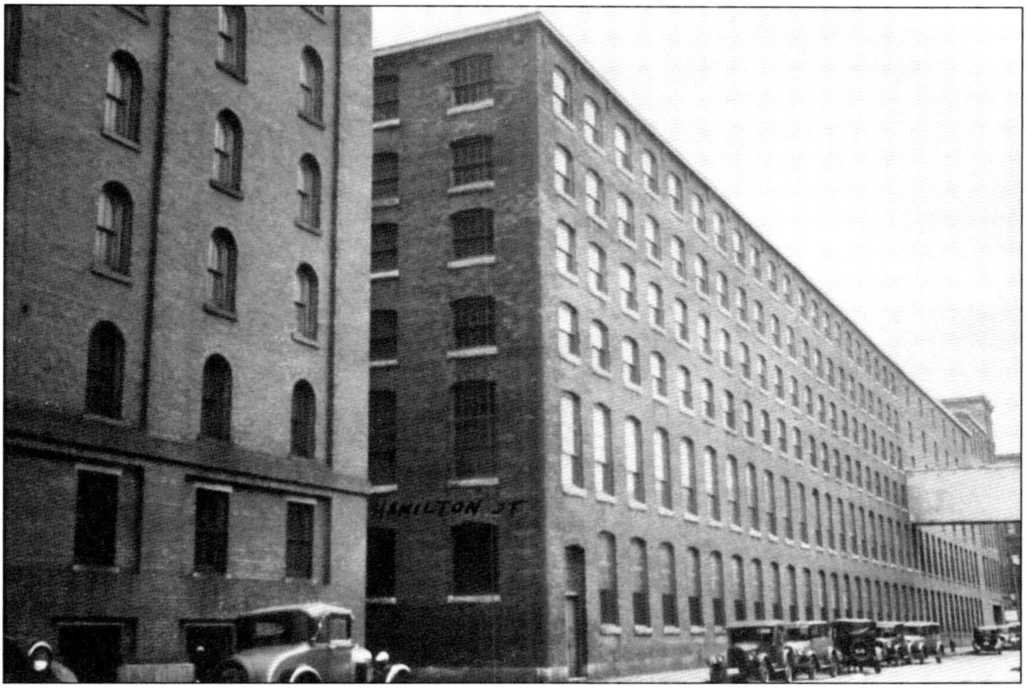

Jackson Street has changed very little in the 1920s. (BK)

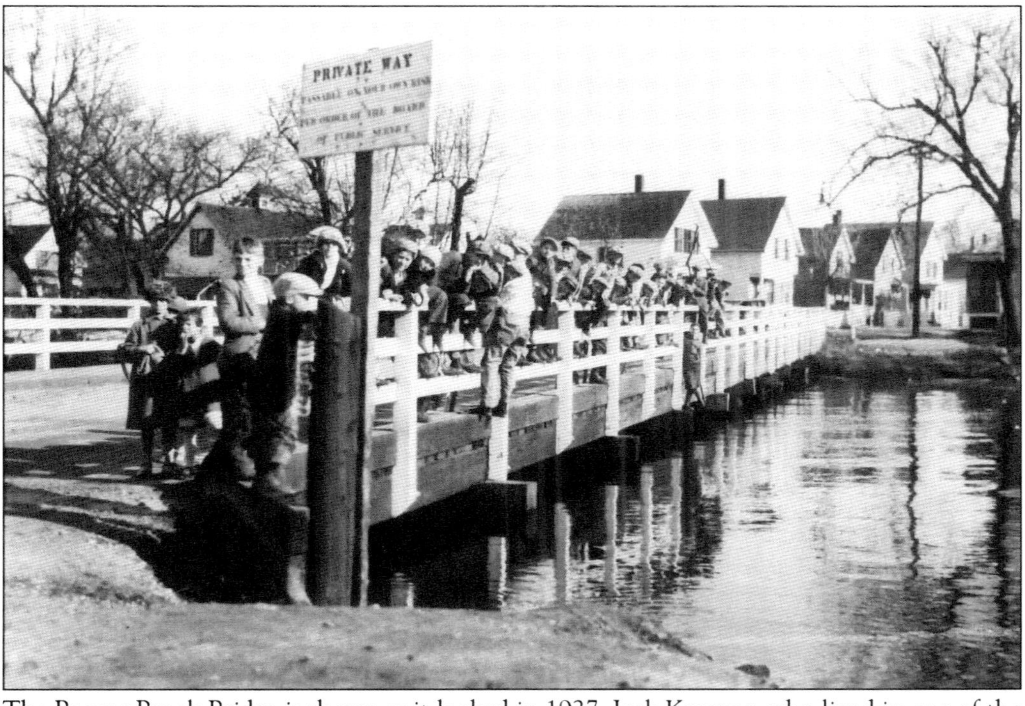

The Beaver Brook Bridge is shown as it looked in 1927. Jack Kerouac, who lived in one of the houses in the background, would have been five years old.(BK)

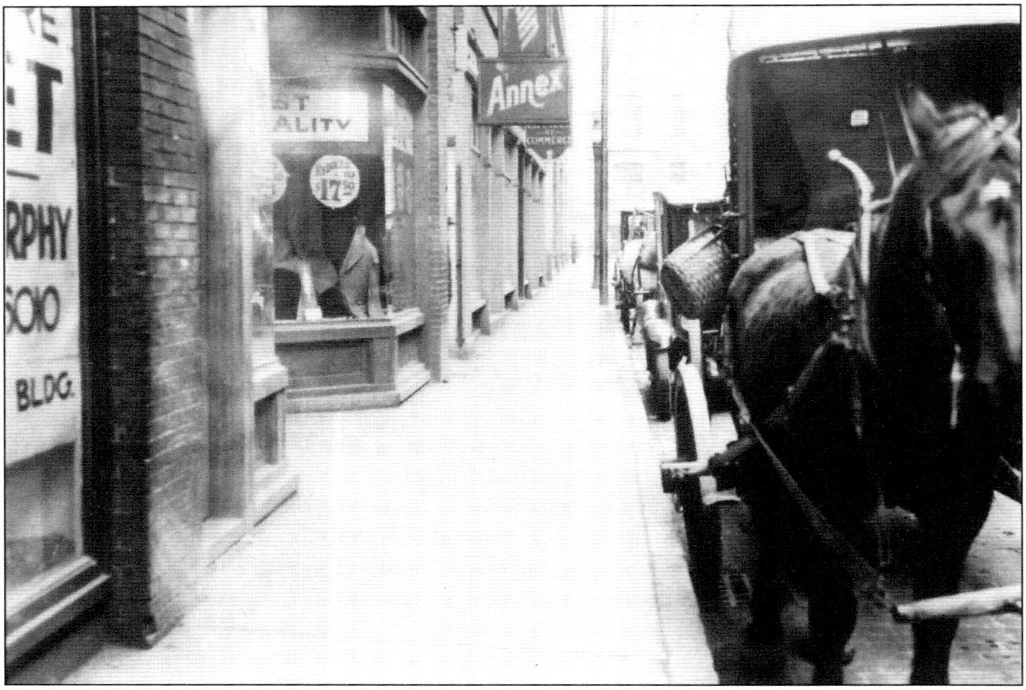

This is Prescott Street on February 17, 1928. There is no parking here today. (BK)

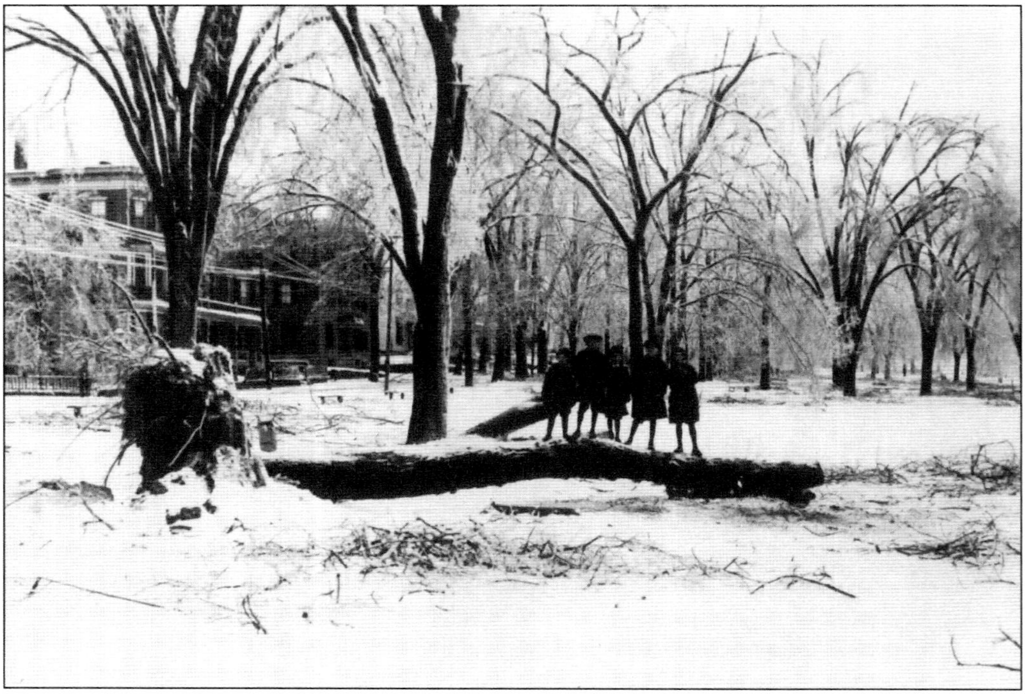

The North Common was photographed on November 24, 1921. (BK)

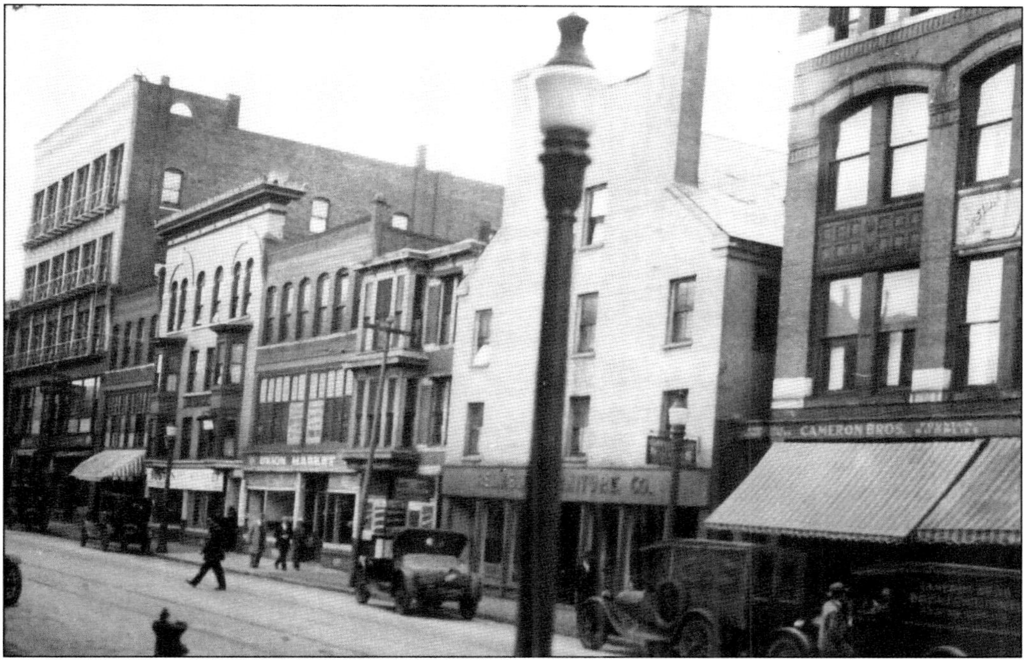

This February 24, 1931 image features Willie Street. The brick building in the right background is still intact. (BK)

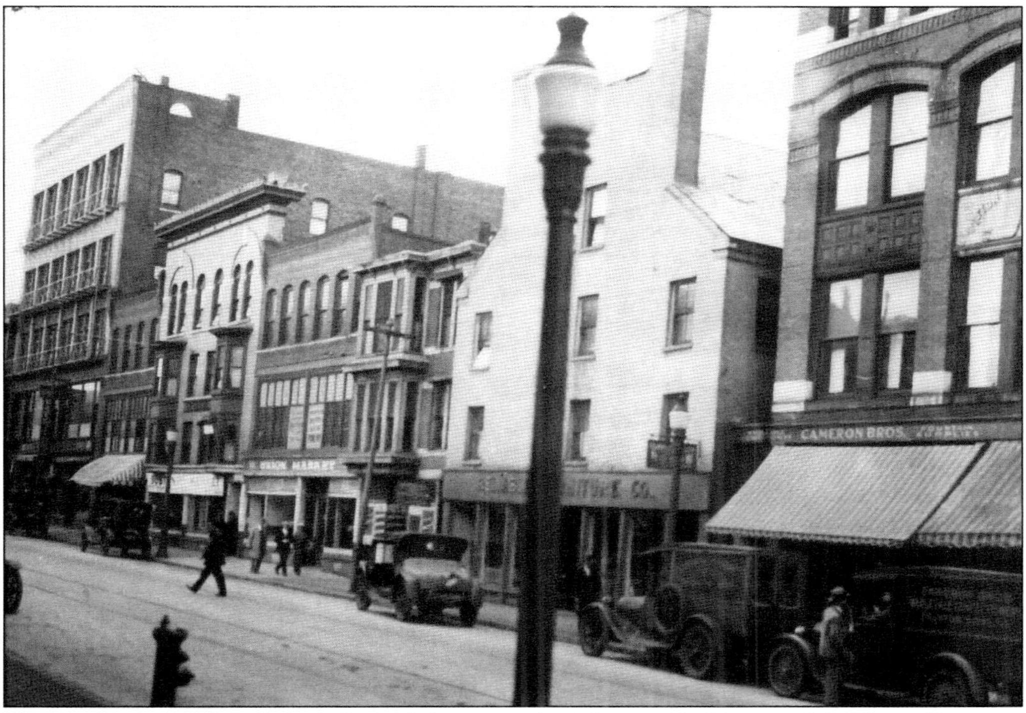

The Cameron Brothers' store (far right) was in the Marston Building on Middlesex Street in 1929. Older Lowellians will remember the street lights.(BK)

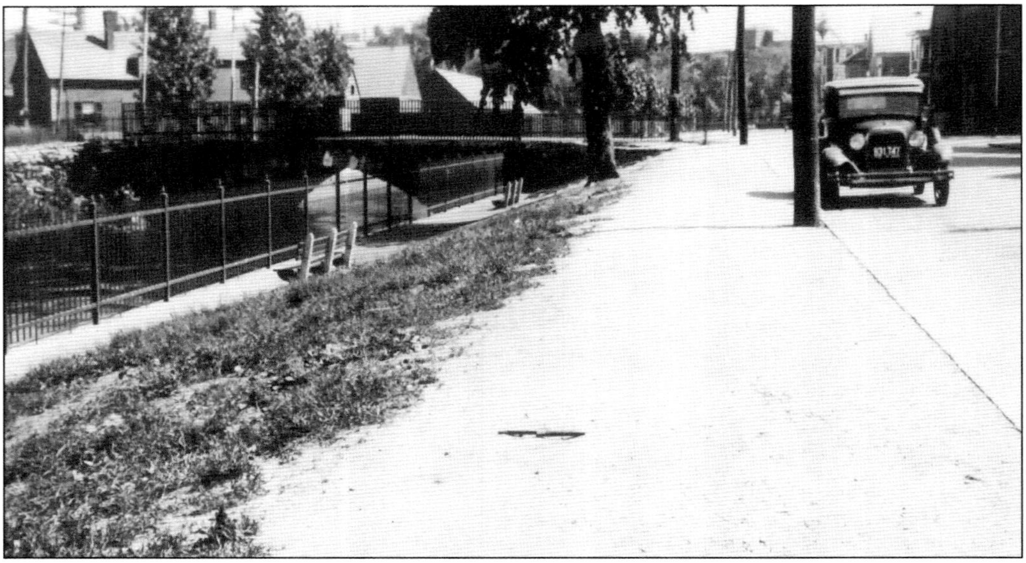

Suffolk Street is shown here on June 16, 1930. Locks and canal buildings, now the site of Macheras Service Mart, are in the background. The bridge in the background is the site of a skirmish between the Irish and the townspeople that took place on May 31, 1831. After three attempts to cross into the Acre to destroy the newly built St. Patrick's Church, the townspeople were chased back downtown. (BK)

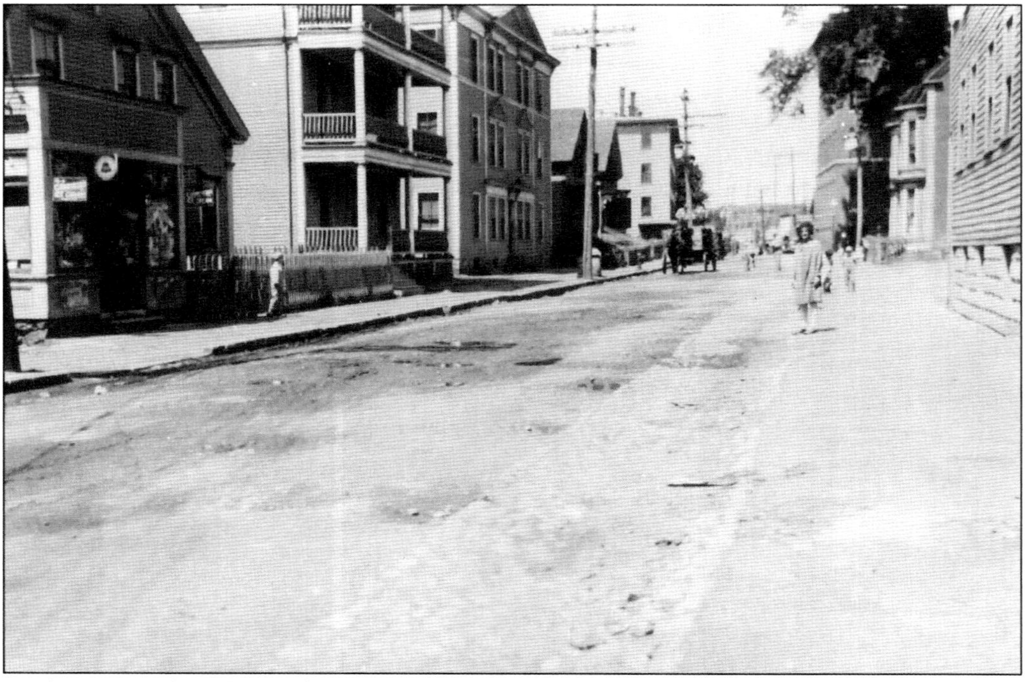

Rock Street is the subject of this June 15, 1928 picture. (BK)

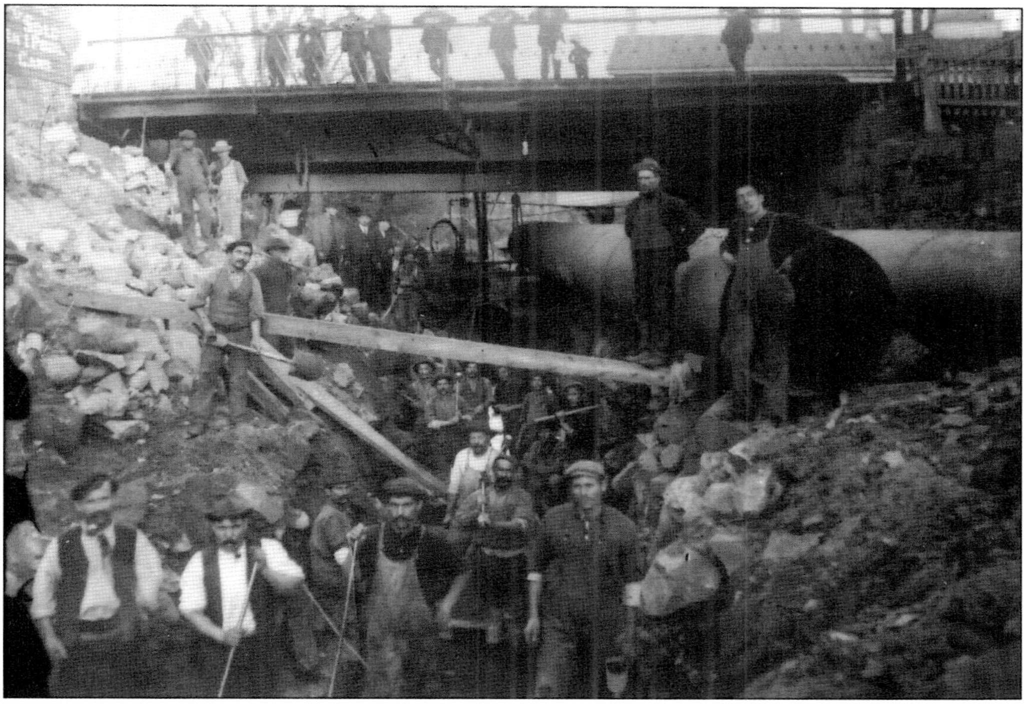

This undated image looks under the School Street Bridge. Onlookers gaze down on workers excavating under the bridge. (JP)

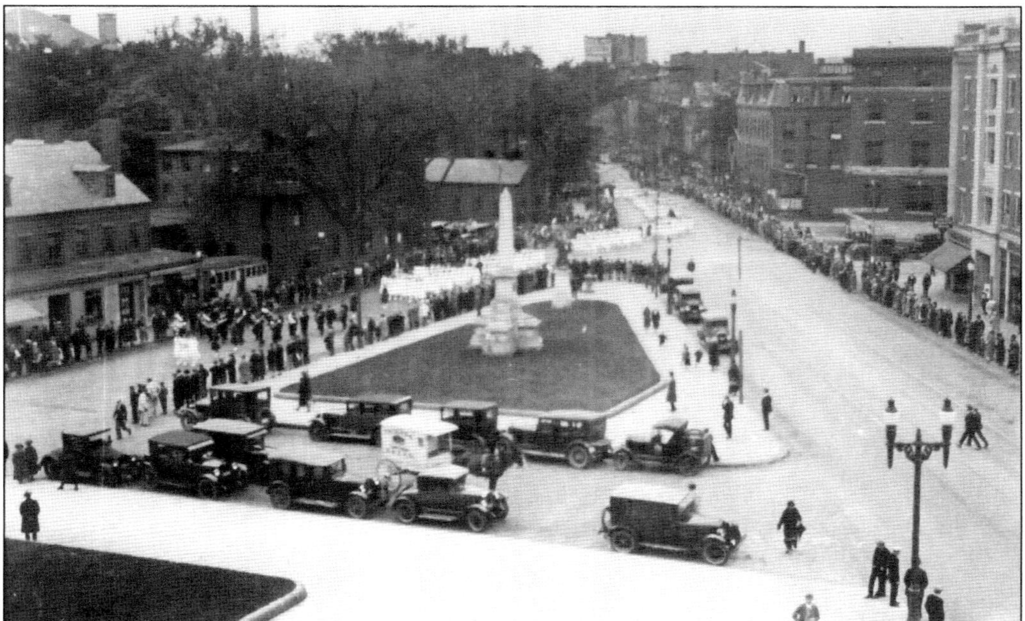

Lowell High School students march up Moody Street. This image, taken from city hall, looks down Merrimack Street on May 27, 1926. (BK)

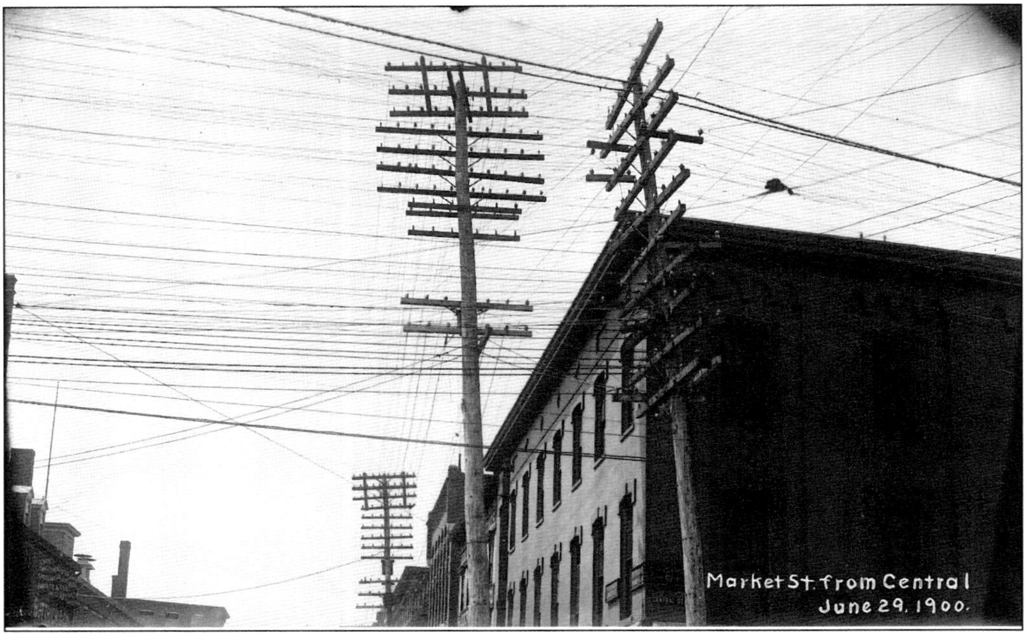

A peculiar angle of Market Street was captured from Central Street on June 27, 1900.

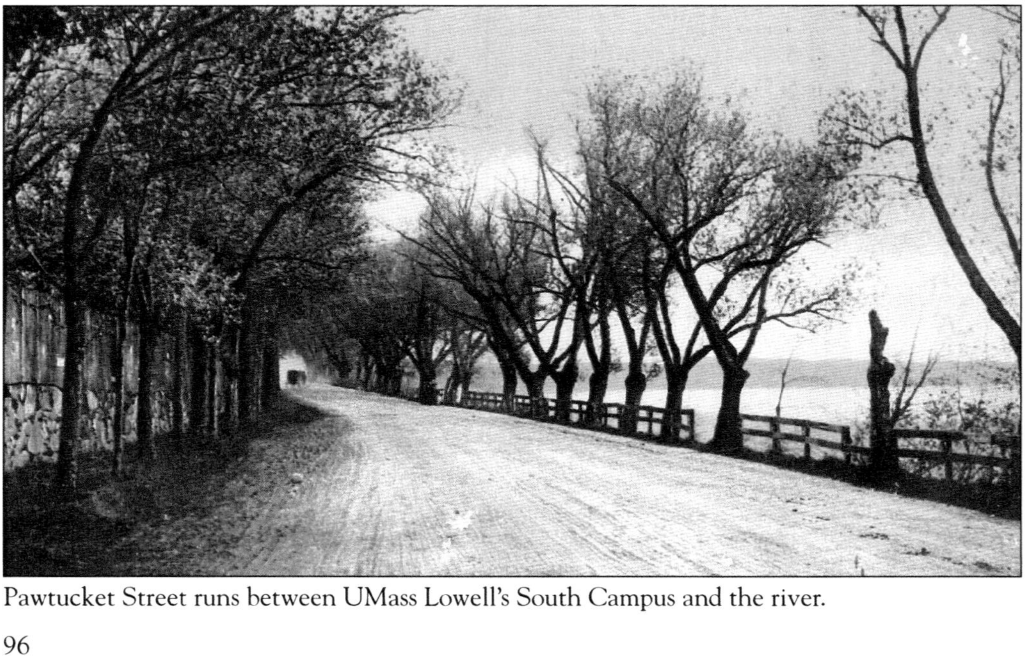

Pawtucket Street runs between UMass Lowell's South Campus and the river.

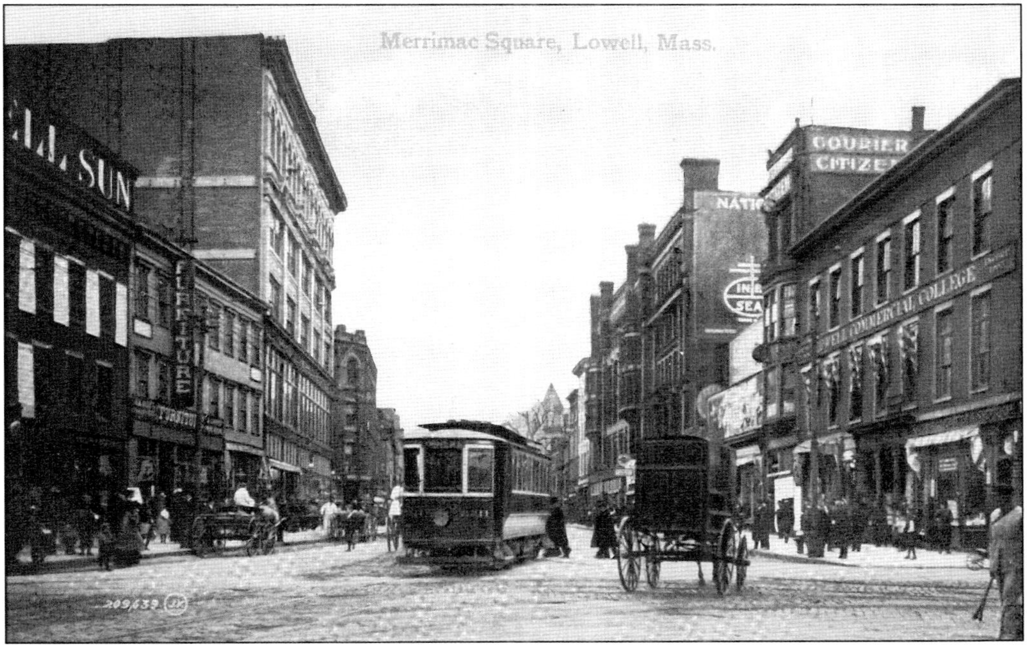

This postcard view shows Merrimac Square in 1910. Note *Lowell Sun*'s Building on the left. It was replaced by the eleven-story yellow brick structure that is still standing in Kearney Square. (CP)

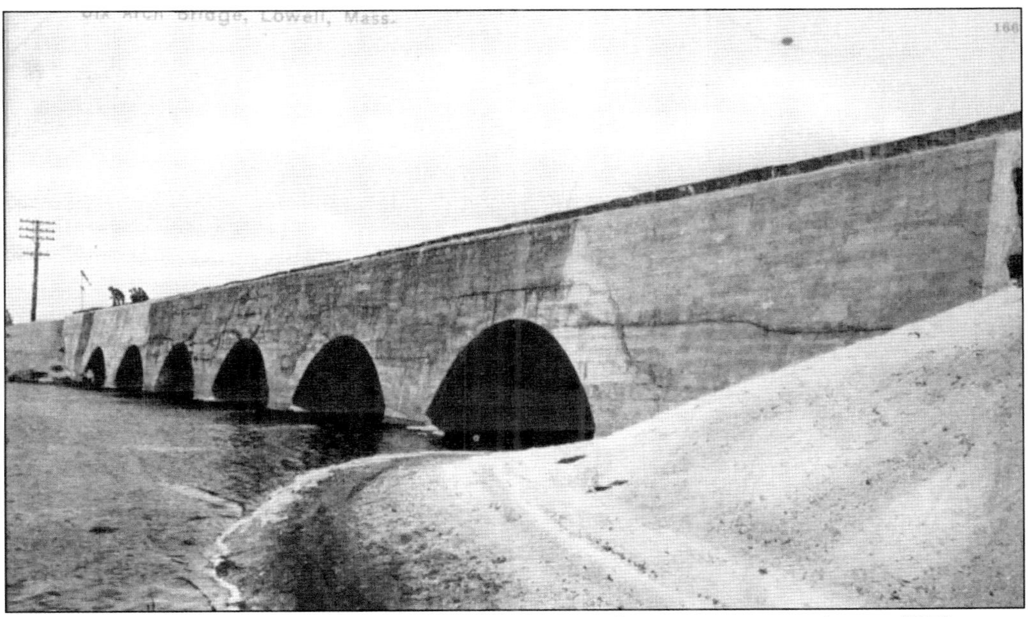

The Six Arch Bridge over the Concord River is seen in this c. 1910 postcard view. (CP)

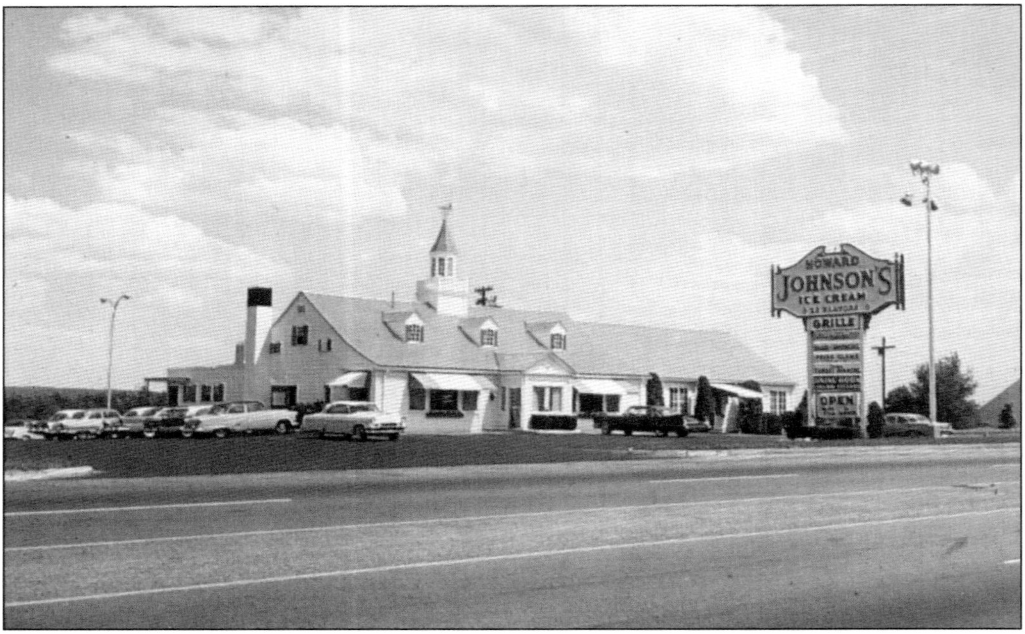

Howard Johnson's was located on Chelmsford Street in Lowell in the late 1950s. (CP)

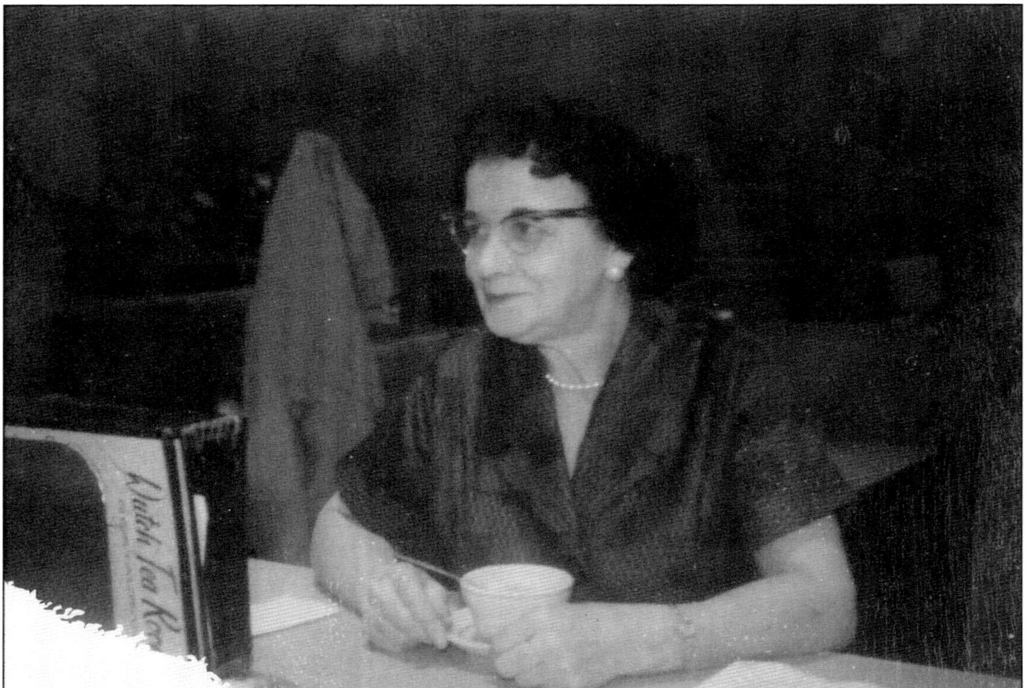

Mrs. Yvette Clancy was the head cashier at the Dutch Tea Room on Merrimack Street in the early 1960s. The Dutch Tea Room was a favorite haunt of Lowell High and Keith Academy students. (DC)

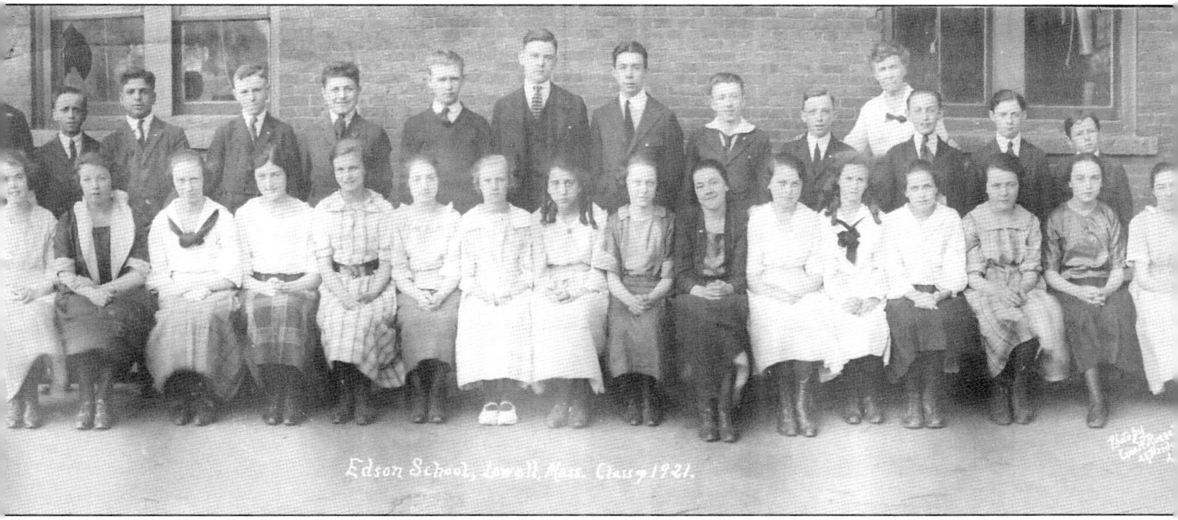

This 1921 image features the Edson School. (HT)

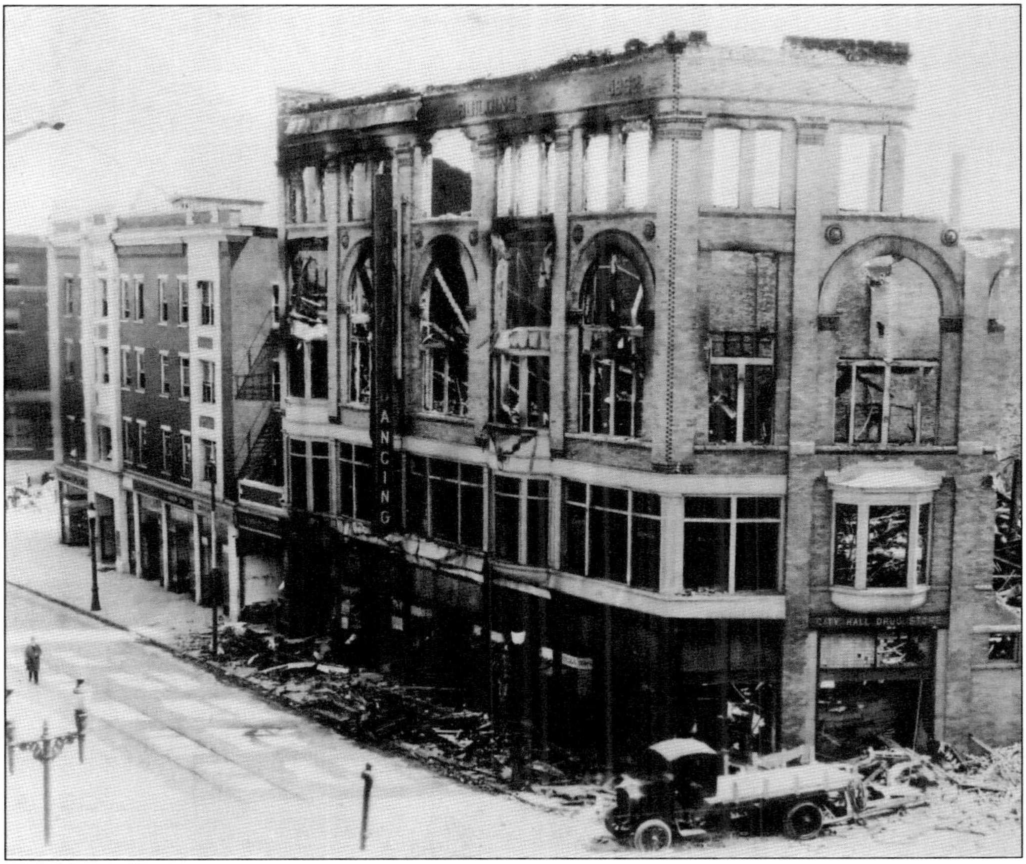

This is a picture of the aftermath of the disastrous Associates Building fire of April 1924. The photograph was probably taken from a second-story, city hall window. (GL)

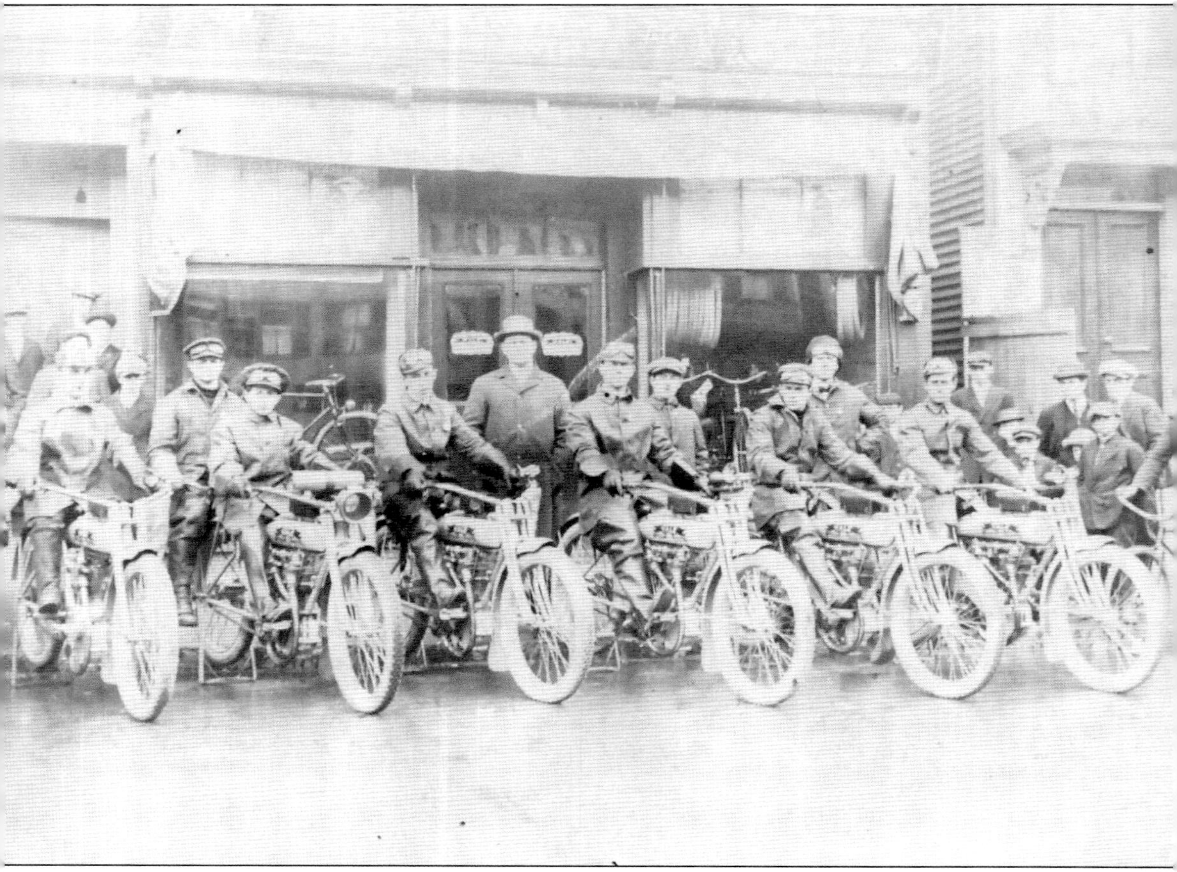

Members of the Lowell Motor Bicycle Club pose in front of Parmentier's Bicycle Shop at 705 Aiken Street in 1910. (DHS)

Local actor Anthony Finneral seems to be making a comment about Lowell's own monster, Sasqua, *c.* 1973. (HF)

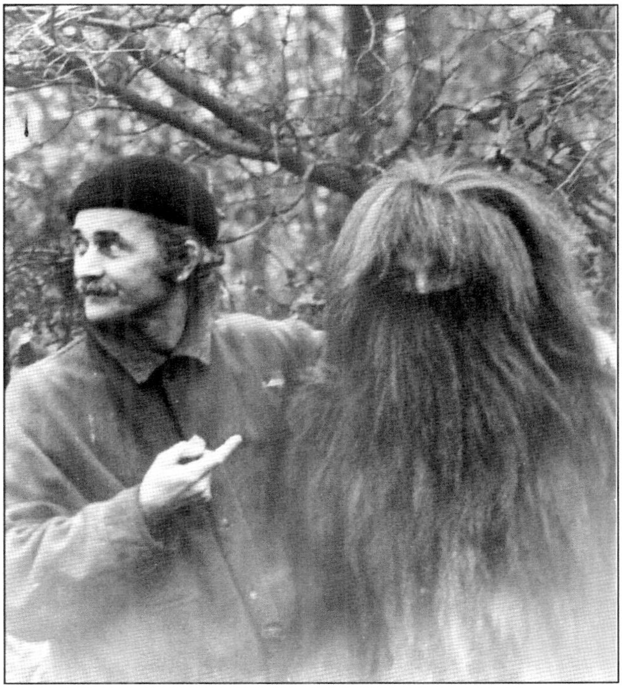

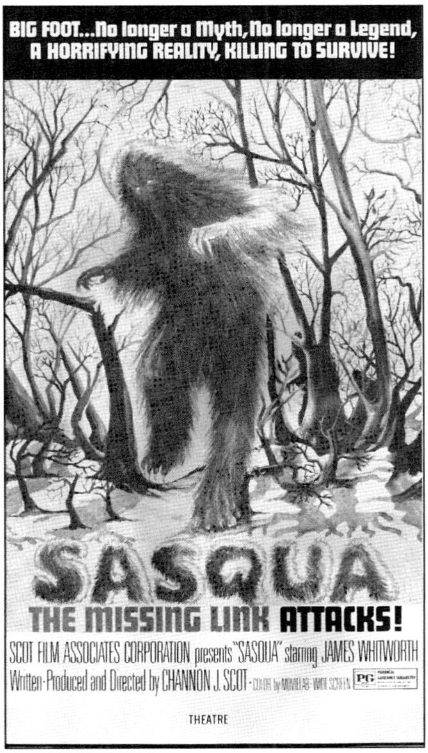

Sasqua was a horrifying reality filmed in Lowell and Dracut. One critic wrote that the movie had "no redeeming qualities." (HF)

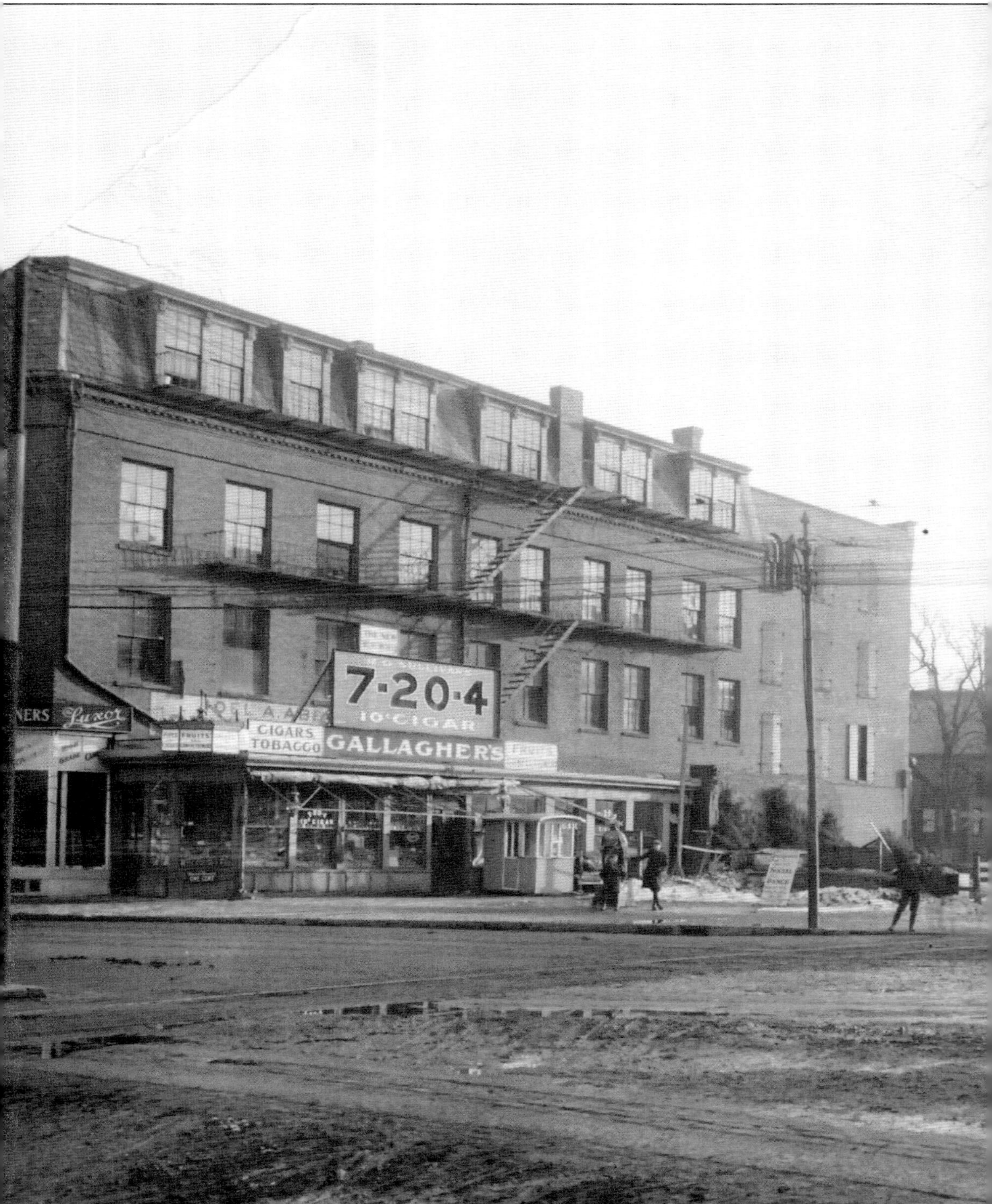

This photograph, taken in 1904, looks down Dutton Street from Merrimack Street soon after the razing of the remains of Huntington Hall and before the construction of the

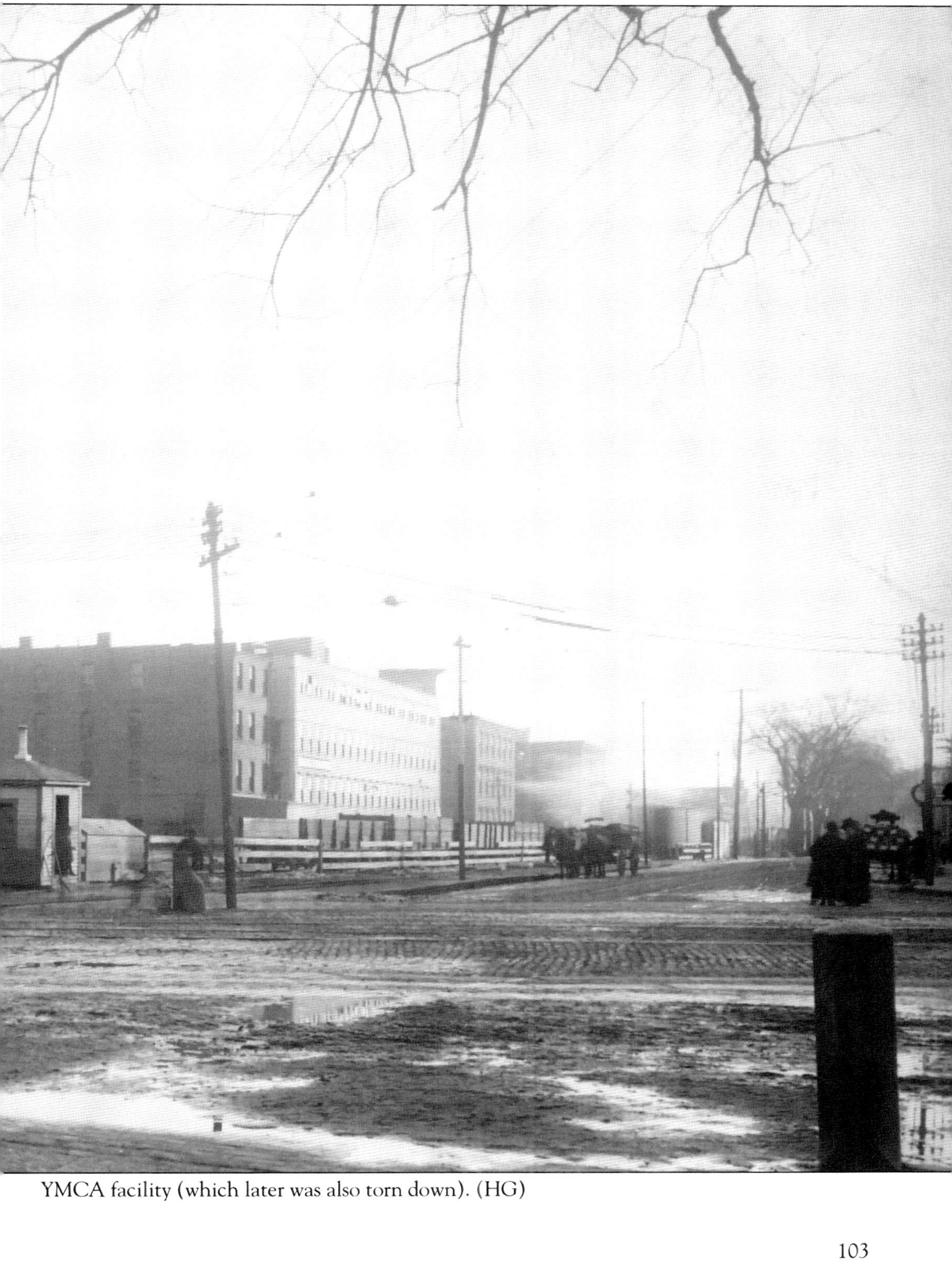

YMCA facility (which later was also torn down). (HG)

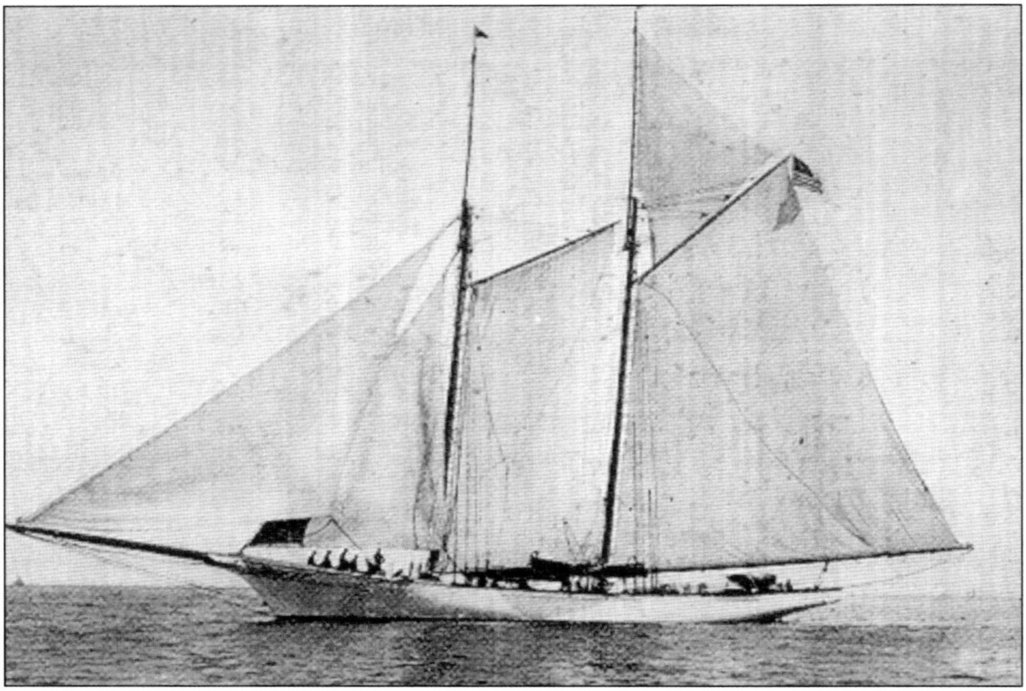

Ben Butler's private yacht, *America*, shown here in the 1870s, was a captured Confederate vessel. Butler acquired it from the Navy for a small sum. The America's Cup racing trophy was named for her. (IHL)

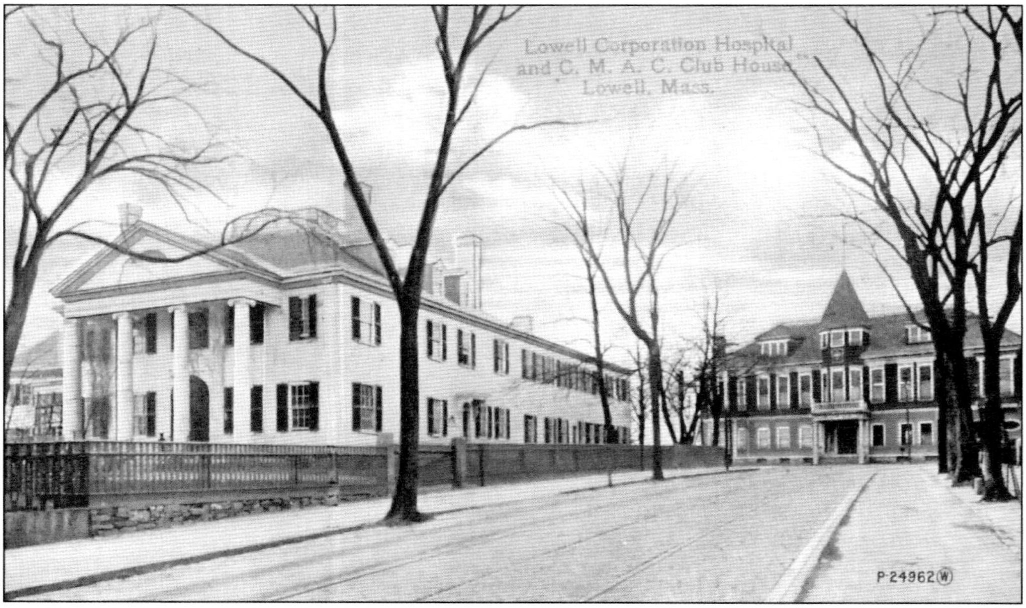

On Merrimack Street in 1918, the Lowell Corporation Hospital (at left) later became the St. Joseph's Hospital building. It was originally known as Kirk Boott's home. The building at the top of the street was built as a French-Canadian fraternal organization. The long-remembered "Bienvenue" sign in bright lights went out permanently in 1997. (CP)

Six

Heroes, Adventurers, Tycoons, Artists, and Others

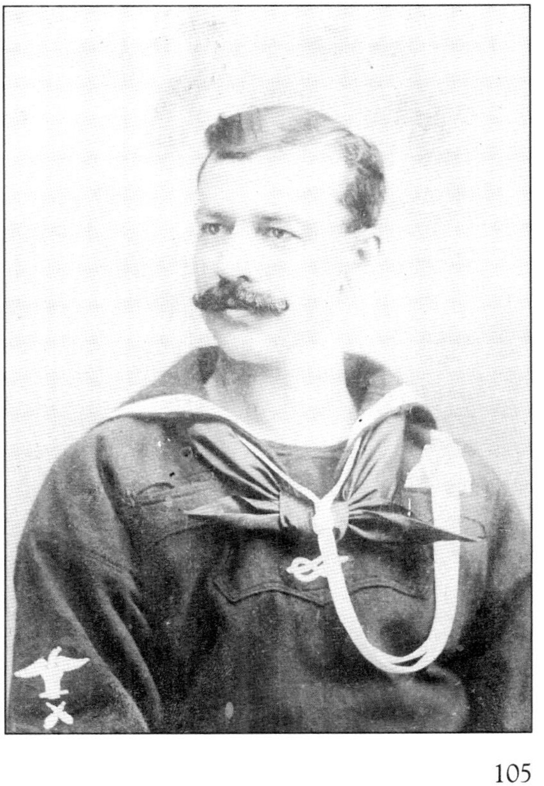

Lieutenant George Charette was awarded the Congressional Medal of Honor for his actions during the Spanish Civil War. He lived at 38 Gorham Avenue. He died in 1938. (JP)

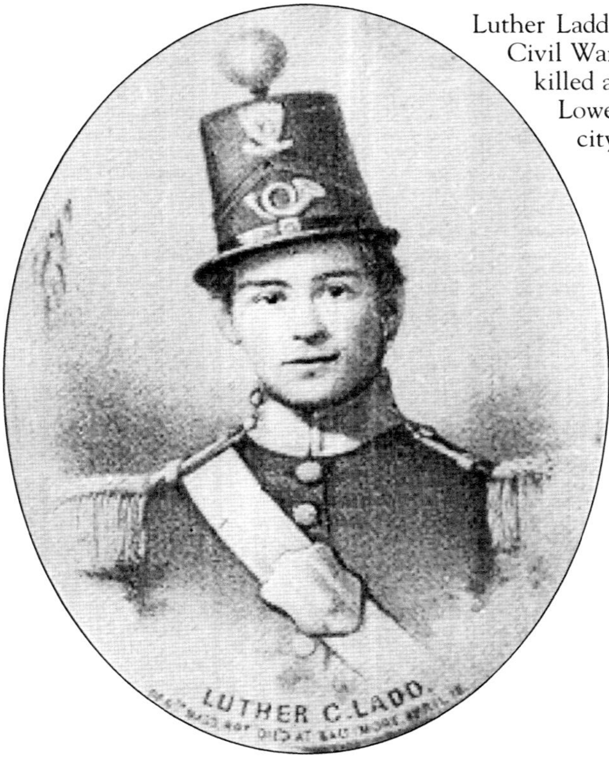

Luther Ladd was one of the first fatalities of the Civil War. He was seventeen years old. He was killed as Baltimore citizens rioted against the Lowell regiment as it marched through the city.(IHL)

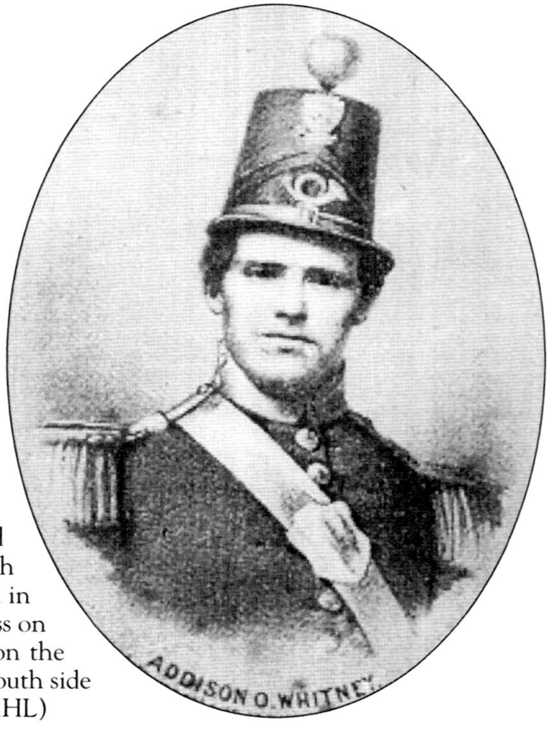

Addison Whitney, another of the first three to die, was twenty-six. One other man, Charles Taylor, was also killed, but his origins have never been traced. On April 15, 1861, orders were given to muster the local regimentation to appear at Boston Common. On the next day, seven hundred men assembled at Huntington Hall on Merrick Street. They marched directly to Baltimore and were greeted with enthusiasm on their route until they arrived in Baltimore. The regiment was required to pass on foot or by streetcar from the train station on the northern side of the city to the one on the south side to continue their progress to Washington. (IHL)

Humphrey Webster was the cousin of Daniel Webster. He lived for a while in a wooden house on the corner of Jackson and Central Streets, then moved his residence to Prescott Street, and finally located to 73 Bridge Street. He built the Appleton Mills Agents House on Appleton Street and the Lowell Machine Shops on Dutton Street (which was torn down). He erected many of the row houses and some of the brick houses still standing on Kirk Street. He was in charge of the carpentry for the old city hall and erected the Central Bridge. (IHL)

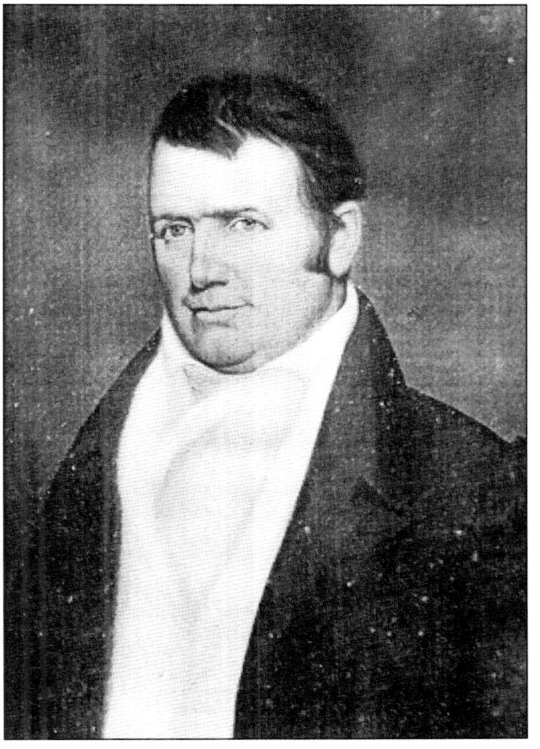

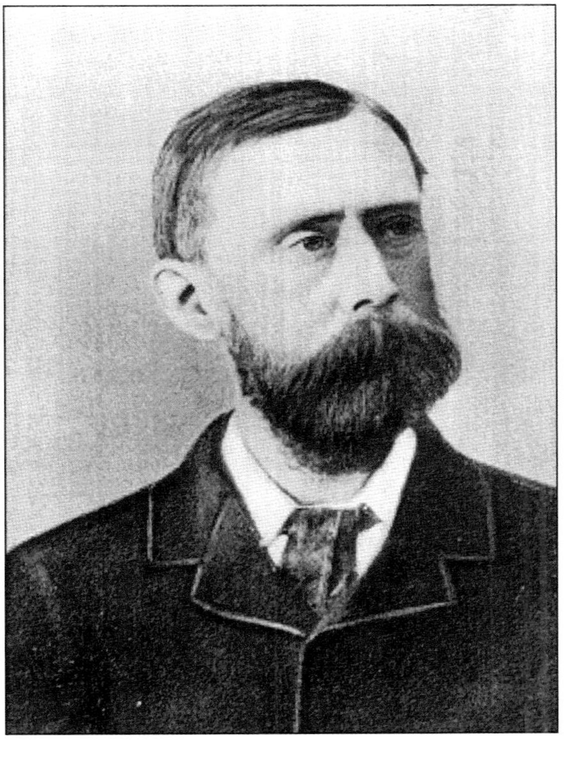

Joseph Ludlam made two extensive sea voyages with his father before he was twenty. He left a ship called the *Atmosphere* in China and became second officer of the *Williamette*, the first American steamer to navigate Chinese waters. During the revolt of Taiping, he served the Chinese government by commanding the gunboats *Zingara* and *Hyson*. In 1870 he served France during the Franco-Prussian War. The Chinese government honored him with induction into the Imperial Order of the Golden Dragon. In 1879 he was appointed agent of the Merrimac Manufacturing Company, a position he held until his death in 1896.

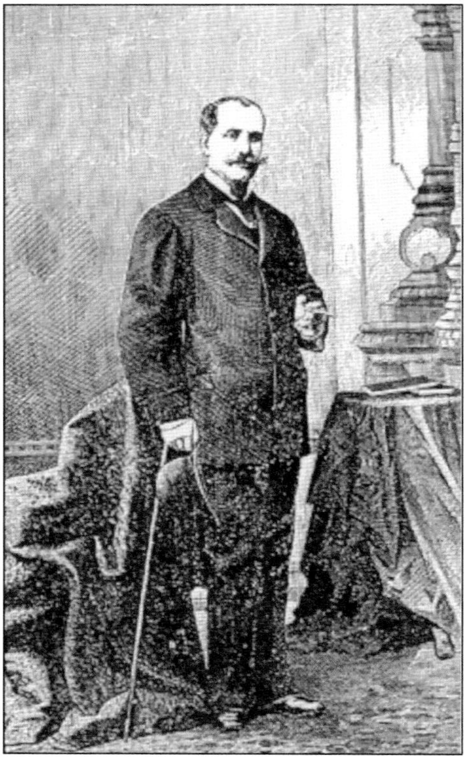

David Neal was born in Lowell in 1838. As a young man, he traveled to Europe to study art and settled in Munich. His paintings received the highest awards in Germany during his day. (IHL)

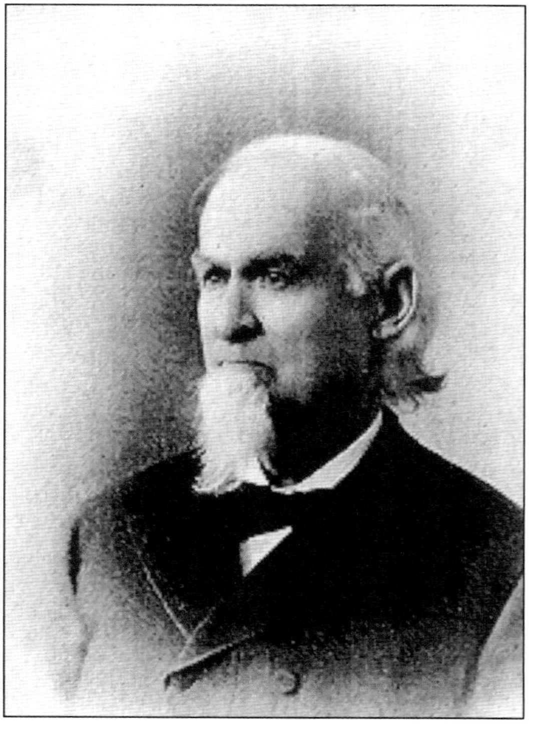

Nathaniel Davis worked on his father's farm in Warner, New Hampshire, until he was twenty-one. He came to Lowell in 1839 and became a granite cutter, cutting all the stone for the county jail (Keith Academy) and the old post office building on the corners of Appleton and Central Streets.

John Amory Lowell was born at the end of the eighteenth century in what would become Lowell. He graduated from Harvard in 1815 at age sixteen and began working for Kirk Boott. In 1835, he built the Boott Mills and was its treasurer and ultimately its president and director. He was a classical scholar, an eminent mathematician, an able botanist, and a rare linguist. He died in 1881. (IHL)

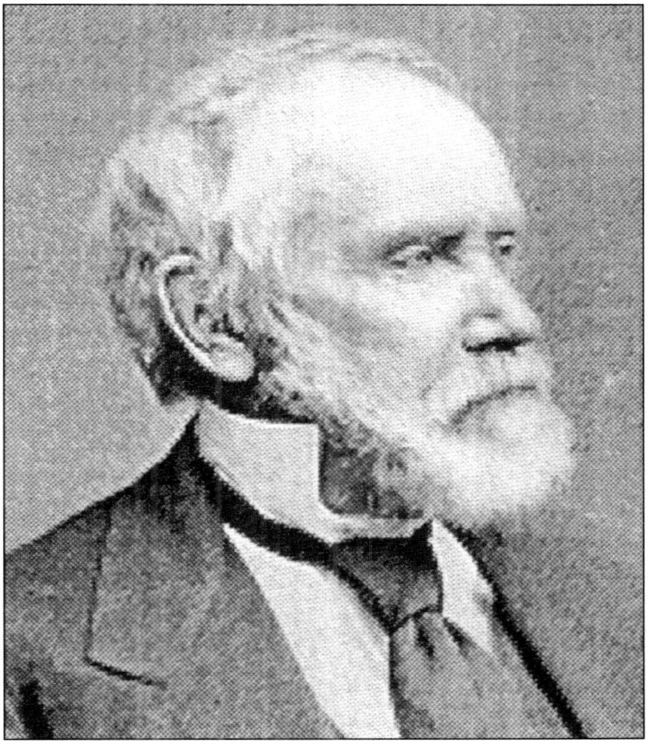

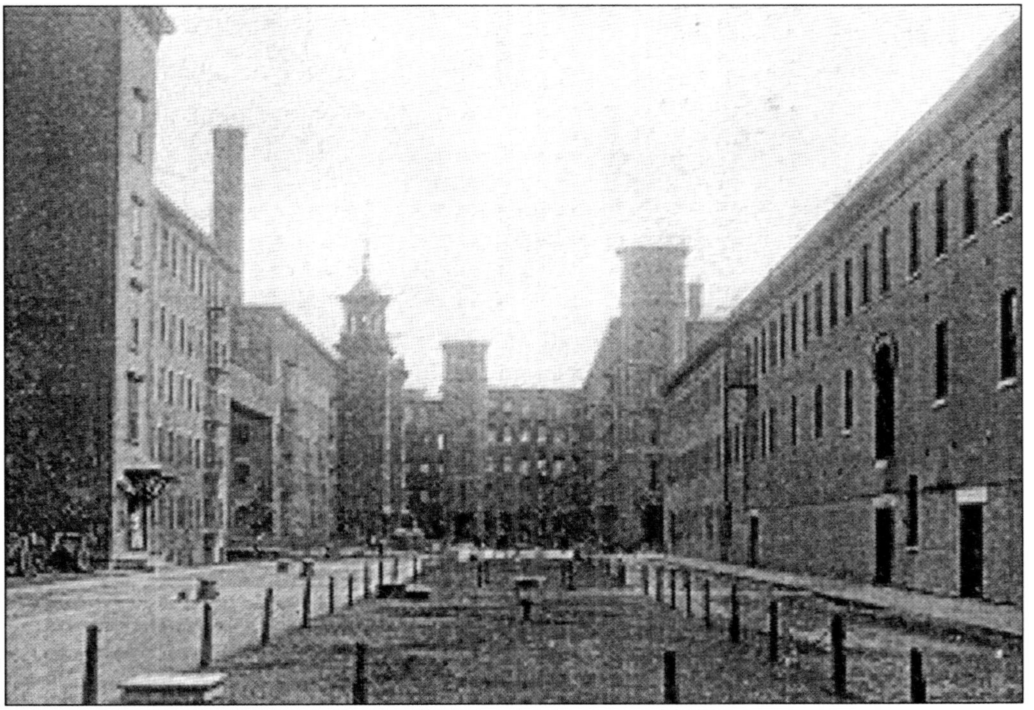

The courtyard of the Boott Mills was photographed *c.* 1880. (IHL)

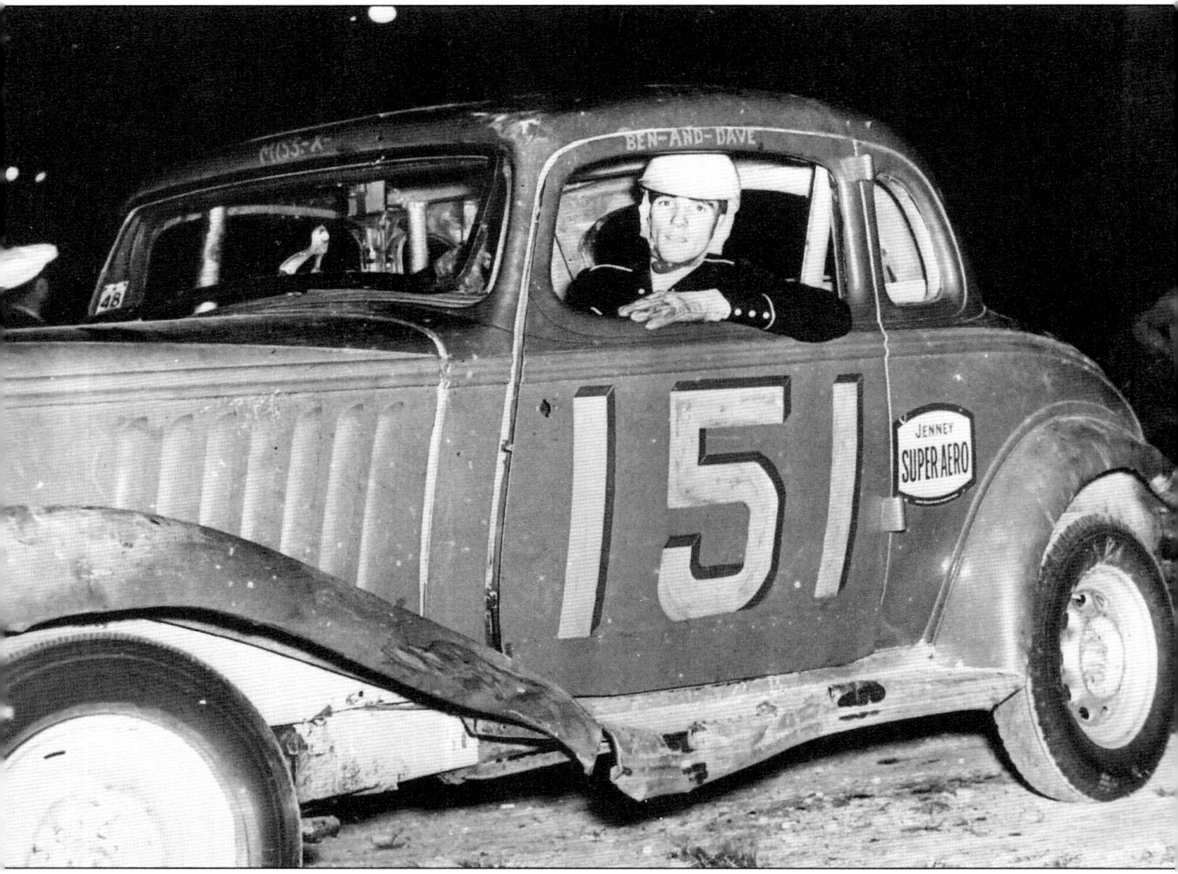

George Poirier sits behind the wheel of a 1928 Hudson Terraplane at the Hudson Speedway just before the race in 1948. The steering was modified to increase speed. George crashed through the guardrails, putting out all the lights at the Speedway, and ending his racing career. His date, later his wife Doris, told the author that her first thought was, "How do I get a ride home?" (GP)

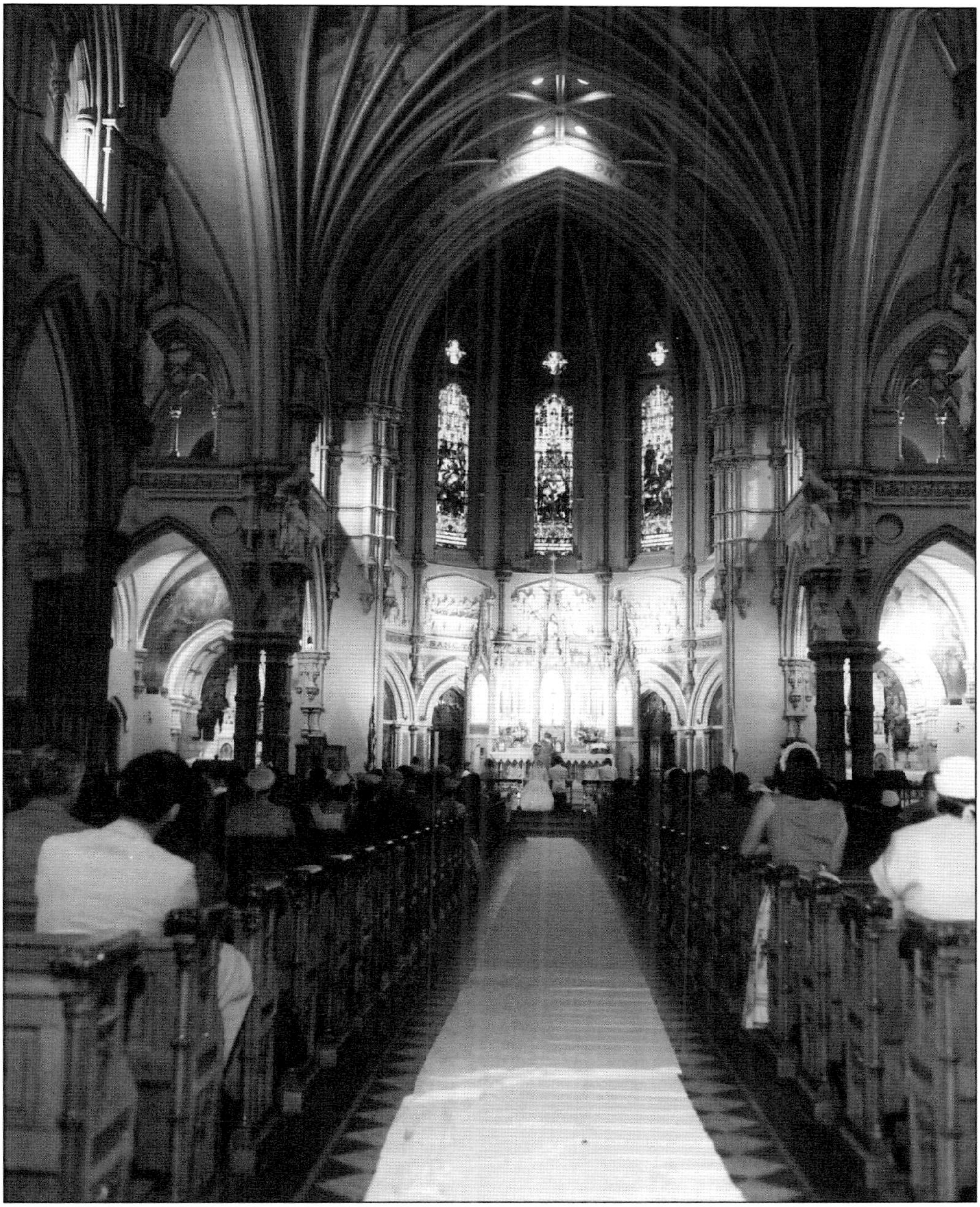

The interior of St. Peter's Church is shown in this 1960s wedding photograph. (GP)

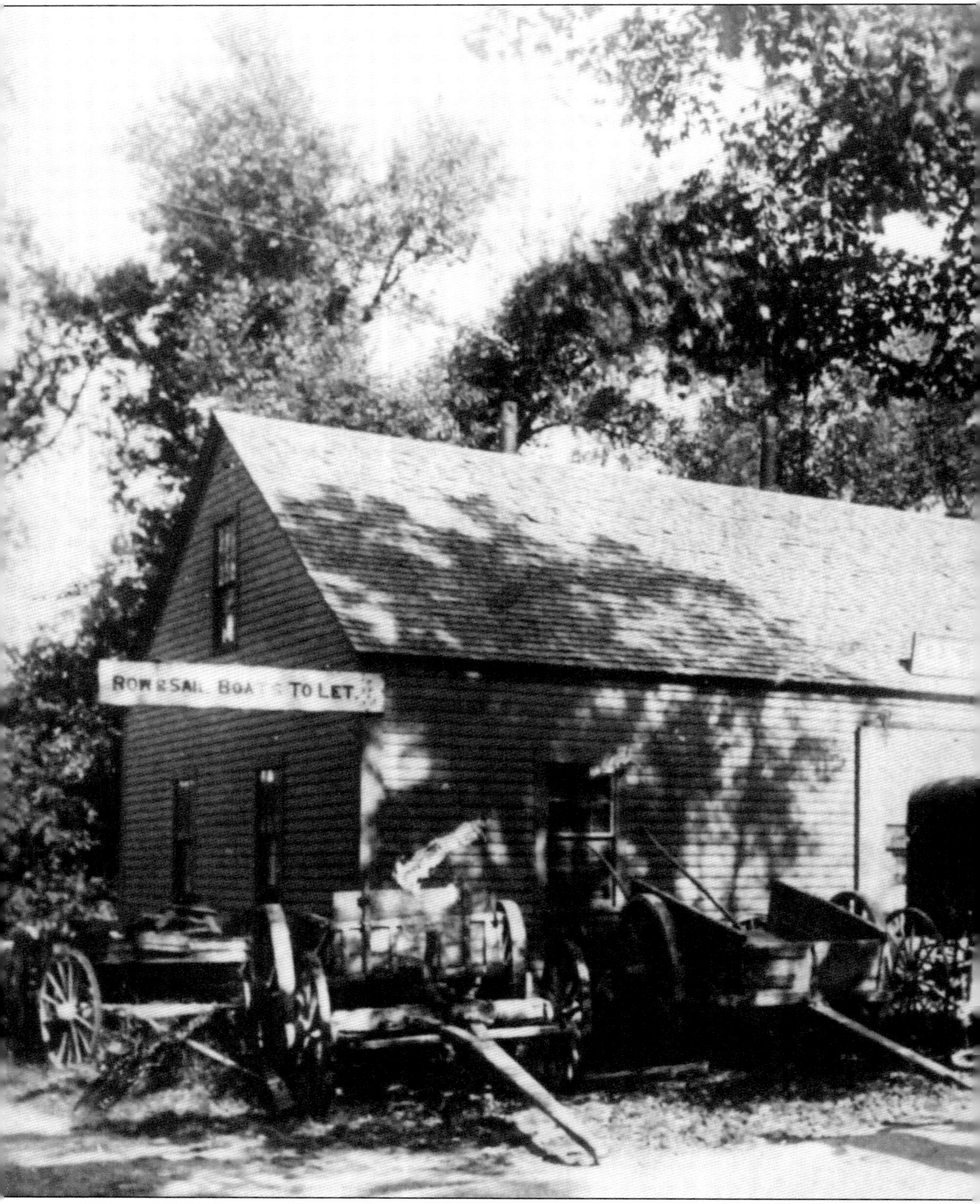

This *c.* 1875 photograph was taken at what is now Sheehy Park along the Merrimac just below the South Campus of UMass Lowell. The tall figure (first on the left) is Edward Francis Dean,

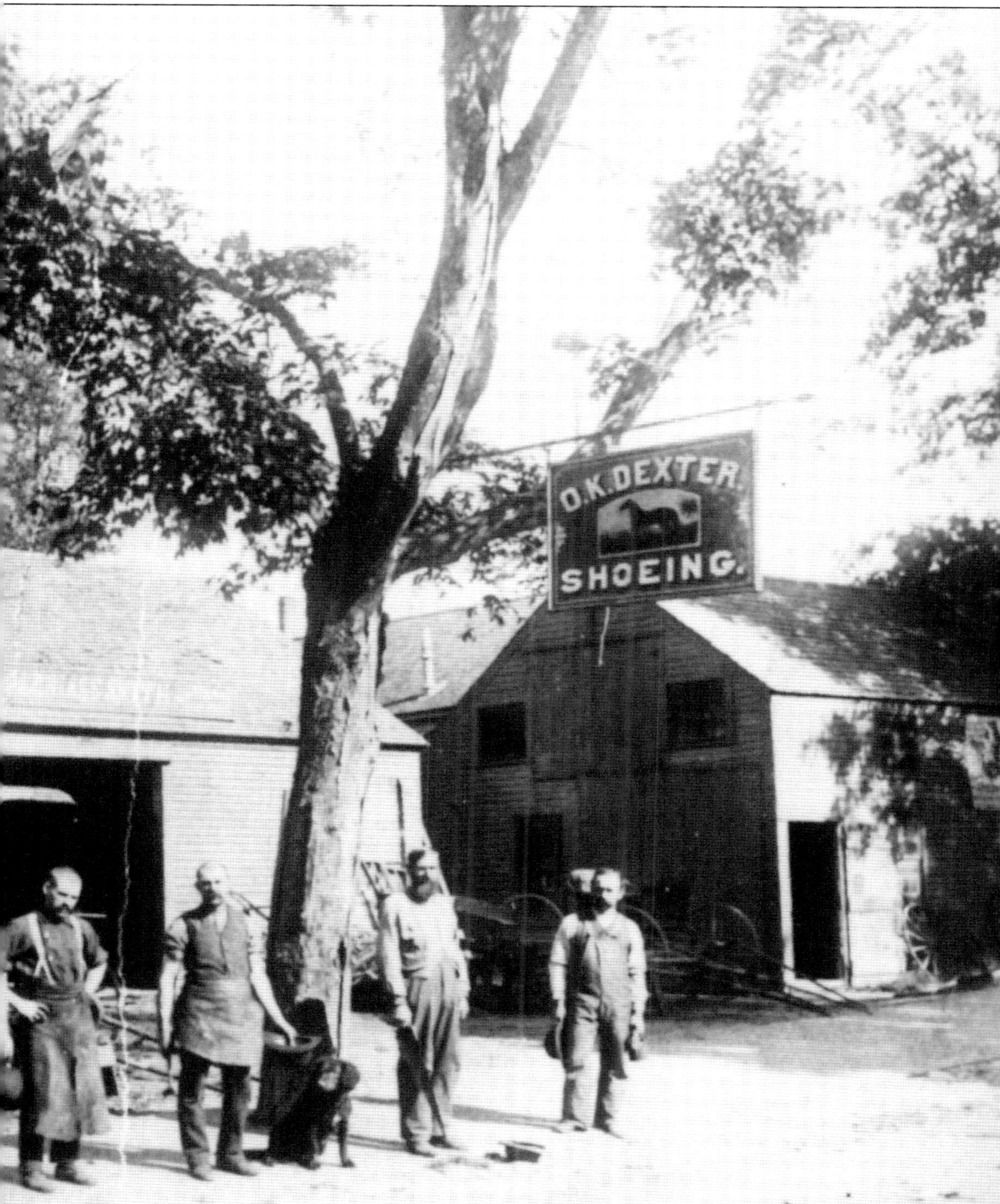

grandfather of Ann Welcome of Fourth Avenue in Lowell. He worked for Daniel Gage, Lowell's leading producer of ice. (AW)

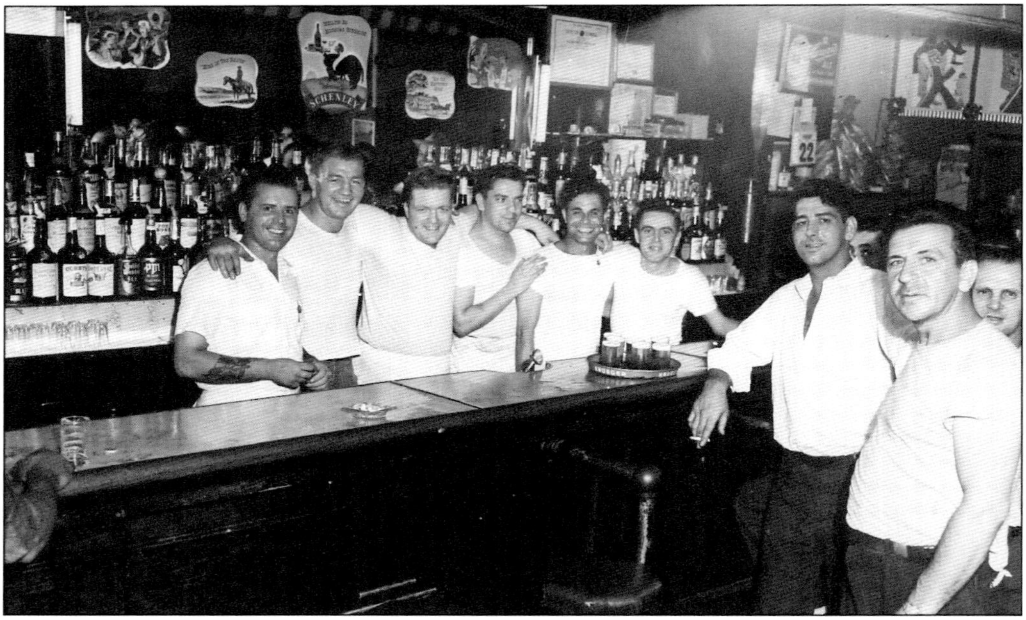

Behind the bar at the Silver Star on Moody Street is Tiny Mulligan (second from left) and Al Cote (fourth in line). The photograph was taken by George Poirier on August 23, 1949. (GP)

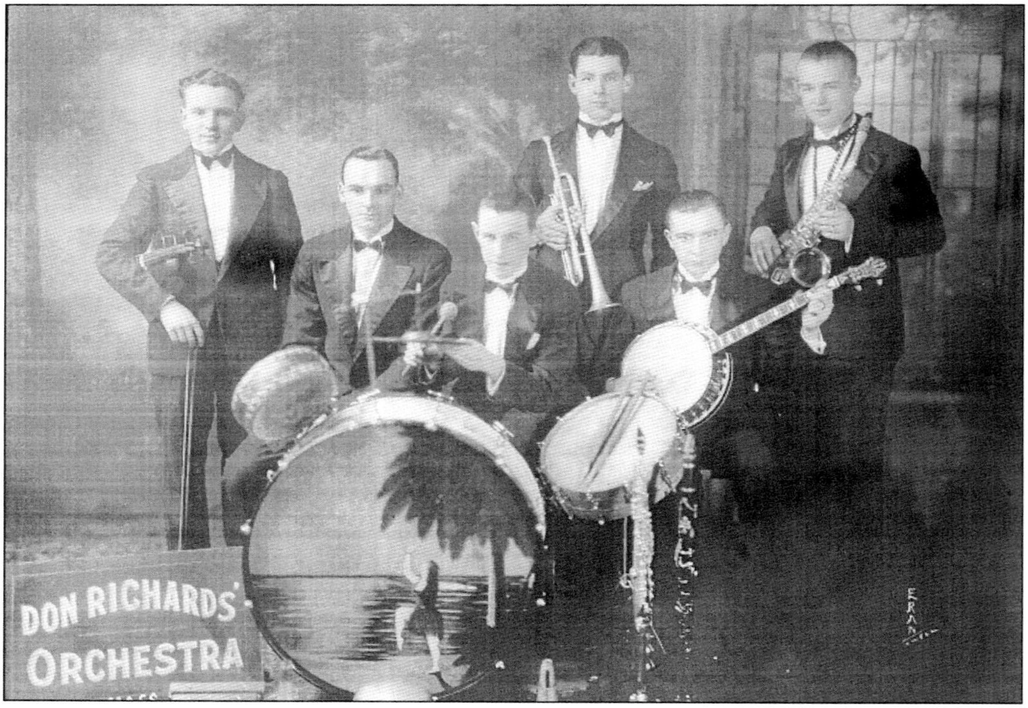

The Don Richards Orchestra played at several local spots, including Lee's Chinese Restaurant on Merrimack Street and the Band Box in Billerica. John Fanning, first on the left, was the pianist. He was also the paymaster for the Mohair Pluch Company. Notice the dancing Indian girl on the drum in this late 1920s photograph. (PF)

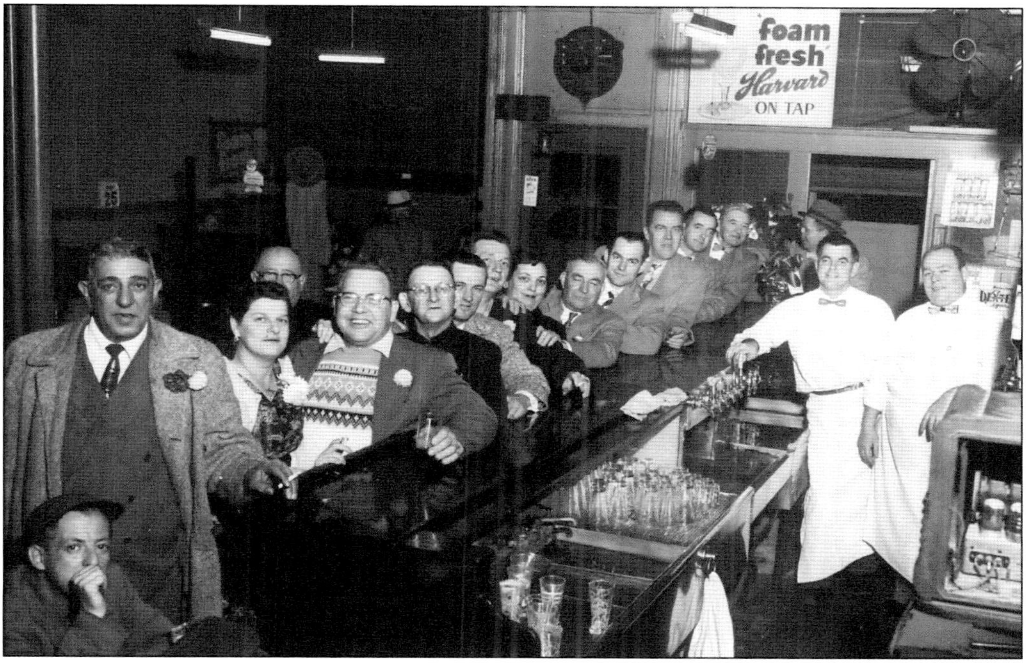

New owners celebrate at the Avon Café on Merrimack Street. Behind the bar are owners Omer Geoffroy and Leandre Marion. Pictured are Blackie Rivet (first man standing on the left and second in line), Leo Fournier (sixth in line), Muggsy Noel (eighth), and (next to Muggsy) Mrs. Leandre (Anita) Marion, her father-in-law, and her brother-in-law. Kit Geoffroy is third from the end. This November 25, 1956 photograph was taken by George Poirier.

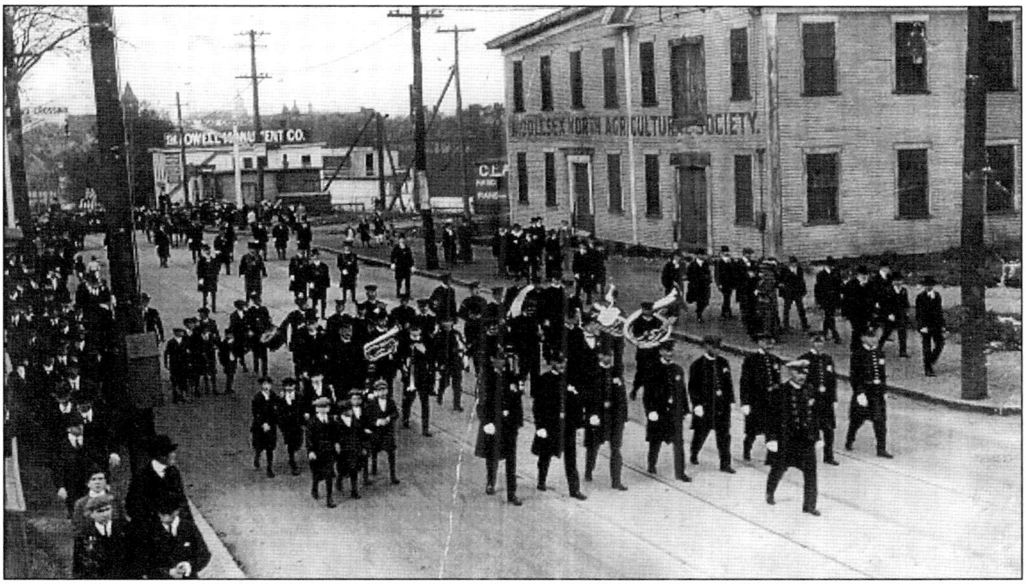

In this c. 1925 postcard, a contingent of Lowell policemen marches down Gorham Street toward the Agricultural Fairgrounds, now Shaughnessy Terrace. Second from the right in the first row behind the captain is one of Lowell's first motorcycle patrolmen, John Fanning. He later suffered serious injuries responding to a late-night call on Merrimack Street.

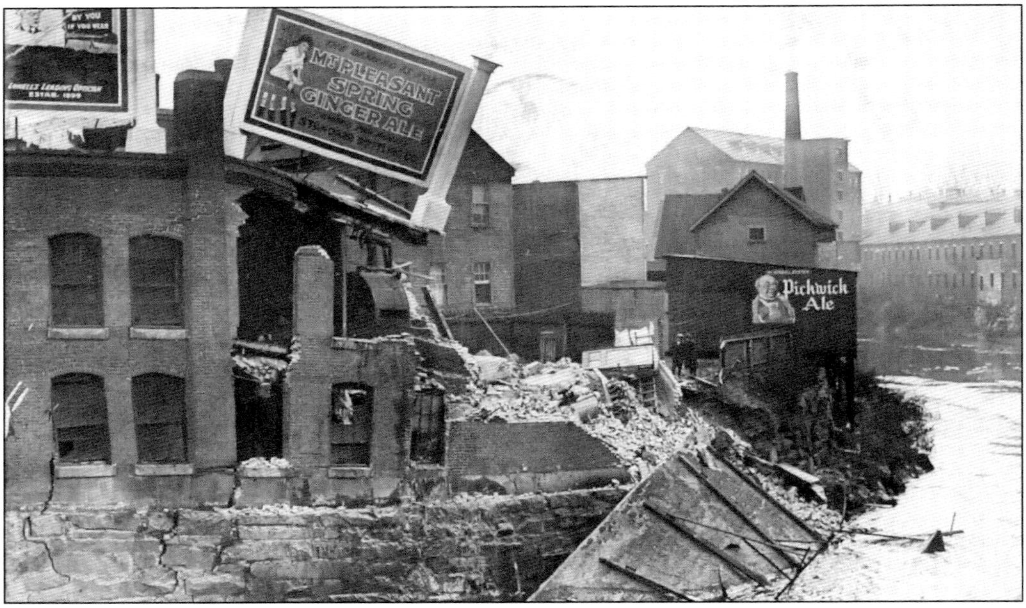

The reverse of this postcard tells the recipient—Corporal Earle Grey, who is on active service in France—the fate of the Dillon Dye Works, which fell into the Concord River after a fire on November 28, 1918. This building was directly across the Concord from the Rex Grille, presently the site of Middlesex Community College. (PF)

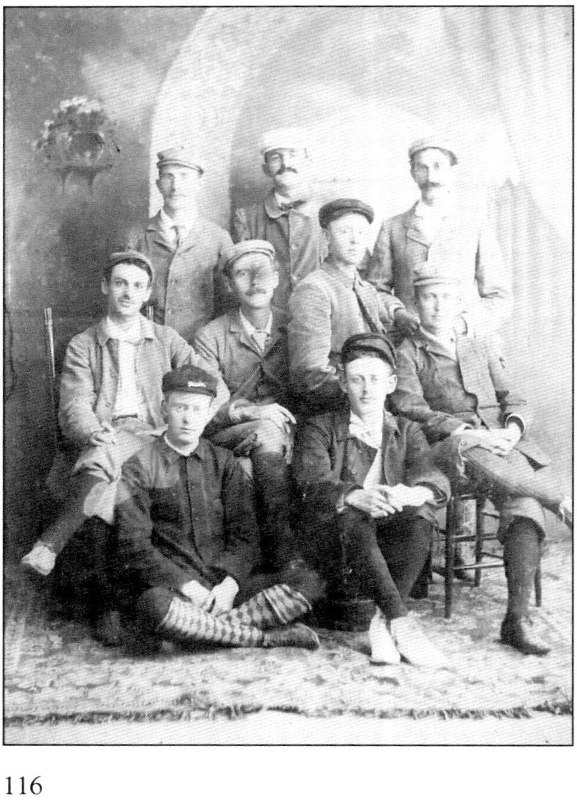

The Lowell Cycle Club was photographed in costume at Freeman's Studio in the Hildreth Building. (PF)

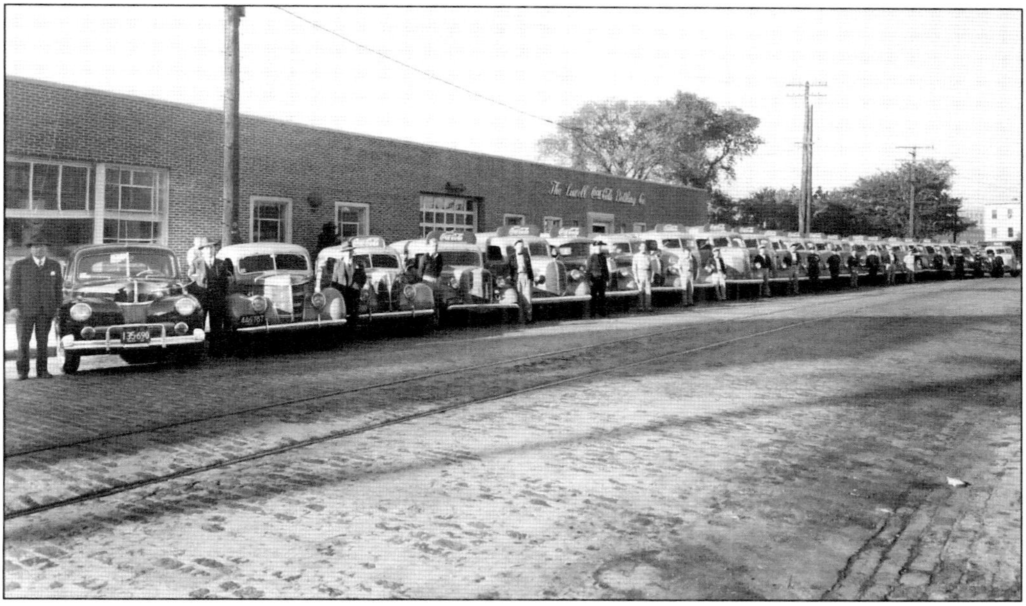

Bert Harliss, owner of the Coca-Cola plant on the Lowell-Lawrence Boulevard, stands next to the first in an impressive fleet of vehicles in this 1942 photograph. (PF)

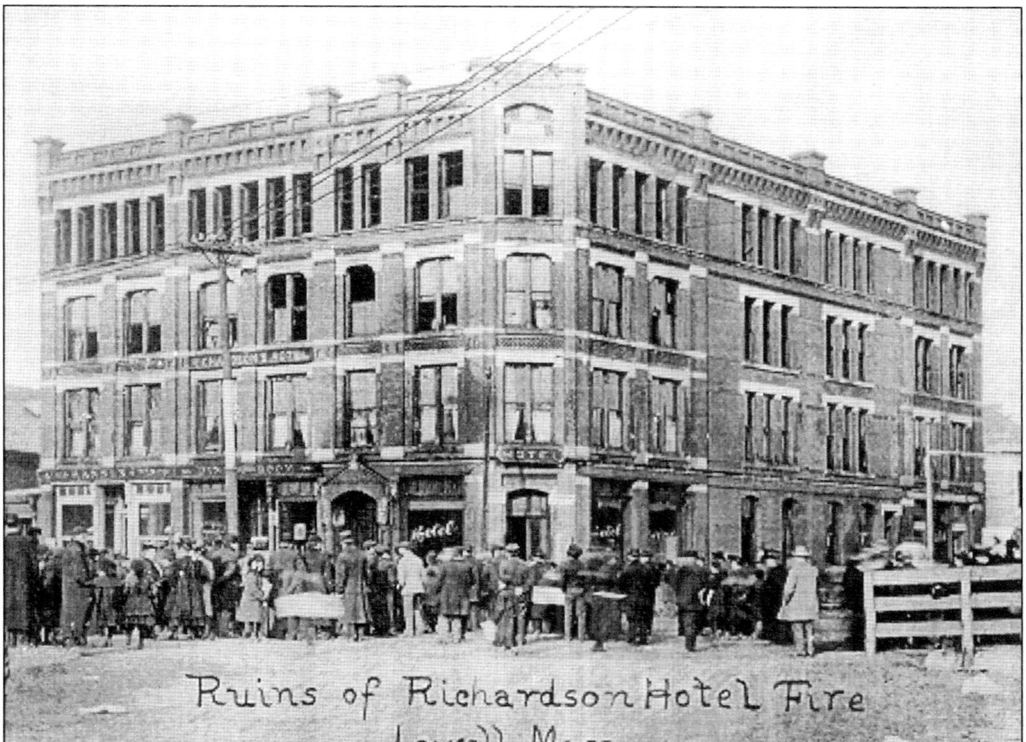

The ruins of the Richardson Hotel at 445 Middlesex Street languished for a long time. (PF)

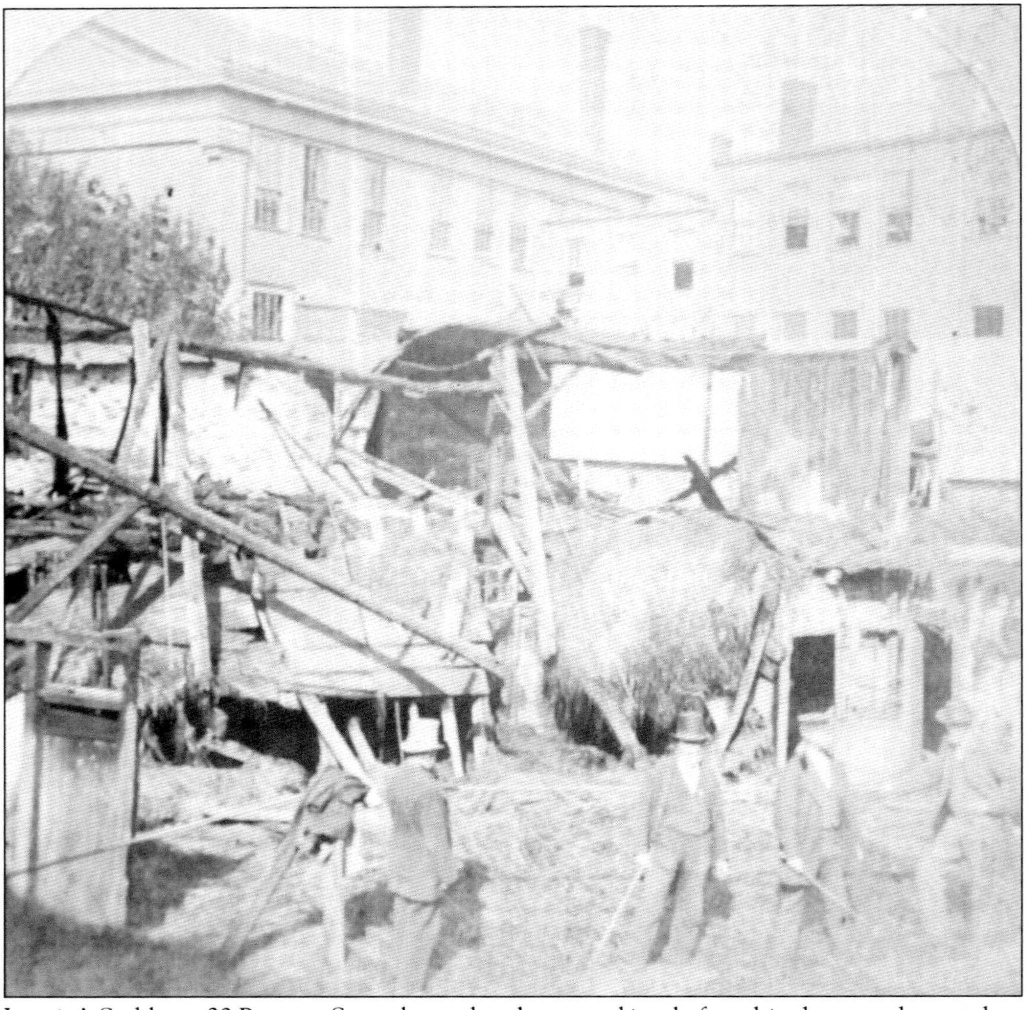

Leavitt's Stables at 32 Prescott Street burned to the ground just before this photograph was taken on October 17, 1870. This is one side of a stereopticon view of the disaster. Daniel Leavitt, who lived on Gold Street near School Street, rebuilt the stables on the same site. (PF)

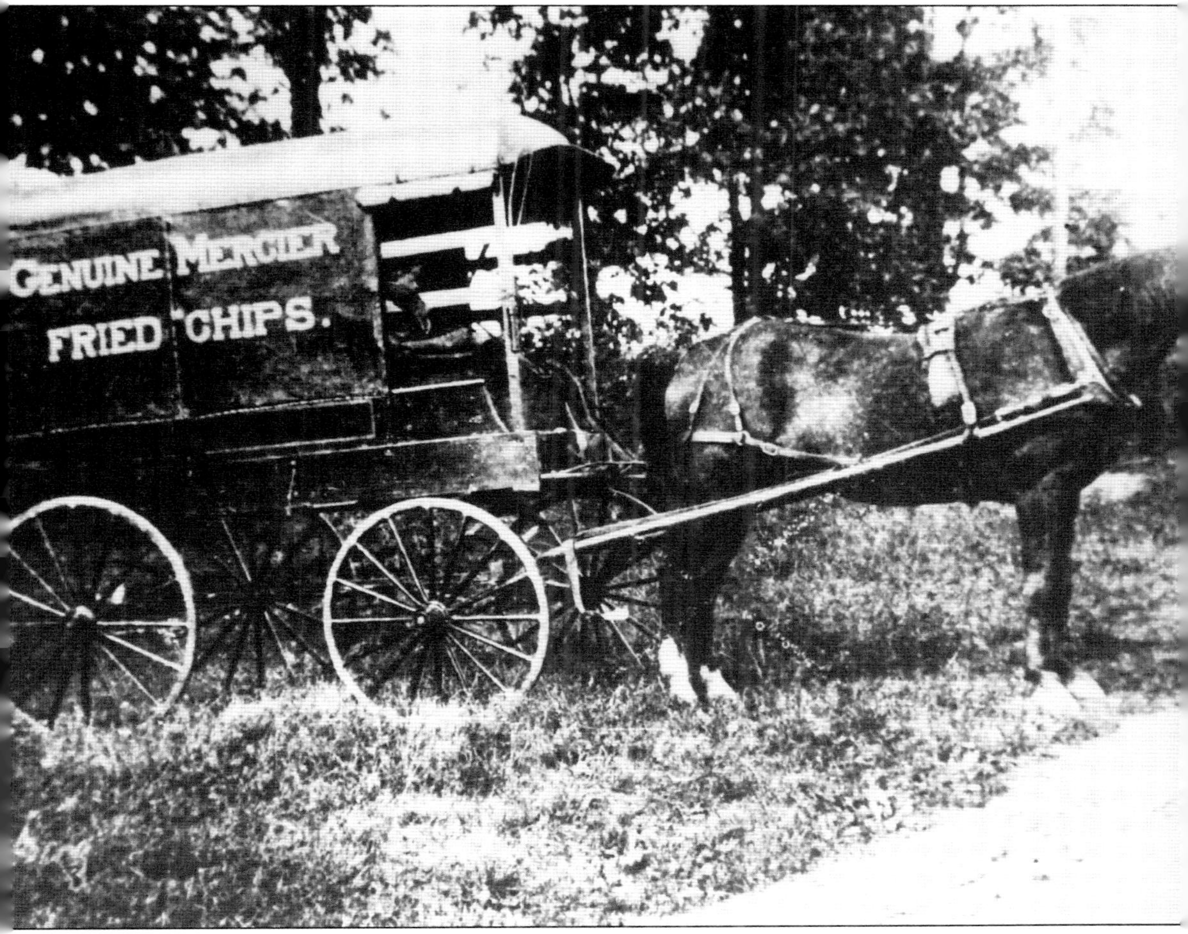

Mercier's Original Potato Chips was founded in 1897 by Alue (Joe) Mercier, who lived on West Eleventh Street and at Campbell Court. His factory was at 16 East Meadow Road. The chips were sliced by hand, deep-fried, and delivered to stores in Lowell, Lawrence, and Haverhill in 50-gallon wooden kegs by three teams of horses which were rotated daily to ease the workload. In 1915, Mr. Mercier sold the company to the Granite State Potato Chip Company of Salem, New Hampshire; that company is still in operation. (GP)

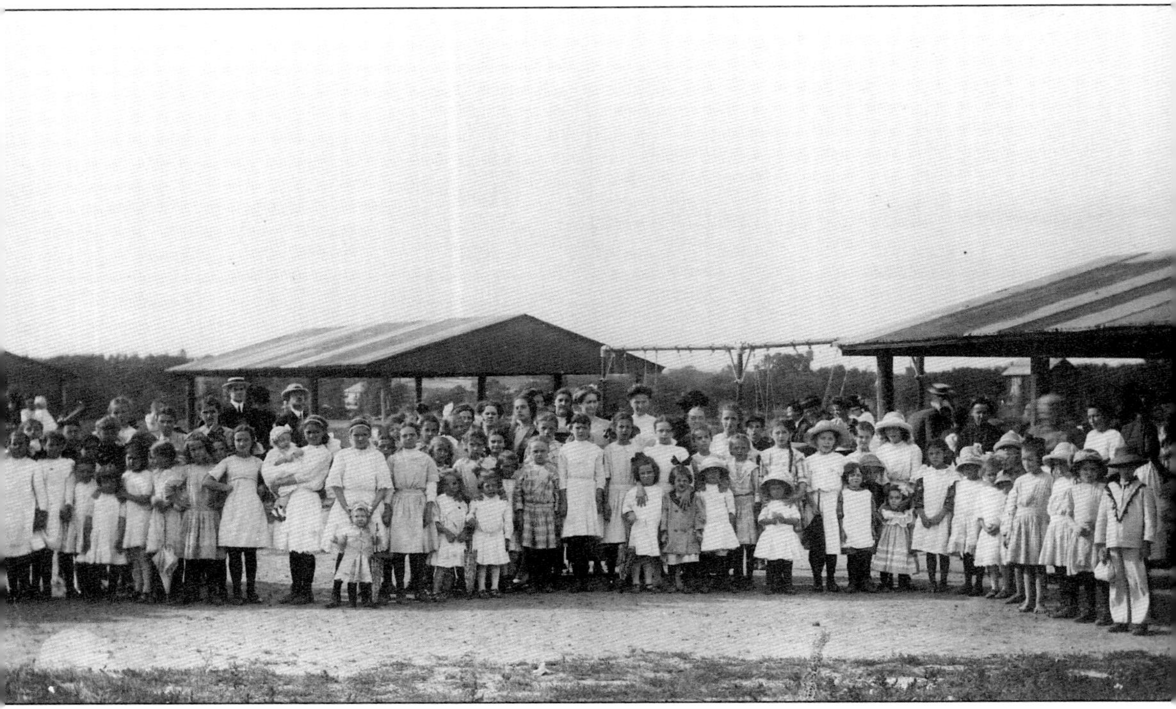

The Aiken Street Playground is pictured here on August 21, 1912, at 3:19 pm. (AT)

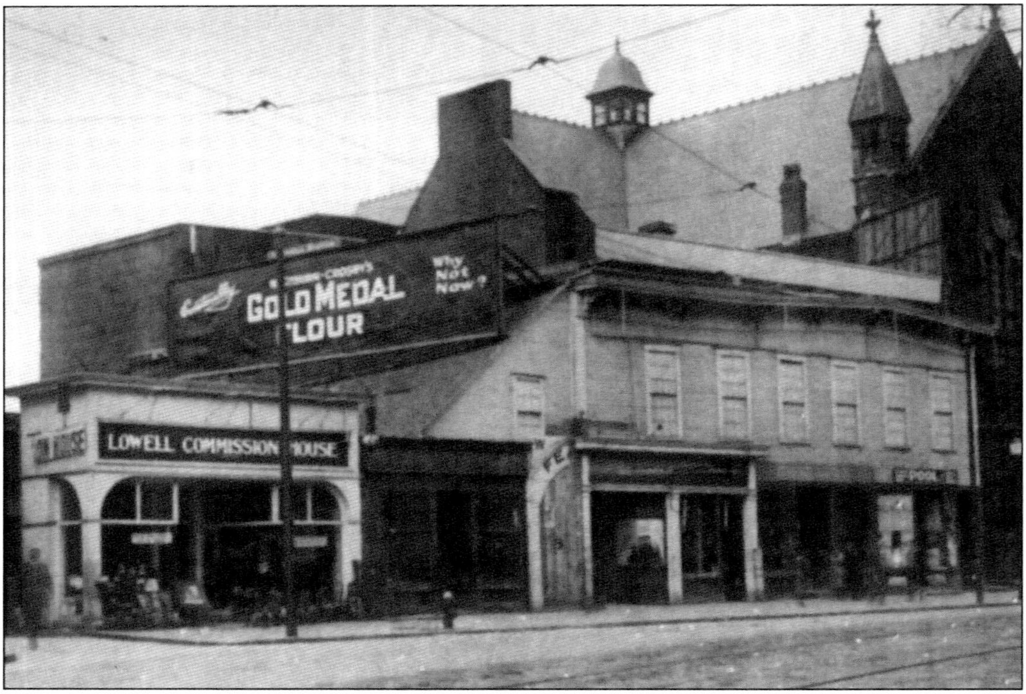

This is a view of Merrimack Street at the present-day location of Cardinal O'Connell Parkway. Notice the Smith-Baker Center at the far right. (HG)

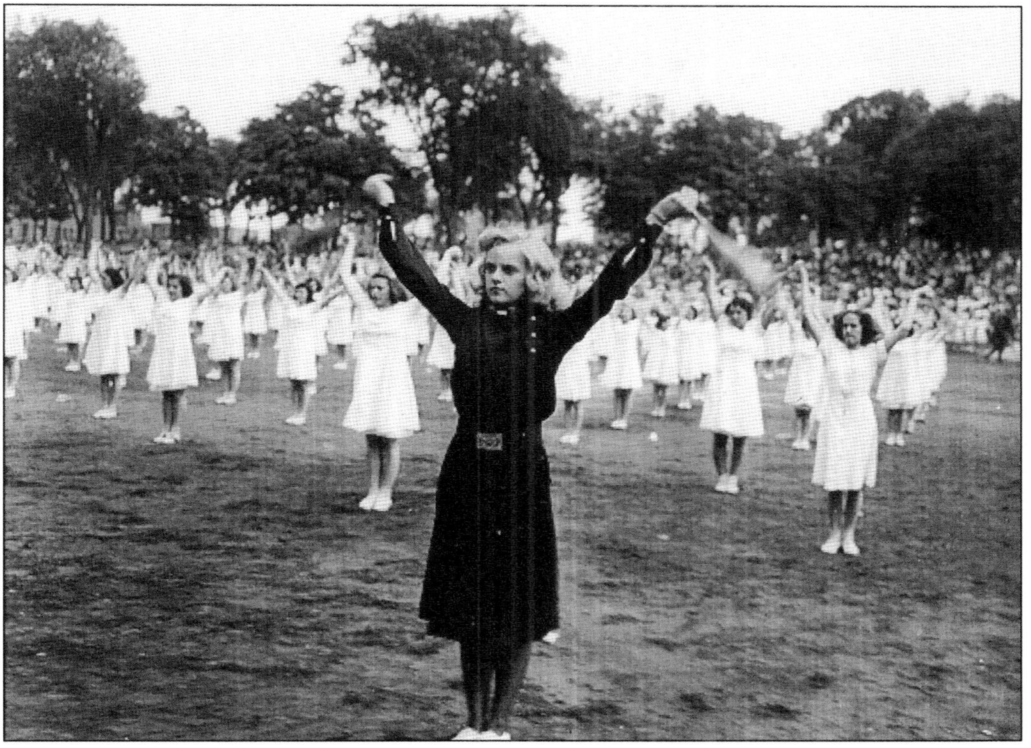

Grace McAllister leads the junior class during Field Day on the South Common on May 27, 1942. (PF)

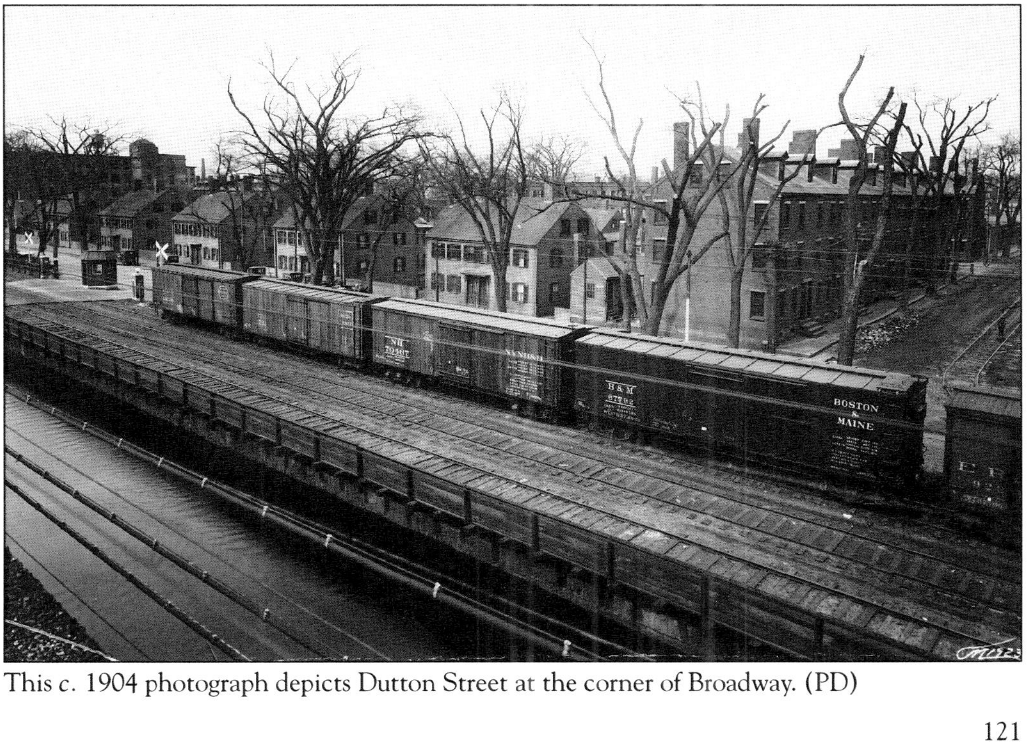

This *c.* 1904 photograph depicts Dutton Street at the corner of Broadway. (PD)

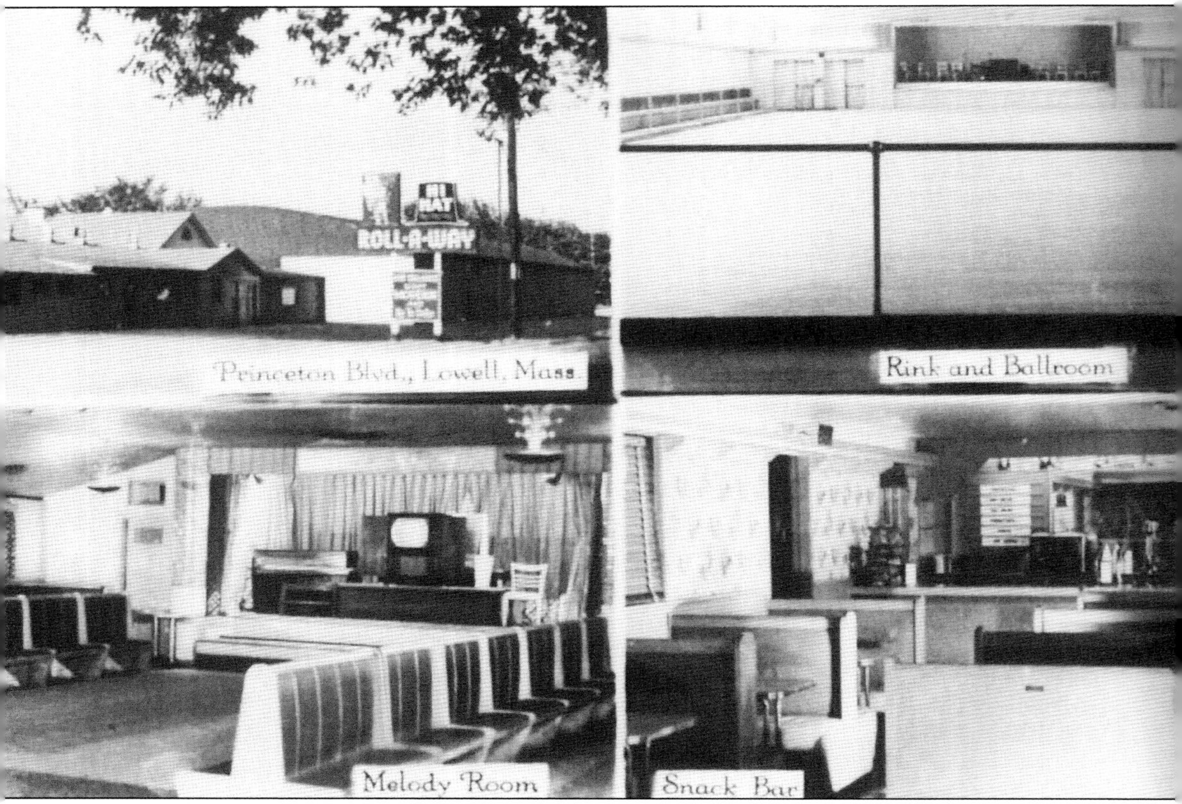

The High-Hat Roll-A-Way is featured on this 1950s postcard. A waitress on roller skates would bring your sandwich. (PF)

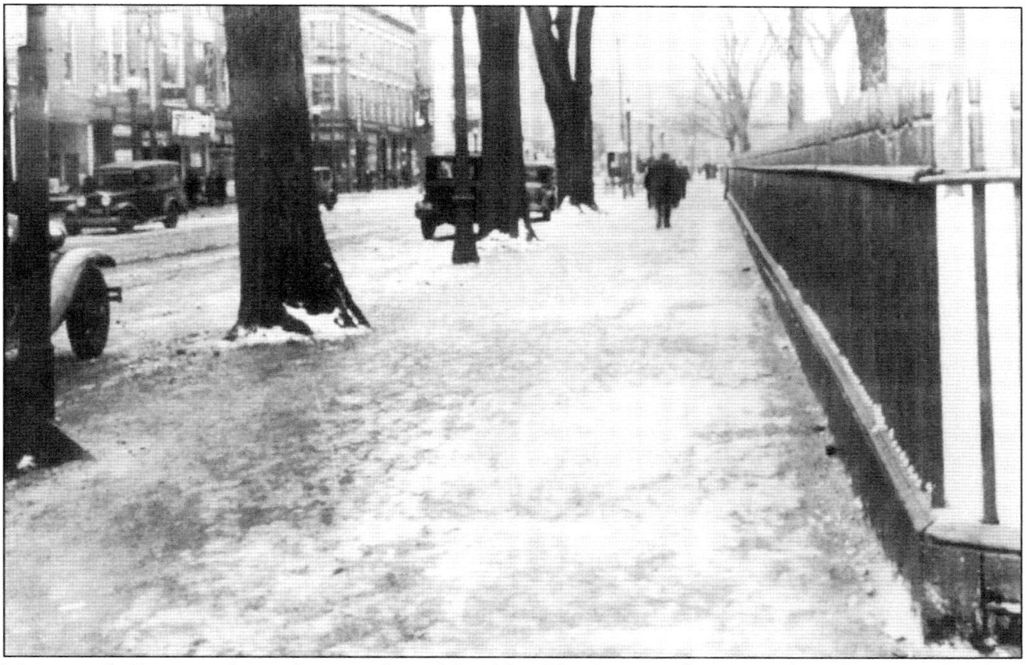

Merrimack Street is shown here on June 23, 1931. The fence still surrounding the grounds of St. Anne's Church is in the right foreground. (BK)

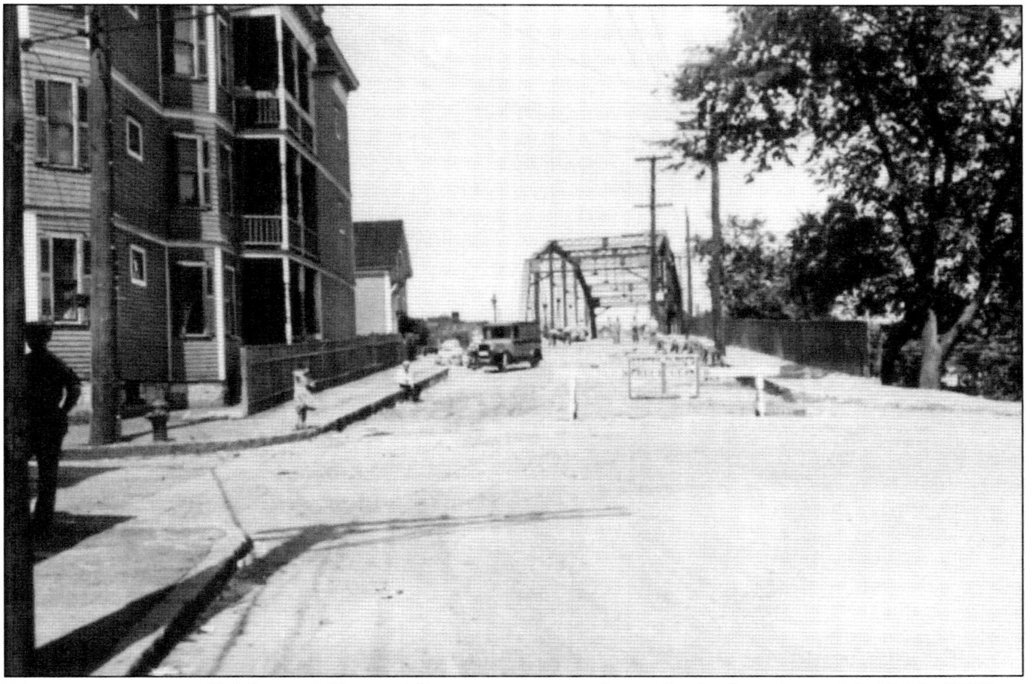

The intersection of Hale and Howard Streets is pictured as it looked on June 26, 1925. (BK)

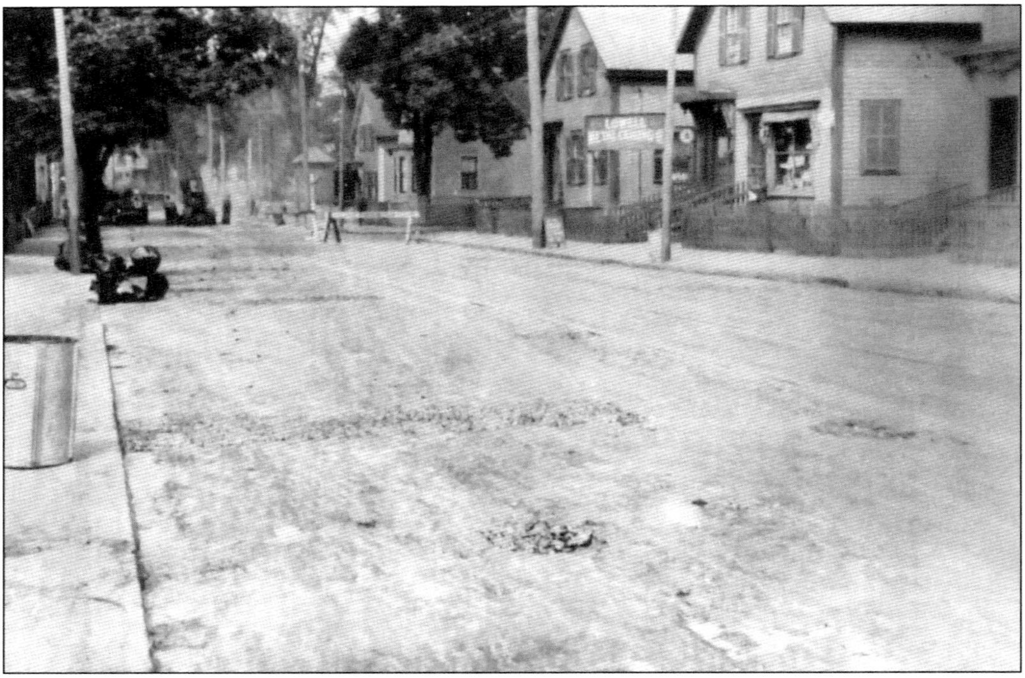

Here we see Broadway opposite Phillips Street on June 23, 1928. (BK)

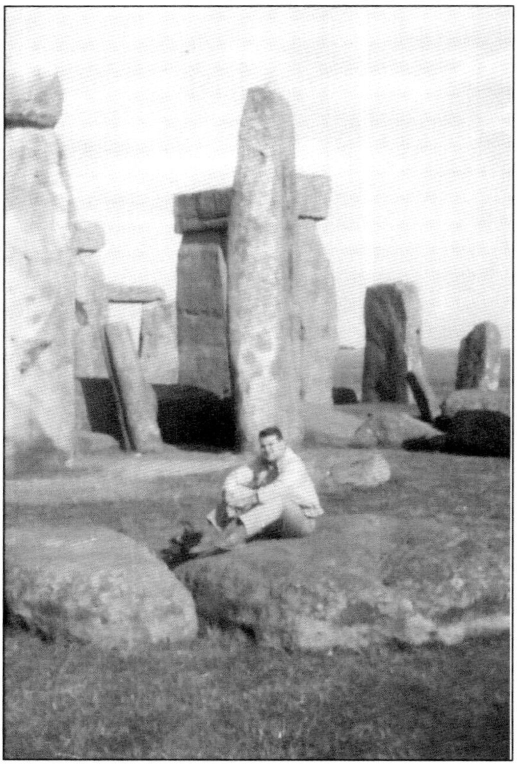

The author is shown here on the North Common, 1961. (JP)

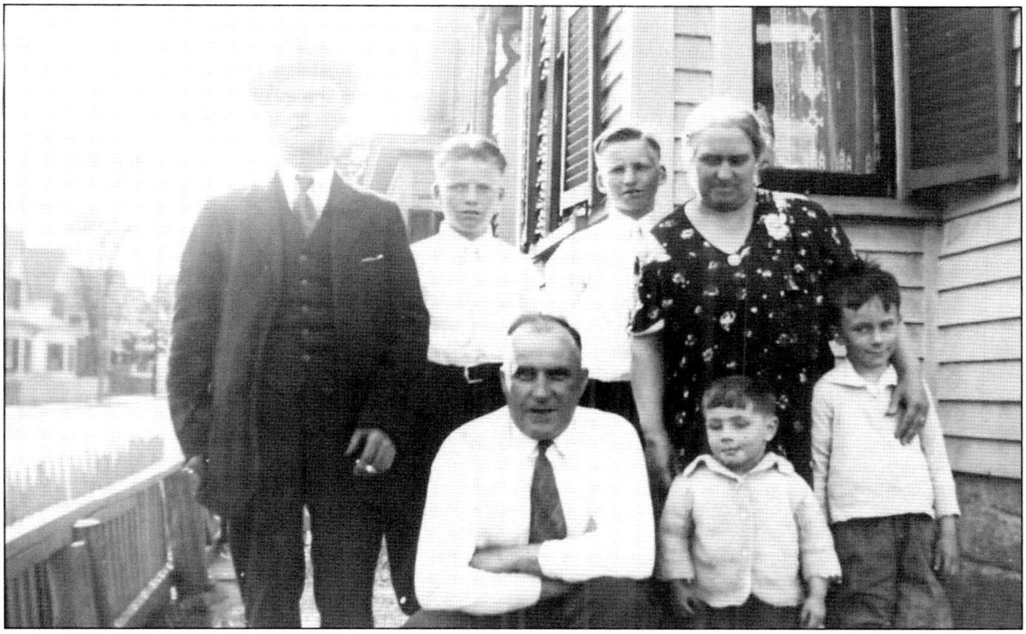

This family group gathered at 123 West Sixth Street in Centralville, *c.* 1932. From left to right are James Quinn; an unknown family friend; John Hogan (crouching in front), Quinn's brother-in-law who was born in Sligo, Ireland, and worked as a driver for Eastern Mass. public transit; Raymond Keefe, who is Quinn's nephew; Margaret Hogan, who is Quinn's sister and John's wife; and two nephews from Dracut, Tommy and Jackie Keefe. (JP)

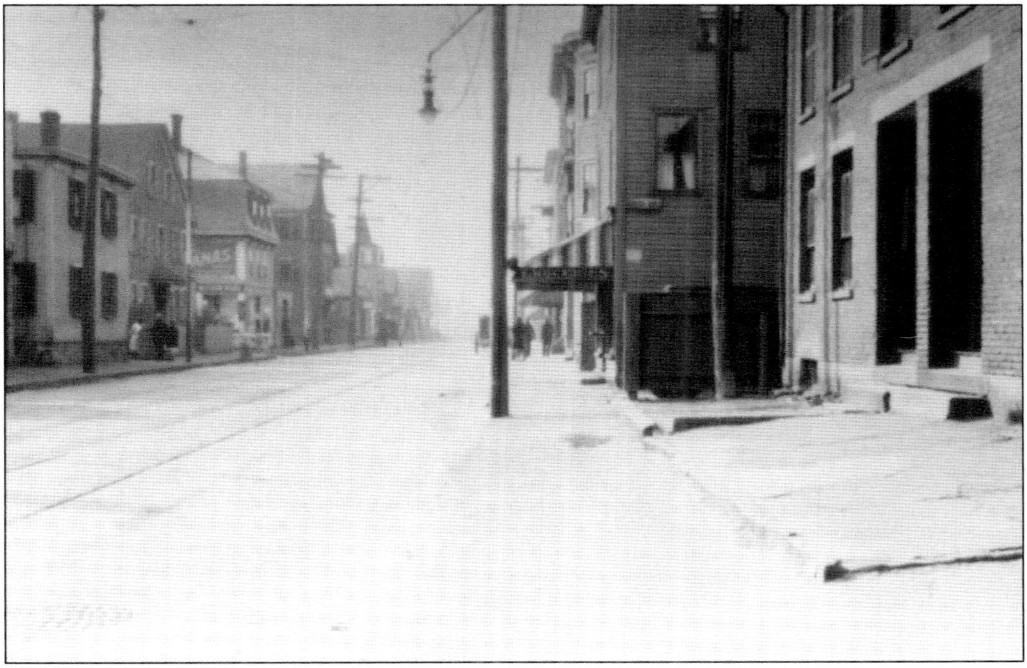

This view is looking down Lakeview Avenue, *c.* 1930. (BK)

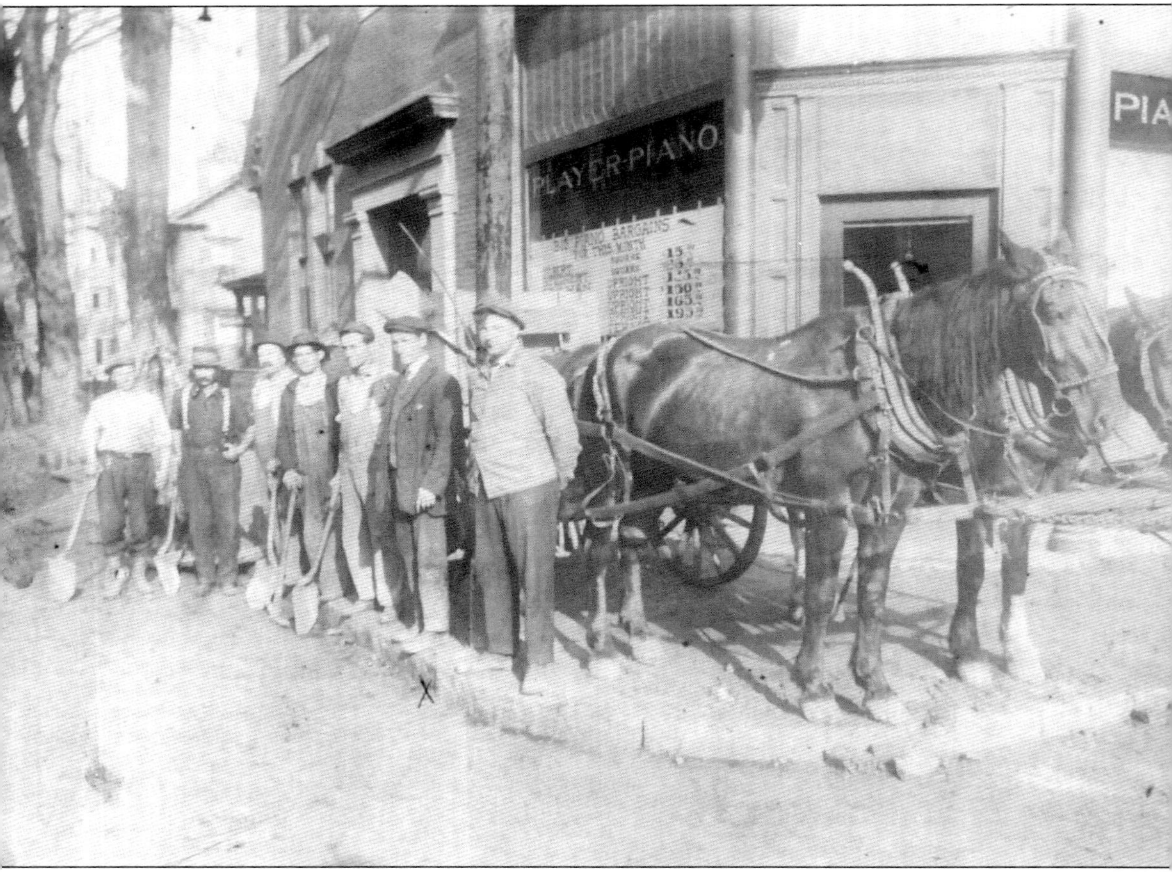

The Delisle Piano Store was located at the corner of Merrimack and Aiken Streets. The Hospital Pharmacy and the Achin Building pictured on page 47 took the place of this building. Zoel Houle is the third man from the right in this *c.* 1915 city road crew. The area is now a parking lot.

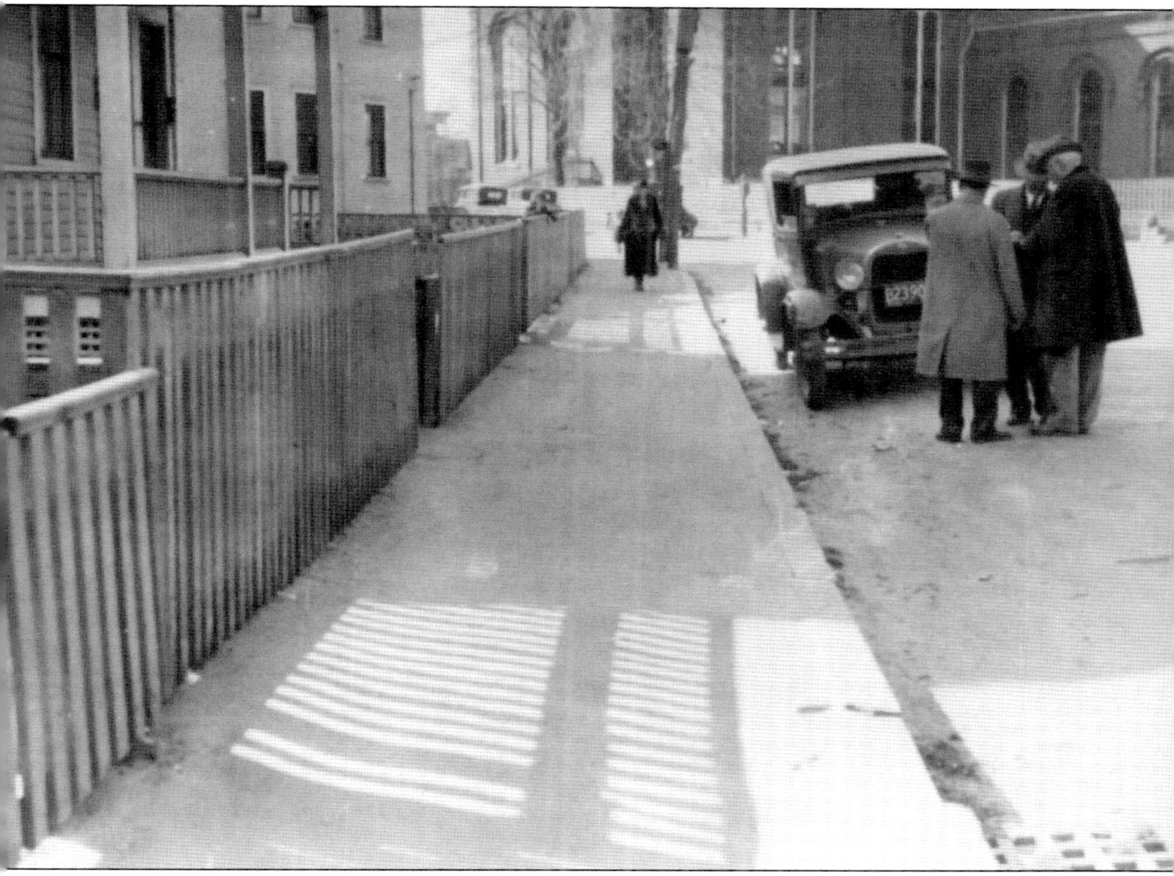

West Sixth Street (with the water works in the background) is shown here as it appeared in April 1931. (BK)

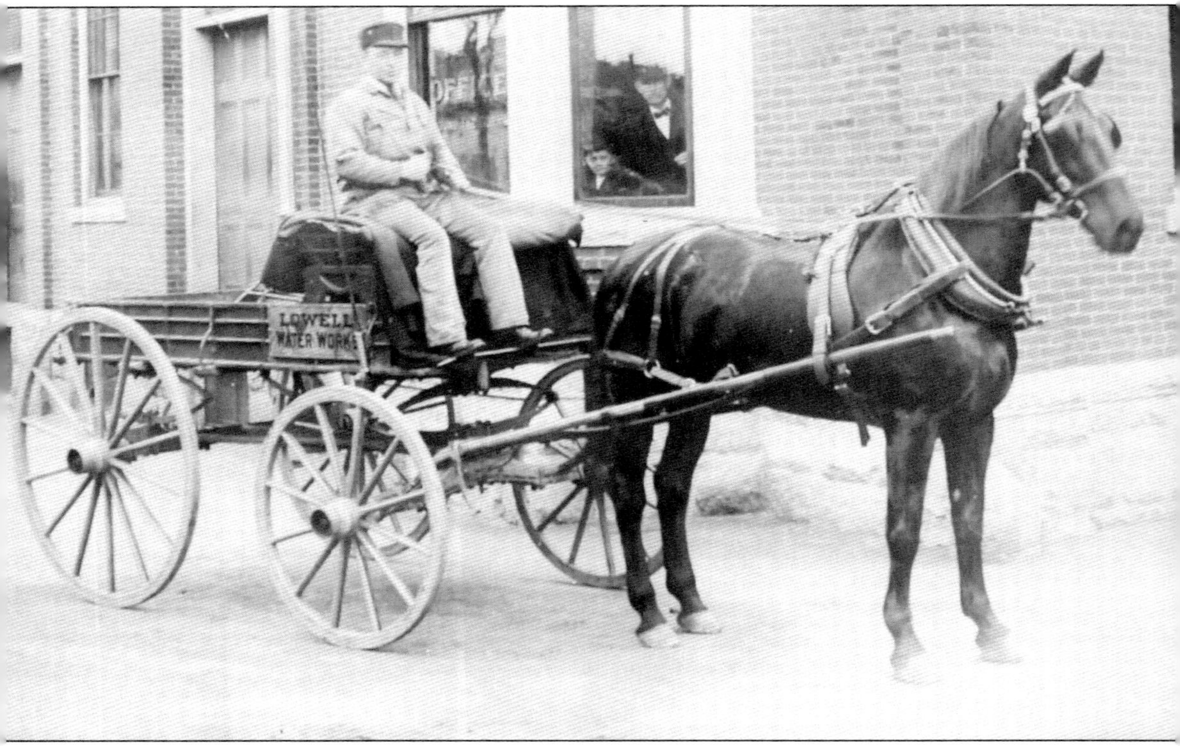

The Lowell Water Works wagon and team are guided by Mr. Sparks. Untreated river water was first distributed through a water works system in 1855. It was believed that although the cities upriver contaminated the water, it would repurify itself as it flowed downstream. A filtration system was adopted in 1870, but typhoid was still a serious problem. (DHS)